Human Resource Management

Gurpreet Randhawa

ATLANTIC
PUBLISHERS & DISTRIBUTORS (P) LTD

Published by
ATLANTIC
PUBLISHERS & DISTRIBUTORS (P) LTD
7/22, Ansari Road, Darya Ganj, New Delhi-110002
Phones : +91-11-40775252, 40775214, 23273880, 23275880
Fax: +91-11-23285873
Web: www.atlanticbooks.com
E-mail: orders@atlanticbooks.com

Printed & bound in India by Atlantic Print Services

To the Almighty

Acknowledgments

In the writing of any book the support and encouragement of many people is naturally required. Same is the case in writing *Human Resource Management*. I am grateful to all those persons who directly or indirectly helped me in accomplishing this great task. I would like to take this opportunity to particularly thank—

- My husband, Manbir for his support, encouragement and interest in this book. He made sure that all I need for writing this book should be available well in time.
- My son, Manraj, for relaxing and refreshing me in the breaks during this work.
- My parents, Dr. S.S. Randhawa and Mrs. Parkash Kaur for their blessings, inspiration and encouragement, which always proved to me a great help.
- My in-laws, Prof. Jamail Singh and Mrs. Jagir Kaur for their moral support and help during this work. Thanks are also due to Kanwal and Savreet for their support.
- Last but not least, Dr. K.R. Gupta, Chairman of Atlantic Publishers & Distributors (P) Ltd., for his guidance and interest in the preparation of this book.

Any suggestions and comments from the readers of this book will be gratefully appreciated.

GURPREET RANDHAWA
dr_grandhawa@hotmail.com

Preface

Strictly speaking, human resource management is a strategic approach to procurement, motivation and development of human resources and conduct of relationship between the employer and the employee in an organization. A dynamic and committed world class workforce is the determining factor in the fulfilment of organization's mission, objectives and goals.

This book on Human Resource Management is a modest but sincere attempt to help the readers to understand human resources in a right perspective. It seeks to provide a comprehensive view on the various functions of human resource management. It provides a detailed analytical discussion on human resource planning, strategic recruitment and selection of workforce, compensation management, placement, training, development, performance management, motivation and industrial relations. In all it contains 24 chapters arranged in a logical sequence. The text matter is very well supported by various examples and exhibits. The book will undoubtedly provide a rewarding and refreshing experience to its readers.

GURPREET RANDHAWA

Contents

Human Resource Management—An Introduction

1

LEARNING OBJECTIVES

After studying this chapter, you should be able to:

1. Define human resource management
2. Understand the nature, scope, objectives and importance of human resource management
3. Know about the various functions of human resource management
4. Design an organisation chart for a human resource department
5. Understand various roles and qualities of a human resource manager
6. Know the challenges faced by human resource management

Every organisation is formed to achieve its primary objectives. As the industrial world is becoming more and more globalised and informationalised, fulfilment of objectives lies in the hands of the people of the organisation. No matter how sophisticated technology, plant and machinery an organisation has, eventually much of the results depend upon human inputs. Out of all the factors of production like land, capital, etc. human factor is a living and an active factor and it activates the passive factors of production. Having superior production facilities or a superior product are usually not enough to sustain an advantage over competition. Physical facilities can be duplicated, cloned or reverse-engineered and no longer provide a sustainable advantage.[1] Thus, a competitive organisation must have highly skilled and knowledgeable workers.

MEANING AND DEFINITION

Human resources are the people who work in an organisation. Human resource management refers to the policies and practices involved in carrying out the 'people' or human resource aspects of a management position, including recruitment, screening, training, rewarding and appraising.[2] The other definitions of human resource management are as follows:

1. Human resource management is the planning, organising, directing and controlling of the procurement, development, compensation, integration, maintenance and separation of human resources to the end that individual, organisational and social objectives are accomplished.[3]
2. Human resource management may be defined as that field of management which has to do with planning, organising and controlling the functions of procuring, developing, maintaining and utilizing a labour force, such that the (a) objectives for which the company is established are attained economically and effectively, (b) objectives of all levels of personnel are served to the highest possible degree, (c) objectives of society are duly considered and served.[4]
3. The management of human resources is viewed as a system in which participants seeks to attain both individual and group goals.[5]
4. Human resource management is the function performed in organisations that facilitates the most effective use of people (employees) to achieve organisational and individual goals.[6]
5. Human resource management is concerned with people dimension in management. Since every organisation is made up of people, acquiring their services, developing their skills, motivating them to higher levels of

performance and ensuring that they continue to maintain their commitment to the organisation are essential to achieving organisational objectives. This is true, regardless of the type of organisation—government, business, education, health, recreation, or social action.[7]

FEATURES OF HRM

The features of human resource management include the following:

1. Comprehensive function

Human resource management (HRM) covers all levels (lower, middle and top) and all categories (unskilled, skilled, clerical, technical, managerial and professional) of employees. It applies to the workers, officers, supervisors, managers, executives and other types of personnel. It covers both organised and unorganised employees.

2. Integral part of the process of management

HRM is the integral part of the management process as a whole. It is embedded in the organisation structure of an organisation. In other words, it is the central sub-system of an organisation and it permeates all types of functional management, i.e. marketing management, financial management and production management.

3. People-oriented

HRM is people-oriented function. In other words, it is concerned with employees both as individuals and as a group in attaining goals. Also, it is concerned with emotional, behavioural and social aspects of personnel in the organisation. It is a process of finding the best arrangement between people and organisations so that the goals of each are met.

4. Individual-oriented

HRM is concerned with the development of human resources, i.e. skills, capability, knowledge, potentialities and attaining employee goals. In other words, in HRM every employee is considered as an individual and the services and programmes are provided to him to facilitate employee satisfaction and growth.

5. Continuous process

HRM is a continuous and never ending process. It cannot be turned on and off like water from a faucet; it cannot be practiced only one hour each day or one day each week. Personnel management requires a constant alertness and awareness of human relations and their importance in everyday operations.[8]

6. Line responsibility and staff function

HRM is a responsibility of all line managers and a function of staff managers in an enterprise. Human resource managers advise the other departments in the organisation on the various issues related with human resources.

7. Pervasive function

HRM is common in all types of organisations. It is not limited to industrial world alone, it is equally applicable to the employees in all types of organisations in the world (service sector, armed forces, sports organisations, government and political departments, religious, social and commerce organisations, etc.). In every organisation, recruitment, selection, training and development and maintenance of people is the integral part. It is the responsibility of all line managers and a function of staff managers in all organisations.

8. Challenging function

HRM is concerned mostly with managing human resources at work. Because of the dynamic nature of the people, managing human resources becomes a challenging task. HRM tries its best to secure unreserved cooperation from all employees in order to achieve its predetermined objectives.

9. Development-oriented

HRM aims to attain the goals of individuals, organisation and society in an integrated approach. As an individual, employee goals include job-security, job satisfaction, status, development opportunity, recognition, etc. HRM is concerned with the overall development of employees in the organisation. As a result of this employees will be satisfied and will contribute their best efforts towards the attainment of organisations' goals.

10. Recent origin

In comparison to the other areas of management, HRM is a young field. It came into existence in the later halves of the nineteenth century.

RELATED TERMS

There are some terms which are used interchangeably with HRM, but there lies a difference.

First of all, there is a term Personnel Management (PM). Historically personnel management preceded HRM. Personnel refer to the persons employed. Personnel Management viewed labour as a tool, the behaviour of which could be manipulated for the benefit of the organisation[9] and replaced when it was worn-out. Thus, in case of PM, the emphasis was only on hiring new employees and just maintaining personnel records. So, it was just limited to the routine activities in the organisation and was never being considered as a part of corporate strategy. However, HRM is broader in scope than PM. HRM viewed employees as human being having psychological, social and economic needs. The difference between the two terms is presented in Table 1.1.

Another term is Human Resource Development (HRD). HRM is a wider term than the HRD. HRD is the development aspect of HRM. So, HRD is a part of HRM. HRD includes performance appraisal, potential appraisal and development, feedback and performance coaching, career planning, training, organisation development or research and systems development, rewards, employee welfare and quality of work life and human resource information.[10] Another term that sometimes creates the problem of semantics is Industrial Relations (IR). IR is basically concerned with relations between management and labour. It deals with grievance handling, settlement of disputes, maintaining harmonious and peaceful relations between the two parties, etc. Thus, IR is one part of HRM.

OBJECTIVES OF HRM

Every organisation exists to attain some purposes which are called its objectives. Objectives are the aims for which individual or group efforts are directed and the standards against which the

Table 1.1: Differences between Personnel Management (PM) and HRM

Dimension	PM	HRM
Beliefs and Assumptions		
Contract	Careful delineation of written contracts	Aim to be 'beyond contract'
Rules	Importance of devising clear rules/mutuality procedures	'Can do' outlook, impatience with 'rules'
Guide to Management action	Norms/customs and practice	'Business-need'
Behaviour referrent		Values/Mission
Managerial task vis-a-vis labour	Monitoring	Nurturing
Nature of relations	Pluralist	Unitarist
Conflict	Institutionalized	De-emphasised
Standardisation	High (e.g. parity is a major issue)	Low (e.g. parity is not seen as relevant)
Strategic Aspects		
Key relations	Labour management	Customer
Initiatives	Piecemeal	Integrated
Corporate plan	Marginal to	Central to
Speed of decision	Slow	Fast
Line Management		
Management role	Transactional	Transformational leadership
Key managers	Personnel/IR Specialists	General/business/line managers
Communication	Indirect	Direct
Standardization	High (e.g. 'parity' an issue)	Low (e.g. 'parity' not seen as relevant)
Prized management skills	Negotiation	Faciltation
Key Levers		
Selection	Separate, marginal task	Integrated, key task
Pay	Job evaluation (fixed grades)	Performance-related
Conditions	Separately negotiated	Harmonization
Labour management	Collective bargaining contracts	Towards individaul contracts
Thrust of relations with stewards	Regulated through facilities and training	Marginalized (with of some bargaining for change models)
Job categories and grades	Many	Few
Communication	Restricted flow	Increased flow
Job design	Division of labour	Teamwork
Conflict handling	Reach temporary truces	Manage climate and culture
Training and development	Controlled access to courses	Learning companies
Foci of attention for interventions	Personnel procedures	Wide ranging cultural structural and personnel strategies

Source: Johan Storey, *Managing Human Resources,* Beacon Books, New Delhi, 1997, p. 35.

performance is evaluated. Objectives indicate the destination of an enterprise. The objectives of HRM are derived directly from the objectives of an organisation.

The main objective of HRM is to ensure the availability of committed and competent workforce in the organisation. The other key objectives of HRM are shown in the Figure 1.1 in the logical sequence and description is also given below:

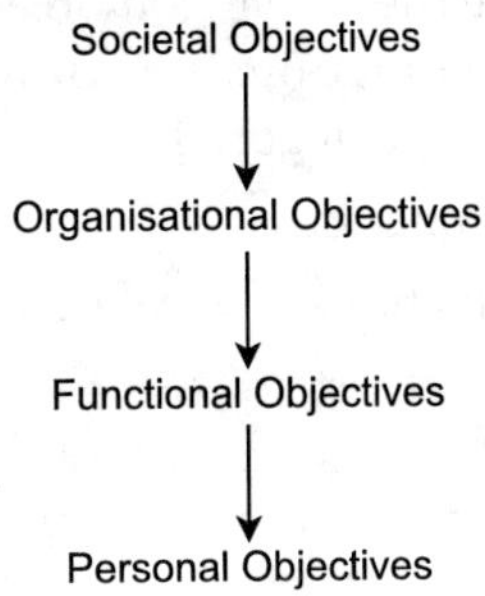

Fig. 1.1: The Objectives of HRM

1. Societal objectives

To be ethically and socially responsible to the needs and challenges of the society while minimising the negative impact of such demands upon the organisation. Organisation should use their resources for the benefit of the society. For example, HR manager must have knowledge of law regarding government's reservation policy while hiring, laws that deal with health, safety and welfare of employees, etc.

2. Organisational objectives

To recognise the role of HRM in bringing about the organisational effectiveness. The department of HRM assists the organisation to achieve its primary objectives.

3. Functional objectives

To maintain the department's contribution at a level appropriate to the organisation's needs. There should be proper alignment between the HRM department's service and the organisation's needs. In other words, HRM should serve well the organisation's demands.

4. Personal objectives

To assist employees in achieving their personal goals, at least in so far as these goals enhance the individual's contribution to the organisation. Personal objectives of employees must be met if workers are to be maintained, retained and motivated.[11]

FUNCTIONS OF HRM

In order to achieve the above said objectives HRM performs some functions. The functions performed by HRM can be classified into two broad categories:

I. Managerial functions

II. Operative functions

Functions of HRM

I. Managerial Functions
1. Planning
2. Organising
3. Staffing
4. Directing
5. Controlling

II. Operative Functions
1. Procurement
2. Development
3. Compensation
4. Integration
5. Maintenance
6. Separation

Fig. 1.2: The Functions of HRM

I. Managerial Functions

HR manager is basically a manager so he performs the basic functions of management which are mentioned below:

1. Planning

It is the primary function of management. It precedes other functions because a manager first plans before he acts. It involves determining in advance, the objectives and goals and selecting a course of action to attain them. Planning means looking ahead and deciding in advance what is to be done, when and where it is be done, how and by whom it is to be done. For the personnel manager, planning means the determination in advance of a personnel programme that will contribute to goals established for the enterprise.[12] Thus, in case of HR manager, planning includes determining HR needs, checking the sources of procuring people, deciding about training and development needs, motivating employees in order to enhance their performance which in turn will increase organisation's performance.

2. Organising

Once the plans are developed and course of action has been determined, the next function is organising. It is the process of establishing harmonious authority-responsibility relationships among the members of the organisation. The network of authority-responsibility is called as organisation structure. This structure serves as the framework within which people can work together effectively for the attainment of organisation's objectives.

Once it has been determined that certain personnel functions contribute toward the firm's objectives, the personnel manager must form an organisation by designing the structure of relationships among jobs, personnel and physical factors.[13] Because of the increasing expertise in this function many top managements are looking to the personnel manager for advise in the general organisation of the enterprise.

3. Staffing

It is a process of manning the organisation and keeping it manned. In other words, staffing is a process concerned with filling all the positions in the organisation with adequate and qualified personnel. As regards HR manager is concerned, he is required to recruit, select, train, place, compensate, maintain, promote and retire the employees of the organisation at the appropriate time and in the most conducive manner.

4. Directing

This function guides, motivates, supervises and lead people towards the attainment of planned targets of performance. Directing is concerned with the execution of plans. In other words, directing includes issuing orders and instructions, supervising people, motivating them, communicating and influencing employees' behaviour. HR manager is required to do all these tasks in a way that people willingly contribute towards organisation's goals.

5. Controlling

It is a process of ensuring that everything is moving in the desired direction. Through controlling functions of management, it is verified whether everything occurs in conformity with the plan adopted, the instructions issued and the principles laid down. Controlling means measurement of actual performance, comparing it with the standards, finding deviations, if any, and taking corrective actions.

II. Operative Functions

The above mentioned management functions are common to all types of managers. On the other hand, operative functions are the specialised functions related to a specific field. In case of HRM, operative functions are related with procurement, development, compensation, integration and maintenance of workforce in the organisations. These functions are also known as "service functions" or "staff functions". Operative functions of HRM are the following:

1. Procurement

It is concerned with obtaining of proper kind and right number of personnel at the right time and at the most economical rates so that organisational goals could be easily accomplished. It deals specifically with such subjects like human resource planning, recruitment, selection, induction and placement. All these activities are presented in detail in Chapters 2 to 8.

2. Development

Once the personnel are obtained, the next step is to develop them. In this era of technological change, realignment of jobs and growing complexities, training and development programmes are unavoidable. Development function is concerned with providing proper training through various methods.

3. Compensation

This function is defined as the adequate and equitable remuneration of personnel for their contribution to organisational objectives.[14] Although non-financial incentives play an important role in raising the morale of employees, yet the importance of monetary compensation cannot be undermined. The compensation function includes job evaluation, wage policies and wage systems.

4. Integration

It deals with the integration of individuals, societal and organisational goals. This function mainly focuses on good labour-management relations, grievance handling, and maintenance of discipline and free flow of communication at all levels.

5. Maintenance

This function of HRM refers to sustaining and improving the already established conditions. This function is concerned with the establishment of proper health, medical and safety measures. Arrangement and proper maintenance of health and safety standards are essential for providing conducive working environment in the organisation.

6. Separation

If the first function of HRM is the procurement of personnel, then logically, the last function is separation of personnel, i.e. return of the person back to the society. Organisations are responsible for meeting certain requirements in the process of separation. This function is concerned with retirement, lay-off, outplacement and discharge.

SCOPE OF HRM

The scope of HRM is indeed very wide. Infact, HRM includes all the major activities in the working life of an individual worker, i.e. starting from his entry into the organisation till he leaves the organisation. The scope of HRM is gradually enlarging. Specifically, the activities included in the scope of HRM are as follows:

- Human resource planning
- Job analysis
- Job design
- Recruitment and selection
- Orientation and placement
- Training and development

- Compensation
- Maintenance
- Motivation
- Managing careers
- Managing industrial relations
- Managing workplace safety and health
- Managing separations.

All these functions are presented in detail in different chapters of this book.

ORGANISATION DESIGN OF HR DEPARTMENT

An organisation can work more effectively if the personnel know the part they are to play in any collaborative endeavour and how their roles relate to each other. An organisation structure should be so designed as to clarify the environment so that every one knows who is to do what and who is responsible for what results.[15] The position of the HR department in the overall organisation structure depends upon the size of organisation, i.e. small or large one. Figure 1.3 shows the organisation structure of a small-scale organisation.

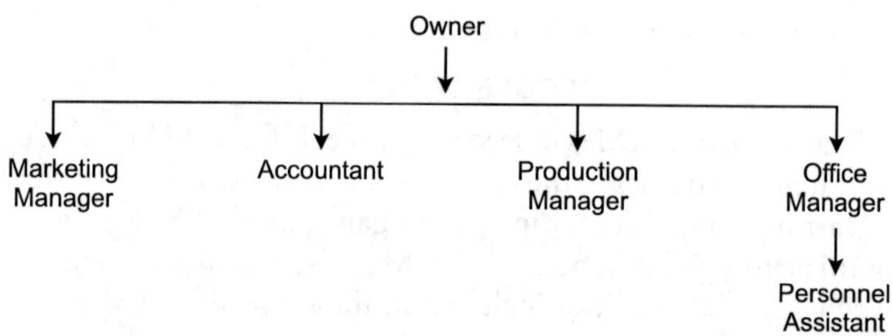

Fig. 1.3: Organisation Structure of a Small-scale Organisation

In case of small-scale organisations, there is usually no separate department of HRM. There may not be a HR manager. Sometimes, services of outsiders are obtained for the maintenance of accounts and records of employees at a nominal fee. Otherwise, a low key placed person is given charge for these tasks.

With the passage of time, increasing complexities, raising status of HR department, things improved over the years.

Realising the importance of human resources along with physical resources, organisations have started providing separate department for HR activities. Figure 1.4 highlights the position of HRM department in the overall organisation structure in case of a large-scale unit.

Fig. 1.4: Organisation Structure of a Large-scale Organisation

Now coming to HRM department itself, again it depends upon the top management's attitude towards its employees and scales of operations. As the scope of HRM is indeed vast, so HRM department's organisation structure is given in Figure 1.5.

ROLE OF THE HR MANAGER

HR manager plays a variety of roles in the organisation. Earlier, the main role of HR manager was to procure and maintain a committed workforce. But with the passage of time, increasingly critical nature of problems and challenges in the effective utilisation of human beings has elevated the status of HR manager. Different roles played by the HR manager are the following:

1. The counsellor

HR manager acts a counsellor for the employees facing problems related with health, work, colleagues, family, supervisors, financial, mental, physical, children education, marriage, etc. Employees discuss their problems with HR manager and he offers suitable suggestions to solve their problems.

2. The advisor

HR manager advises the management regarding human resource planning, recruitment, selection, training and development, appraisal, compensation, integration, separation, etc. HR manager advises management in case of industrial disputes, etc. On the other hand, he also provides assistance to the workers by conveying their problems to the management.

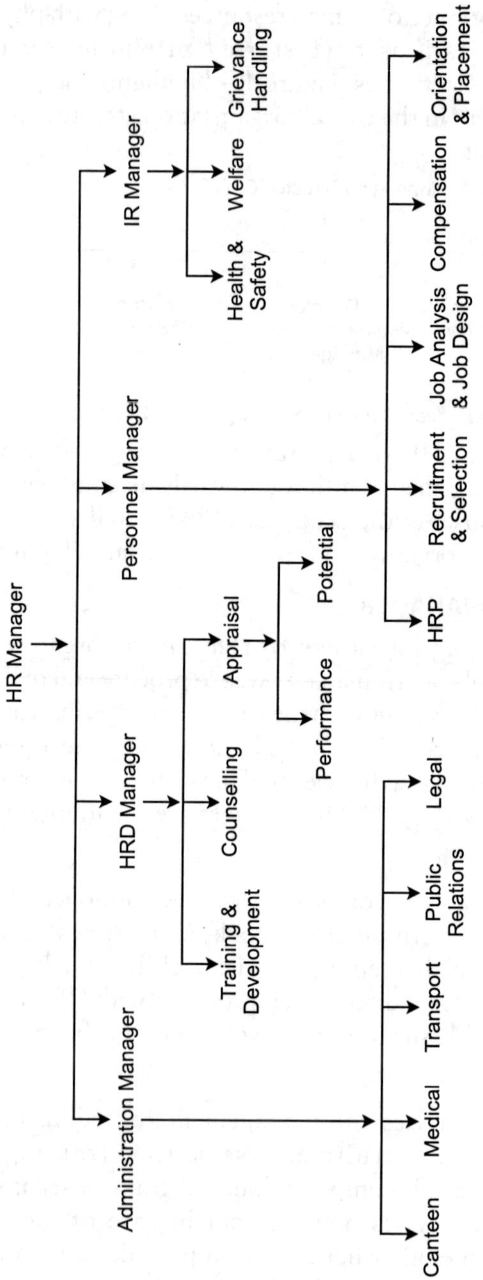

Fig. 1.5: HRM Department's Composition

3. The mediator

In case of some conflicts and disputes, HR manager plays the role of peacemaker between management and employees.

4. The conscience role

This role is that of a humanitarian who advises management of its moral and ethical obligations to its employees.

5. The liaison role

Generally, HR manager acts as spokesman for or representative of the organisation.

6. The change agent

He acts as a catalyst in introducing new changes in the organisation.

7. The problem solver

Problems related with HR in any part of organisation are tackled by HR manager.

8. The welfare role

As per The Factories Act, 1948, where 500 or more workers are employed, one welfare officer should be appointed. Otherwise, HR manager acts as a welfare officer. He is concerned about facilities like creche, canteen, shelter, lunch and restrooms, etc.

9. The legal role

HR manager plays a vital fire-fighting role during grievance handling procedure, settlement of industrial disputes, collective bargaining, handling disciplinary action, joint consultation etc.

The other roles performed by HR manager are depicted in Figure 1.6.

QUALITIES OF A HR MANAGER

HR manager should be a blend of many talents such as good negotiator, psychologist, strategist, adviser, statistician, etc. Specifically, generally applicable qualities are as follows:

1. Intelligence

It is concerned with mental ability, tactfulness while dealing with others, etc.

Personnel Role	*Welfare Role*	*Clerical Role*	*Fire-Fighting Legal Role*
(a) Advisory—advising Management on effective use of human resources	(a) Research in personnel and organisational problems	(a) Time keeping	(a) Grievance handling
(b) Manpower planning-Recruitment, Selection, etc	(b) Managing services canteens, grain shops, transport co-operatives cereals, etc	(b) Salary and wage Admistration, Incentives	(b) Settlement of dispute.
(c) Training and development of linemen	(c) Group dynamics-Group counselling, Motivation, leadership, communication, etc	(c) Maintenance of records.	(c) Handling disciplinary actions
(d) Measurement of assessment and individual and group behaviour		(d) Human Engineering Man-Machine relationship	(d) Collective bargaining
			(e) Joint consultations

Fig. 1.6: Roles of the HR Manager

Source: P. Subba Rao, *Personnel and Human Resource Management*, Himalaya Publishing House, Mumbai, p. 26.

2. Educational skills

He should possess learning and teaching skills, as he himself has to learn and teach workers about organisation's growth and development.

3. Communication skills

HR manager should have good command over the language especially the local language, listening skills, interpretation skills etc.

4. Executive skills

This refers to the speedy and accurate execution of management policies and programmes by HR manager.

5. Human skills

This refers to the HR manager's successful dealing with employees.

6. Leadership skills

This includes ability to motivate, direct and create enthusiasm among employees.

7. Decision skills

HR manager should possess analytical ability, good judgement, etc.

8. Free from bias

HR manager should be free from biasness. He should be neither pro-workers nor pro-management. He should be well-balanced and honest person.

IMPORTANCE OF HRM

HRM is important as it is needed for the better alignment of individual and organisational goals. HRM is considered important because of the following reasons:

1. In order to maintain harmonious and peaceful industrial relations.
2. To have committed and willing workforce in organisation.
3. In order to attract and retain best people in organisation.
4. To improve the quality of work life.
5. To manage and develop human resources.
6. Due to change in government/political attitude towards HRD.
7. To cope with changing technological development.

EVOLUTION AND GROWTH OF HRM

HRM is a term of recent origin. Very earlier, Kautilya's *Arthashastra* written in 400 BC dealt with the important aspect of human resource management. In those days, government adopted techniques of HRM as suggested by Kautilya. Later on, in 1931 it was Royal Commission on Labour which recommended the appointment of labour officers to deal with the recruitment of labour and to settle their grievances. But in modern sense, HRM has developed only since independence. According to The Factories Act, 1948 if a factory employs more than 500 workers then appointment of a welfare officer becomes obligatory. The important phases in the evolution of HRM in India are mentioned in the Table 1.2.

Table 1.2: Evolution of HRM in India

Period	Development Status	Outlook	Emphasis	Status
1920s-1930s	Beginning	Pragmatism of capitalists	Statutory, welfare, paternalism	Clerical
1940s-1960s	Struggling for recognition	Technical, legalistic	Introduction of techniques	Administrative
1970s-1980s	Impressing with sophistication	Professional, legalistic, impersonal	Regulatory conformance, imposition of standards on other functions	Managerial
1990s	Promising	Philosophical	Human values, productivity through people	Executive

Source: C.S. Venkata Ratnam and B.K. Srivastava, *Personnel Management and Human Resources*, Tata McGraw-Hill, New Delhi, p. 5.

Among the other important development aspects of HRM in India was the formation of Indian Institute of Personnel Management (IIPM) and National Institute of Labour Management (NILM). The headquarters of IIPM was at Kolkata and that of NILM was at Mumbai. Later on, in 1980, these two bodies merged together to form National Institute of Personnel Management (NIPM).

CHALLENGES TO HRM

Challenges to HRM can be understood by studying the environment of HRM. Environment refers to all those factors/ forces which have bearing on the proper functioning of the HR department. HR manager should always be aware of the changes in his external and internal environment. Some of the important challenges faced by HRM are as follows:

1. Technological developments

As a result of technological advances made in almost all fields, jobs have become more intellectual. Modernisation ends with problems like retrenchment, lay-offs, unemployment, dislocation of workers, etc. Thus, HR manager has to make proper assessment of manpower needs, retraining, skill upgradation, etc.

2. Changes in the political and legal environment

In order to meet the changes in political and legal environment, awareness of legislation at state and central level becomes necessary for proper utilisation of human resources.

3. Globalisation

As the industrial world is becoming globalised and informationalized, HR managers are expected to play more competitive roles. They should be aware about employees and company's needs in foreign market, designing suitable compensation packages, planning about spouse's job and children's education in other country, if needed making arrangements of training in foreign country's local language, etc.

4. Socio-cultural factors

Organisations' do not operate in isolation. Thus, organisations have to be alert always before taking any decision. The HR manager should evaluate beforehand the impact of any business action upon the society so that the peoples' beliefs, morals, customs, ethics, values, etc. do not hurt.

5. Changing mix of workforce

Another challenge to HR manager is increasing workforce diversity. This includes more young and highly educated people in organisations, more female employees, increasing levels of married female workers, etc. Prohibition of discrimination and the need of positive action for redressing the imbalances in workforce have made job of HR manager more challenging.

6. Trade unions

Trade union refers to any combination of workers for a common cause. Trade unions act as a challenging force for HR manager in decisions like signing of agreements, recruitment, selection, training and development programmes, retrenchment, etc.

7. Management of human relations

The new workforce is educated, talented, well-qualified and conscious than their predecessors. So, HR manager has to be conscious and tough while leading and motivating, winning employees' commitment, etc.

KEY TERMS

Human resource development (HRD)	Managerial functions
Human resource management (HRM)	Operative functions
Industrial relations (IR)	Personnel management (PM)

QUESTIONS

1. Define HRM and describe its objectives.
2. Differentiate between the terms HRM, PM and HRD.
3. Explain the various roles performed by HR manager.
4. Discuss the scope of HRM.
5. Describe the challenges faced by HRM.
6. What are the functions of HRM?
7. Describe in brief the growth of HRM in India.

ENDNOTES

1. Quinn, James B., Thomas L. Doorley and Penny C. Paquette, "Beyond Products: Service-Based Strategy," *Harvard Business Review*, 90, No. 2, 1990, pp. 58-67.
2. Gary Dessler, *Human Resource Management*, Pearson Education, Ninth Edition, Delhi, 2004.
3. Edwin B. Flippo, *Personnel Management*, Sixth Edition, McGraw-Hill, New York, 1984, p. 5.
4. Michael J. Jucius, *Personnel Management,* Richard D. Irwin, Inc., Homewood, Illinois, 1971, p. 5.
5. Dale Yoder, *Personnel Management & Industrial Relations*, Prentice-Hall of India, New Delhi, 1975.
6. Ivancevich and Glucck, *Personnel Management.*
7. David A. Decenzo and Stephen P. Robbins, *Personnel/HRM,* Third Edition, Prentice-Hall of India, New Delhi, 1989, p. 3.
8. George R. Terry, *Personnel Management.*
9. K. Aswathappa, *Human Resource and Personnel Management*, Tata McGraw-Hill, New Delhi, 2006, p. 5.
10. T.V. Rao and Uday Pareek, *Recent Experiences in HRD,* Oxford and IBH, New Delhi, 1985.

11. K. Aswathappa, *Human Resource and Personnel Management*, Tata McGraw-Hill, New Delhi, 2006, p. 7.
12. Edwin B. Flippo, *Personnel Management*, Sixth Edition, McGraw-Hill, New York, 1984.
13. *Ibid.*
14. *Ibid.*
15. Harold Koontz and Cyril O'Donnell, *Management: A Systems and Analysis of Managerial Functions*, McGraw-Hill Kogakusha., Tokyo, 1976.
16. D.C. Sharma and R.C. Sharma, *Personnel Management &Industrial Relations*, First Edition, S.J. Publications, Meerut, p. 26.
17. Edwin B. Flippo, *Personnel Management*, Sixth Edition, McGraw-Hill, New York, 1984, p. 5.

Human Resource Planning

2

LEARNING OBJECTIVES

After studying this chapter, you should be able to:

1. Understand the need and importance of human resource planning
2. Identify the factors affecting human resource planning
3. Understand the process of human resource planning
4. Identify the barriers to human resource planning
5. Identify the pre-requisites for successful human resource planning

Human resource planning (HRP) is the first step in the HRM process. In the earlier chapter, we had discussed about the nature and scope of HRM. The real HRM process starts with the estimation of the number and kind of people required by the organisation for the coming period. HRP is also known by other names such as 'Manpower Planning', 'Employment Planning', 'Labour Planning', 'Personnel Planning', etc. HRP is a sub-system in the total organisational planning. In other words, HRP is derived from the organisational planning just like production planning, sales planning, material planning, etc.

MEANING AND DEFINITION

The following definitions of HRP will make its concept more clear:

1. Human resource planning is the process by which an organisation ensures that it has the right number and kind of people, at the right place, at the right time,

capable of effectively and efficiently completing those tasks that will help the organisation achieve its overall objectives. HRP translates the organisation's objectives and plans into the number of workers needed to meet those objectives.[1]

2. Human resource planning is a process of determining and assuring that the organisation will have an adequate number of qualified persons available at the proper times, performing jobs which meet the needs of the enterprise and which provide satisfaction for the individuals involved.[2]

NEED AND IMPORTANCE OF HRP

The following points highlight the need and importance of HRP in the organisations:

1. Assessing future personnel needs

Whether it is surplus labour or labour shortage, it gives a picture of defective planning or absence of planning in an organisation. A number of organisations, especially public sector units (PSUs) in India are facing the problem of surplus labour (see Exhibit 2.1). It is the result of surplus labour that the companies' later on offer schemes like Voluntary Retirement Scheme (VRS) to eliminate surplus staff. Thus, it is better to plan well about employees in advance. Through HRP, one can ensure the employment of proper number and type of personnel.

Exhibit 2.1: Milkfed: VRS For Non-Core Sector Staff Sought

Realizing that it has surplus staff, Milkfed has asked the Punjab Government to allow a voluntary retirement scheme for its employees in the non-core sector. Milkfed is identifying crucial posts that will not be covered under the VRS. This will primarily include technical personnel like dairy technologist. Several big private companies like Reliance Retail Limited are offering jobs to employees in Milkfed, in the recent past. Milkfed will require about Rs. 32 crore and nearly 700 employees can opt for the VRS. The Government of India has agreed to pay 50 percent of the cost subject to the Punjab Government paying the rest.

Source: *The Tribune*, August 22, 2006.

2. Foundation for other HRM functions

As discussed in Chapter 1, HRP is the first step in all HRM functions. So, HRP provides the essential information needed for the other HRM functions like recruitment, selection, training and development, promotion, etc.

3. Coping with change

Changes in the business environment like competition, technology, government guidelines, global market, etc. bring changes in the nature of the job. This means changes in the demand of personnel, content of job, qualification and experience needed. So, HRP will help the organisation in adjusting to new changes.

4. Investment perspective

As a result of change in the mindset of management, investment in human resources is viewed as a better concept in the long run success of the enterprise. Human assets can increase in value as opposed to physical assets. Thus, HRP is considered important for the proper planning of future employees.

5. Expansion and diversification plans

During the expansion and diversification drives, more employees at various levels are needed. Through proper HRP, an organisation comes to know about the exact requirement of personnel in future plans.

6. Employee turnover

Every organisation suffers from the labour turnover may be of small or extreme nature. This is high among young graduates in the private sector. This necessitates again doing manpower planning for further recruiting and hiring.

7. Conformity with government guidelines

In order to protect the weaker sections of the society, the Indian Government has prescribed some norms for organisations to follow. For example, reservation for SC/ST, BC, physically handicapped, ex-servicemen, etc. in the jobs. So, while planning for fresh candidates, HR manager takes into consideration all the Government guidelines.

8. International expansion strategies

International expansion strategies of an organisation depend upon HRP. Under International Human Resource Management (IHRM), HRP becomes more challenging. An organisation may want to fill the foreign subsidiary's key positions from its home country employees or from host-country or from a third country. All this demands very effective HRP.

9. Having highly talented manpower inventory

The jobs have become upgraded and intellectual, as a result, highly skilled, talented and knowledged workers are required in the organisation. HR manager should be able to attract and retain well-qualified staff.

10. Cost-effective

Employees costs may be less as the management, with the help of proper HRP, can anticipate the imbalances before they become expensive and unmanageable.

OBJECTIVES OF HRP

The main objectives of HRP are:

1. Proper assessment of need of human resources in future.
2. Anticipation of shortage or surplus and taking the corrective action.
3. To create a highly talented personnel in the organisation.
4. To protect the weaker sections of the society.
5. To manage the challenges in the organisation due to modernisation, restructuring and re-engineering.
6. To facilitate the realisation of the organisation's objectives by providing right number and types of personnel.
7. To lower the costs associated with personnel by proper planning.
8. To determine the future skill requirement.
9. To do career planning for individual employee.
10. Providing a better view of HR dimensions to top management.

11. Determining the training and development needs of employees.

FACTORS AFFECTING HRP

Several factors influence HRP. The important factors are (1) type and strategy of organisation, (2) organisational growth cycles and planning, (3) environmental uncertainties, (4) time horizons, (5) type and quality of forecasting information, (6) nature of jobs being filled, and (7) off-loading the work.[3]

1. Type and strategy of organisation

Depending upon the type of organisation requirement, the number and type of human resources at managerial and supervisory levels are decided. For example, whether production process is involved or service providing organisation. In the latter case organisations are simple in comparison to where manufacturing process is involved.

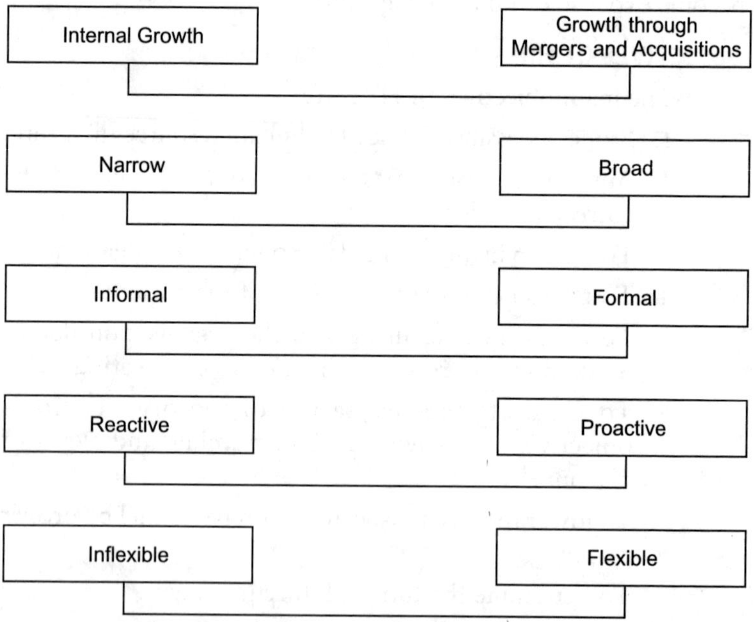

Fig. 2.1: Continual Strategic Choices in HRP

Source: K. Aswathappa, *Human Resource and Personnel Management,* Tata McGraw-Hill, New Delhi, 2006, p. 69.

Corporate strategic decisions affect the HRP decisions in the enterprise. Figure 2.1 summarises the key concepts in this regard.

An organisation will often tend to be to the left or to the right on all continua rather than to the left on some and to the right on other, although there could be exception.[4] If an organisation wants to adopt the strategy of internal growth, then more personnel are required. On the other hand, in case of Mergers and Acquisitions (M&As), HR manager must plan regarding lay-offs, retrenchment, etc.

In determining the breadth of the plan, organisation can choose a narrow focus by planning in just one or two areas of HR like recruitment and selection. Otherwise, it can choose a broad focus by planning in all HR areas including training and development, compensation, maintenance, etc.

Regarding the formality of the plan, an organisation can have an informal plan that is not well-written, just in the talks of managers. On the other hand, an organisation can have a formal plan, which is written very much in detail and equally supported by documentation and data.

An organisation can adopt the reactive or the proactive approach to HRP. In the proactive approach, an organisation will anticipate the personnel needs and plan and take action well in advance. On the other hand, in the reactive approach, an organisation will take action only when need arises.

Lastly, an organisation should take decision regarding flexibility. Flexible approach means the ability of HR plan to anticipate and deal with uncertainties. With the help of forecasting and other prediction techniques, the organisation tries to reduce the uncertainties. By this, organisation becomes easily adjustable and adaptable to its environment.

2. Organisational growth cycles and planning

The various stages of organisational growth cycles influence the HRP. In the inception stage of the organisation, there may not be any personnel planning. When the organisation enters the growth stage, then HR forecasting becomes necessary. More people are needed. When an organisation becomes mature then growth slows down. There is less flexibility and more formalized plans are there. Organisation may be planning about issues like retirement, etc. In the last stage, declining stage, the focus of HRP is different. Here, planning is done about lay-offs, retrenchment and offering VRS scheme.

3. Environmental uncertainties

An organisation does not operate in isolation. Environmental factors such as economic, political, socio-cultural, international conditions, etc. affect all organisations and thus HRP. All this necessitates changes to be made while formulating recruitment, selection and training and development programmes.

Table 2.1: The Degree of Uncertainty and Length of Planning Period

Short Planning Period-Uncertainty/Instability	Long Planning Period-Certainty/Stability
Many new competitors	Strong competitive position
Rapid changes in social and economic conditions	Evolutionary, rather than rapid social, political and technological change
Unstable product/service demand patterns	Stable demand patterns
Small organizational size, poor management practices (Crisis Management)	Strong management practices

Source: E.H. Burack and N.J. Mathis, *Human Resource Planning—A Pragmatic Approach to Manpower Staffing and Development,* Illinois, Brace-Park, 1987, p. 129.

4. Time horizons

Time factor also affects HRP. Planning about human resources will be different in case of a short-term period (ranging from six months to one year) and in case of a long-term plan (which spread from three to ten years). Table 2.1 highlights this point.

5. Type and quality of forecasting information

Organisations' strategic decisions and general information affects HRP decisions. Table 2.2 presents the type and levels of forecasting information beneficial for HRP.

6. Nature of jobs being filled

Vacancies in the organisation may be due to retirement, promotion, transfer, demotion, expansion and diversification

Table 2.2: Various Levels of HRP Information

Strategic Information	General Organisational Information	Specific Information Necessary for HRP
Product mix	Organisational structure	Job analysis
Customer mix	Information flows	Skills inventories
Competitive emphasis	Operating and capital budgets	Management inventories
Geographic limits of market	Functional area objectives	Available training and development programmes
	Production schedules	Recruitment sources
	Distribution channels	Labour market analysis
	Sales territories	Compensation programmes
	Production processes	Constitutional provisions and labour laws
	Level of technology	Retirement plans
	Planning horizons	Turnover data

Source: T.L. Leap and M.D. Crino, *Personnel/Human Resource Management,* Macmillan, New York, 1990, p. 161.

decisions. HR manager should be well aware in advance regarding the nature of job. For example, it is relatively easy to fill the vacancies of low-level workers than any managerial position.

7. Off-loading the work

Off-loading the work to other/outside parties through outsourcing, etc. is a regular feature in today's business environment. Thus, it affects decisions like further hiring, offering VRS to surplus labour, etc.

THE PROCESS OF HRP

The main steps involved in HRP are the following:

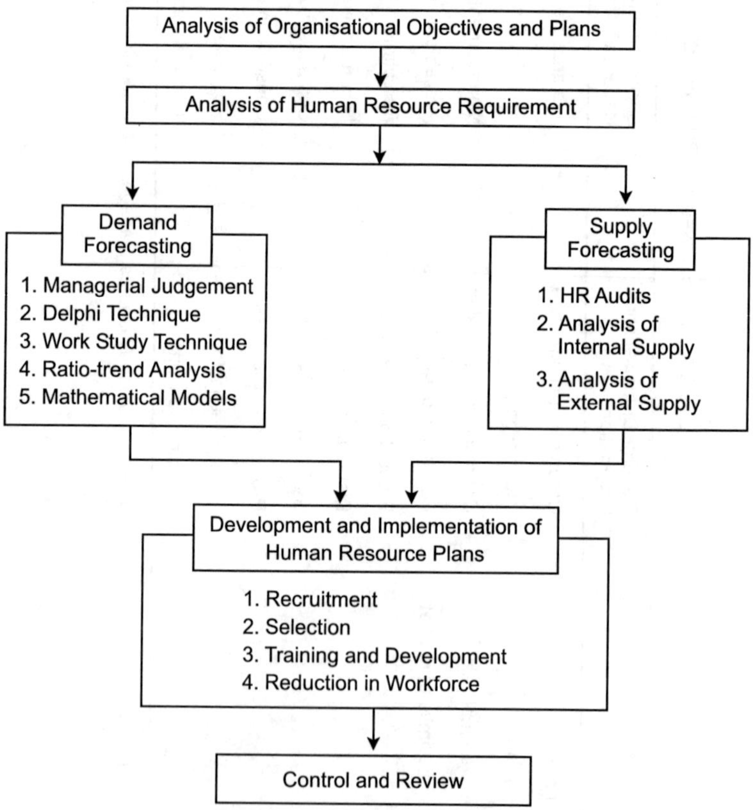

Fig. 2.2: The Human Resource Planning Process

I. Analysis of Organisation's Objectives and Plans

Firstly, the HR manager should consider the organisation's overall objectives and policies as the HRM objectives are derived from them. HR plans should be align with the organisation's plans for the success of the organisation. Consideration of the factors such as time period, organisation's strategic decisions (e.g. growth through M&A's or internal growth), flexibility, formality, etc. should be taken into account while formulating HR plans. The ultimate mission or purpose is to relate future human resources to future enterprise need so as to maximize the future return on investment in human resources.[5]

II. Analysis of HR Requirements

Manpower requirement can be analysed with the help of information provided by existing job analysis and job design information and future business objectives. The analysis can be divided into 2 parts:

(a) Demand Forecasting

(b) Supply Forecasting

(a) *Demand Forecasting*

It is the process of estimating organisation's future quantity and quality of people required. Overall business plans and annual budget acts as a base for demand forecasting. Various other environmental factors are also considered while forecasting such as expansion and growth, management philosophy, business forecasts, government policy, competition, etc.

The various forecasting techniques are:

1. Managerial judgement

This is one of the simplest forecasting technique. In this the managers judge about the future demand of the personnel. Managers who are experienced, well-acquainted with the requirements of jobs like workload, ability of employees, future capability, etc. discuss together and reach at the figure of demand of labour. After the estimation, the lower level managers submit their requirement to the higher level managers for consideration and revision if necessary.

2. Delphi technique

In this, estimates of personnel needs are obtained with the help of group of experts. Face-to-face contact is avoided. The HR manager acts as intermediaries, they obtain the responses from experts and re-consider them and report back to the experts. Again, the feedback is obtained from the experts through survey method. This technique is considered as qualitative demand forecasting technique.

3. Work study techniques

These techniques are more suitable where there is a possibility of work measurement. This is also called as workload analysis. In this, the volume of workload for the forthcoming years are analysed and on this basis, analysis of personnel requirement is done. Allowances are also made for absenteeism, idle time, labour turnover, etc.

4. Ratio-trend analysis

In this technique, the past ratios are studied and future ratios are forecasted after making some allowances for changes. Availability of past records and estimate of future changes is essential for using this technique.

5. Mathematical models

These are also used for demand forecasting. The commonly used technique is the following:[6]

$$E_n = \frac{(Lagg + G_n)^{1/x}}{y}$$

where

E_n = estimated level of personnel demand in n planning periods(e.g. years)

G_n = total growth in business activity anticipated through period n in today's rupees

Lagg = aggregate level of current business activity in rupees

x = average productivity improvement anticipated from today through planning period n

y = conversion figure relating today's overall activity to personnel required. It reflects the level of business activity per person.

(b) *Supply Forecasting*

Demand forecasting provides the HR manager the estimation of number and type of personnel required. Supply forecast provides information regarding the ability of organisation to procure the required number of personnel. It is concerned with the availability of personnel from within and outside an organisation. The supply forecast includes:

1. HR audits

This analyses the present employee's skills and abilities. The audits of managers are known as management inventories whereas that of non-managers are called as skill inventories. This gives the HR planners a detailed summary of the capabilities available in the organisation.

2. Analysis of internal supply

This involves the consideration of the following aspects:

(i) *Absenteeism*

According to Labour Bureau, Simla,[7] "Absenteeism is the total manshifts lost because of absences as a percentage of the total number of manshifts scheduled to work". Absenteeism refers to unauthorized absence from the work. In other words, it is the failure of a person to come to work when he is scheduled to work. Allowances should be made for the impact of absenteeism on the future supply of personnel. The management should find out the causes of absenteeism and take remedial measure. Algebraically, it may be expressed as follows:

Absenteeism Rate =

$$\frac{\text{Number of mandays lost}}{(\text{Average number of persons}) \times (\text{number of workdays})} \times 100$$

(ii) *Employee turnover*

HRP has an important aspect of labour turnover. Turnover is the rate of displacement of the personnel employed due to resignation, retirement, etc. Turnover refers to the movement into and out of an organisation by the workforce. This movement is an index of the stability of the workforce.[8] The measurement of turnover is important for determining the number of persons to be recruited at a particular time. It may be determined by separation rate method or replacement rate method.

Algebraically, it may be expressed as follows:

Turnover Rate =

$$\frac{\text{Number of separation (or replacement) in a period}}{\text{Average number of workers in the period}} \times 100$$

For example, if average workforce per month is 100 and there are 20 separations during that period then turnover rate:

$$\frac{20}{1000} \times 100 = 2 \text{ per cent}$$

Turnover is very costly for the organisation and management should take every effort to keep its level as low as possible.

(iii) *Productivity*

The productivity levels of the employees influence HR requirements. Rise in productivity of personnel will reduce the requirement and vice-versa.

(iv) *Analysis of inflows and outflows*

Analysis of inflows in an organisation (e.g. promotions, transfers) and outflows (e.g. resignations, retirements, discharges, promotions, transfers) provide an estimate of personnel requirement in the organisation.

(v) *Movement among the jobs*

Some jobs are sources of personnel for the other jobs, for example, secretaries may be obtained by the promotion of typists, branch managers are obtained from a pool of section managers.[9] Thus, anticipation of these movements among jobs from the past records will help to determine the personnel needed in future.

3. Analysis of external supply

Alongwith the internal supply analysis, there is a need to look for the prospective employees from the external sources. It is important to have new blood and new experience in the organisation. There are numerous sources of external supply such as universities, technical and management institutes, etc.

III. Development and Implementation of HR Plans

After the demand and supply forecast of the personnel, the next logical step is to obtain and maintain a balance between these two. This will ensure that organisation fills up its vacancies by the right number and right kind of employees at the right time. This is done by developing HR programmes and implementing them. Implementation refers to converting HR plans into action. As a part of HR plan implementation, there may be series of actions to be taken. Depending upon the situation programmes like recruitment, selection, training and development, retention, etc. are planned. Planning depends upon the situation. Like, if there is a situation of surplus labour in the organisation then management should not go for fresh hiring, offer schemes like VRS to its employees, plan gradually about retrenchment, etc. On the other hand, if it is the situation of shortage of employees then organisation can proceed for fresh recruitment, hire full-time and contractual employees, ask for overtime, etc.

IV. Control and Review

This is the final phase of HRP process. HRP need considerable amount of financial resources along with staff and time. Thus, a HR plan should have set targets to be achieved. Regular monitoring will reveal the deficiencies in HR plan so that corrective action should be taken well in time.

BARRIERS TO HR PLANNING

The major problems in the process of HRP are the following:

1. Time-consuming

People raise questions on the utility of comprehensive and time-consuming human resource planning. From management point of view, lot of man-hours go wasted while preparing an elaborate plan for human resources.

2. Expensive

As HRP is time-consuming, so it is an expensive exercise.

3. Inaccuracy

HRP involves forecasting the demand and supply of personnel required. Its effectiveness depends upon accurate projection which are not cent per cent accurate. Factors such as time, absenteeism, labour turnover, resignations, turbulent business environment, etc. bring inaccuracy in the final HR plan.

4. Lack of top management support

In an organisation, top management support is essential for the success of every plan. Availability of essential resources (e.g. funds) and willingness of everyone towards the HRP depends upon top management's interest and commitment. But, in case of HRP, management's unwillingness to commit funds makes it an unimportant task.

5. Employees resistance

Workers and tradc unions often resist the comprehensive and detailed HRP because of apprehensions such that it will end in increase in their workload, retrenchment and lay-offs.

6. Incompatibility

Often there is improper alignment between HR plans and corporate strategic plans. Information provided through HR plans is incompatible with the information used in the business strategy formulation. Importance wise top management stresses upon the financial forecasting rather than HR forecasting.

7. Approach conflict

Usually, there arises a conflict between the two approaches towards HRP, i.e. qualitative and quantitative. People following the quantitative approach consider it as a number game. On the other hand, people following the qualitative approach emphasize upon career development, promotions, training and development, etc. A proper balance is needed between both the approaches in HRP.

8. Environmental changes

Recent changes in the business environment (e.g. market fluctuations, technological development, new government rules) are the uncertainties which affect the estimates of human resources.

9. Lack of involvement

Lack of involvement of at least managers at all levels in the organisation makes HRP ineffective. Proper coordination is required among all managerial positions in the different departments for knowing the actual number and kind of personnel required. Usually, operating managers are not included in the exercise and this makes HRP ineffective.

PREREQUISITES FOR A SUCCESSFUL HRP

1. There should be a proper linkage between HR plan and organisational plan.
2. Top management support is essential.
3. Proper balance should be adopted between the qualitative and quantitative approaches to HRP.
4. Involvement of operating managers is necessary.
5. Proper alignment between short-term HR plans and long-term HR plans.
6. HR plan should have in-built flexibility in order to adopt environmental uncertainties.
7. Time period of HR plan should be appropriate to needs and circumstances of the organisation.

KEY TERMS

Absenteeism
Delphi technique
Demand forecasting
Human resource planning (HRP)
Labour turnover
Management inventories
Skills inventories
Supply forecasting

QUESTIONS

1. What do you mean by HRP and why it is important?
2. What are the objectives of HRP?
3. Explain the process of HRP.
4. What are the barriers to effective HRP?
5. What are the prerequisites for a successful HRP?
6. Discuss the factors affecting HRP.

ENDNOTES

1. David A. Decenzo and Stephen P. Robbins, *Personnel/HRM*, Third Edition, Prentice-Hall of India, New Delhi, 1989, p. 79.

2. Dale S. Beach, *Personnel—The Management of People at Work,* Fourth Edition, Macmillan, New York, 1980.
3. Terry L. Leap and Michael D. Crino, *Personnel/Human Resource Management,* Macmillan, New York, 1990, p. 159.
4. William P. Anthony, et al., *Strategic Human Resource Management*, Dryden Press, New York, 1993, p. 179.
5. A.F. Sikula, *Personnel Administration and Human Resource Development*, 1978, p. 148.
6. Eelmer H. Burack and Robert D. Smith, *Personnel Management—A Human Resource Systems Approach,* West Publishing, Minnesota, 1977, p. 128.
7. Indian Labour Statistics, Bureau of Labour, Simla, 1962, p. 16.
8. Edwin B. Flippo, *Personnel Management*, McGraw-Hill, New York, 1976, p. 127.
9. *Ibid.*

Job Analysis

3

LEARNING OBJECTIVES

After studying this chapter, you should be able to:

1. Understand the nature of job analysis
2. Identify the products and uses of job analysis
3. Understand the process of job analysis
4. Identify the problems associated with job analysis

Before the recruitment takes place it is essential to determine (1) the duties, responsibilities and requirements of a particular job (job description) and (2) the minimum acceptable human qualities essential to perform the job properly (job specification). This information is obtained with the help of job analysis. Exhibit 3.1 highlights the importance of job analysis.

Exhibit 3.1: Implementing the new strategy at U.S. Bank

U.S. Bank's new customer service and retention manager, Todd Berkley, discovered that focusing the bank's competitive strategy on customer service affected every aspect of the bank. Employees must now perform a multitude of new tasks. When they meet with customers closing their accounts, service reps now have to try to understand the customer's reason for leaving, and keep detailed records of frequent complaints. The bank is installing complaint identification initiatives to identify, track, and solve complaints in all branches, call centers and websites. Salesperson's must gather more information about customer preferences when they open new accounts. Employees across the bank have had to learn how to use the bank's new complaint-monitoring software. The bank designed new jobs to place care calls when customers complain. The bank is developing a new customer assurance unit, which will swing into action when high-value accounts are in danger of leaving.

All of which means Todd and his colleagues had to reanalyze all of the bank's jobs, from teller to guard to vice-president; add duties like those above to current lists of job functions; and create several new jobs (such as customer assurance manager), Todd and his colleagues found, in other words, they could not implement the bank's new strategy without a keen understanding of job analysis.[1]

Source: Gary Dessler, *Human Resource Management,* Pearson Education, 9th ed., Delhi, 2004, p.85.

KEY TERMS

Job analysis is a combination of two words 'job' and 'analysis', i.e. to analyse the job. Before discussing the term job analysis, first there is a need to clarify certain key terms.

Position

A position is a group of tasks assigned to one individual. There are as many positions in a firm as there are personnel.[2]

Job

It is defined as the collection or aggregation of tasks, duties and responsibilities which as a whole, are regarded as a regular assignment to individual employees.[3] In relation to positions, job can also be defined as a group of positions that are similar as to kind and level of work.[4] Thus, a job may include many positions. An employee has his position, but many positions may involve the same assignment of duties and constitute a single job.[5]

Occupation

Another related term is occupation. An occupation is a group of jobs that are similar as to kind of work and are found throughout the industry or the entire country.[6] So, occupation is a category of work found in many firms. In other words, occupation refers to a group of jobs with common characteristics.[7]

MEANING AND DEFINITION

Job analysis is the complete study of the job. It is a procedure by which facts with respect to each and every aspect of the job are discovered systematically. It refers to anatomy of the job. Some definitions of job analysis are given below:

1. Job analysis is the process of studying and collecting information relating to the operations and

responsibilities of a specific job. The immediate products of this analysis are job description and job specification.[8]

2. Job analysis is the process of getting information about jobs; specially what the worker does; how he gets it done; why he does it; skill, education and training required; relationship to other jobs, physical demands; environmental conditions.[9]

PRODUCTS OF JOB ANALYSIS

Job analysis is basically a process of data collection. The information collected after the job analysis can be divided into two categories. These are known as job description (JD) and job specification (JS). Figure 3.1 presents the products of job analysis in detail.

Job description is an organized factual statement of the duties and responsibilities of a specific job.[10] In other words, it provides information like job identification (titles, code numbers, etc.),

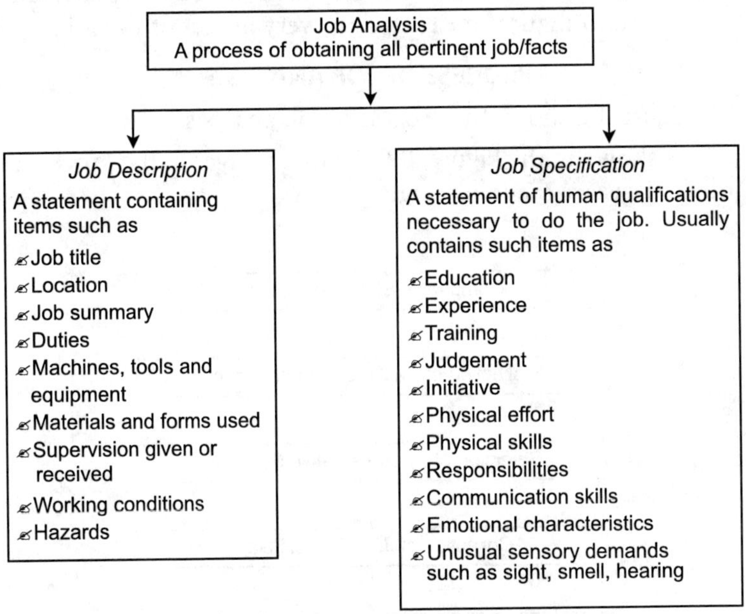

Fig. 3.1: Products of Job Analysis

Source: Dale S. Beach, *Personnel—The Management of People at Work*, Macmillan, New York, 1980, p. 166.

distinctive characteristics of the job (details regarding its location, physical setting, etc.), what the typical worker does (specific operations and tasks), what materials and equipment will be used by the workers, how the job is performed (operations involved). Whereas job specification is a statement of the minimum acceptable human qualities necessary to perform a job properly.[11] In other words, job specification refers to the personal attributes required.

OBJECTIVES OF JOB ANALYSIS

The major objectives of job analysis are as follows:

1. To clarify the methods and operations involved in a job.
2. To determine the minimum acceptable qualities of personnel required.
3. To provide information for other HRM functions like recruitment, selection, training and development etc.
4. To simplify the processes involved by providing information for each and every aspect of the job.

PROCESS OF JOB ANALYSIS

Figure 3.2 shows the process of job analysis.

As shown in the Figure 3.2, the basic stages in the process of job analysis are the following:

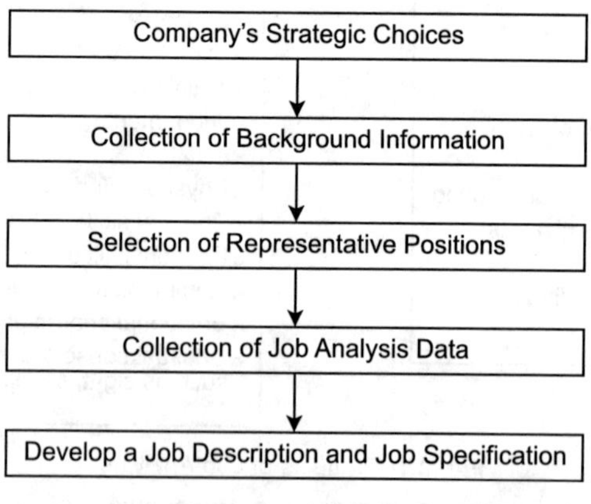

Fig. 3.2: The Process of Job Analysis

1. Company's strategic choices

Business strategies are the basis for any activity in an organisation including job analysis. Regarding job analysis, the companies have to make four strategic choices.

1. The extent of employee involvement in job analysis
2. The levels of details of job analysis
3. Timing and frequency of analysis, and
4. Past-oriented v/s future-oriented job analysis.[12]

2. Collection of background information

Now, review relevant background information such as organisation charts, process charts and job descriptions.[13] Organisational charts show how the job in question relates to other jobs and how it fits in the overall organisation. A process chart shows the flow of inputs to and outputs from the job under analysis. Lastly, the existing job description provides a starting point for making the revised job description.

3. Selection of representative positions

Analysis of all the jobs in a company will be very time-consuming and difficult. Moreover, there may be lot of similar jobs for analysis. Thus, it is logical to select few representative positions. For example, for the analysis of 350 assembly workers, a sample of 25 jobs will be sufficient.

4. Collection of job analysis data

This is the stage of actually analysing a job. This is done by collecting data on various job activities, working conditions, human abilities and required human behaviours.

5. Developing job description and job specification

These are the two visible products of job analysis. Job description is a document which is basically descriptive in nature and contains very vital information about the job. Job description is a written statement that describes the duties and responsibilities of the job. On the other hand, job specification summarises the human qualities, skills, traits and background essential for getting the job done.

WHO WILL PERFORM JOB ANALYSIS

Depending on the technique selected, job analysis is performed either by a member of the HR department or by the job holder/job incumbent (the person who is currently assigned to the job in question).[14] Person assigned for job analysis is known as job analyst.

METHODS OF COLLECTING JOB DATA

There are several methods to collect information on the duties, responsibilities and activities of a job. Data can be collected by using only one method or by combination of methods. Few factors like cost associated and job complexity will influence the selection of the method. Following are some methods of data collection:

1. Interviews

It is probably the most widely used method of data collection. The interviewer gathers complete and accurate data by conducting structured interview. Managers use three types of interviews to collect job analysis data—individual interviews with each employee, group interviews with groups of employees who have the same job and supervisor interviews with one or more supervisor who know the job.[15] Group interviews are where a large number of employees are performing similar or identical work. Whichever kind of interview method is adopted, the interviewer should create favourable conditions for the conduct of interviews. The important interview guidelines are the following:

- First, the job analyst and supervisor should work together to identify the workers who know the job best.
- Secondly, quickly establish rapport with the interviewee.
- Third, follow a structured guide, one that lists questions and provide space for answers.
- Fourth, when duties are not performed in a regular manner then ask the worker to list his/her duties in order of importance and frequency of occurrence. This will ensure that the important aspects are not overlooked.
- Finally, after completing the interview review and verify the data. Specifically, review the information with

the worker's immediate supervisor and with the interviewee.[16]

2. Observation

Here, the job analyst observes the jobholder actually performing the job and then records the key job characteristics from observation. Direct observation is good in case where the job is of routine nature and consists of mainly observable physical ability, for example, job of mechanic, draftsman, etc. This method is usually not appropriate where a job involves lot of mental activity (e.g. design engineer, lawyer, etc.).

3. Questionnaires

In this case well-drafted questionnaires are given to jobholders to fill them up. The questionnaires ask a series of questions about the job's knowledge, skills and ability requirements (KSAs), duties and responsibilities. Each question is associated with a quantitative scale that measures the importance of the job factor or the frequency with which it occurs. A computer can then tally the scores on the questionnaires and creates a printout summarising the job's characteristics.[17]

4. Diary method

In this method, the jobholders are asked to maintain diaries daily showing their job activities and also record the time spent on each activity. Later on, the job analyst will analyse the records and arrive at the job's characteristics.

5. Job/work performance

In this case, in order to get the first hand experience, the job analyst himself performs the work. But the use of this technique is very limited. This is a very time consuming method.

TECHNIQUES OF JOB ANALYSIS

Table 3.1 lists four major techniques of job analysis.

1. Position Analysis Questionnaire (PAQ)

It is a structured job analysis questionnaire which consists of 194 different items. Using a five-point scale, the PAQ seeks to determine the degree to which the items or job elements are

Table 3.1: Techniques of Job Analysis

Technique	Employee Group Focused on	Data Collection Method	Analysis Results
1. Position Analysis Questionnaire (PAQ)	Any	Questionnaire	Rating of 194 job elements
2. Management Position Description Questionnaire (MPDQ)	Managerial	Questionnaire	Checklist of 208 items
3. Functional Job Analysis (FJA)	Any	Questionnaire/ Group interview	Rating of how job incumbent relates to people, data, and things
4. Critical Incident Technique	Any	Interview	Behavioural description

Source: Adapted from Gomez Mejia et al., *Managing Human Resources*, Perason Education, Delhi, 2003, p. 67.

involved in performing a particular job.[18] The 194 job elements are grouped into six categories. These are as follows:

(i) **Information input**—Where and how a worker gets information needed to perform the job.

(ii) **Mental processes**—The reasoning, decision making, planning and information processing activities involved in performing the job.

(iii) **Work output**—The physical activities, tools and devices used by the worker to perform the job.

(iv) **Relationship with other persons**—The relationships with other people required in performing the job.

(v) **Job context**—The physical and social contexts in which the work is performed.

(vi) **Other characteristics**—The other activities, conditions and characteristics relevant to the job.[19]

2. Management Position Description Questionnaire (MPDQ)

MPDQ is a highly structured questionnaire containing 208 items relating to managerial responsibilities, restrictions, demands and other miscellaneous position characteristics.[20] The 208 items are organised into 13 sections as shown in Table 3.2.

Table 3.2: Management Position Description Questionnaire

1. Product, marketing and financial strategy planning.
2. Co-ordination of other organisational units and personnel.
3. Internal business control.
4. Products and services responsibility.
5. Public and customer relations.
6. Advance consulting.
7. Autonomy of actions.
8. Approval of financial commitments.
9. Staff service.
10. Supervision.
11. Complexity and stress.
12. Advanced financial responsibility
13. Broad personnel responsibility.

Source: Lloyd L. Byars and Leasile W. Rue, *Human Resource Management*, Irwin, 1997, p. 92.

3. Functional Job Analysis (FJA)

This is a worker-oriented approach. It attempts to describe the whole person on the job. FJA collects information on the following aspects of the job:

1. What the job incumbent does to people, data and things.
2. The methods and techniques the job incumbent uses to perform the job.
3. The machines, tools and equipment used by the job incumbent.
4. The materials, projects or services produced by the job incumbent.[21]

4. Critical Incident Technique

The critical incident technique is used to develop behavioural descriptions of a job.[22] In this, the employees and supervisors generate behavioural incidents of job performance. This technique involves the following four steps:

(i) Generate dimensions
(ii) Generate incidents

(iii) Retranslate

(iv) Assign effectiveness values.[23]

In the first step, dimensions refer to the various aspects of performance. Then, employees and supervisors generate critical incidents of behaviour which represents high, moderate and low levels of performance on each dimension. Finally, the last two steps ensure that critical incidents generated in the earlier two steps are commonly viewed by the same way by other workers.

USES OF JOB ANALYSIS

The products of job analysis, i.e. job description and job specification are necessary ingredient for all the HRM functions. The main uses of job analysis information are as follows:

1. Organisation audit

Job information obtained by job analysis often reveals instances of poor organisation in terms of factors affecting job design.[24] Thus, the process of job analysis constitute a kind of organisation audit.

2. Human resource planning

It determines the number and kind of personnel required in future. And number and kind of personnel required are determined by the jobs which needs to be staffed. Job analysis provides for the proper human resource planning.

3. Recruitment and selection

Job analysis provides information to manager regarding the required skills, qualifications, etc. in future for doing jobs. So, this helps in selecting the right number and kind of people at the right place.

4. Training and development programmes

Job description information regarding duties and responsibilities acts as a base for the content of training and development programmes.

5. Job evaluation

Job description and job specification of human requirements are evaluated in terms of worth. And the ultimate goal is to know the rupee value.

6. Performance appraisal

Job analysis information helps performance appraisal by fixing standards for work performance. Actual performance is compared and assessed in relation to set standards. This assessment acts as a base for promotions and training.

7. Induction

Job description is the most helpful tool for new employee's induction programme.

8. Compensation

Job analysis is the base for job evaluation. Compensation package depends upon job evaluation.

9. Safety and health

Job description informs regarding the unsafe and unhealthy conditions, hazardous substances, etc. So, corrective measures should be taken in advance.

10. Industrial relations

A job description is a standard of function. If an employee attempts to add to or subtract from the duties listed therein, the standard has been violated.[25] So, conflict, controversies and misunderstandings may arise. Written record of standard job description is essential in solving such disputes.

PROBLEMS IN JOB ANALYSIS

The main problems during the conduct of job analysis are as follows:

1. Lack of top management support

It is required from the top management to make it clear to all the employees that their whole-hearted participation is very important for the process of job analysis. But this is missing in most of the cases.

2. Dependence on a single method

Often the job analyst relies on only single method of data collection. However, the best results are provided by the combination of two or more methods.

3. Lack of training and motivation

Jobholders are the important source of information but they are neither trained nor motivated to generate quality information for job analysis. Moreover, they are very rarely made aware of the importance of providing accurate data.

4. Distorted activities

In the absence of any training or preparation, job holders will submit distorted information, may be intentionally or inadvertently.

Apart from these internal problems in job analysis, there are also external issues which affect the importance of job analysis, for example, flexible work system, Total Quality Management (TQM), team building and dejobbing. Dejobbing refer to broadening the responsibilities of the company's jobs and encouraging employees not to limit themselves to what's on their job descriptions.[26] Dejobbing has triggered broader HR issues. For example, "you must find people who can work well without the cue system of job descriptions".[27] Exhibit 3.2 provides an insight into dejobbing.

Exhibit 3.2: Job Analysis and Dejobbing

In British Petroleum's exploration division—the need for more efficient, faster acting, flatter organisations and empowered employees inspired management to replace job descriptions with matrices listing skills and skill levels.[28] Senior managers wanted to shift employees' attention from a job description/"that's-not-my-job" mentality to one that would motivate them to obtain the new skills they needed to accomplish their broader responsibilities. The emphasis is no longer on specific job duties. Instead, the focus is on developing the new skills needed for the employees' broader, empowered and often relatively undefined responsibilities.

Source: Gary Dessler, *Human Resource Management,* Pearson Education, 9th ed., Delhi, 2004, p. 84.

KEY TERMS

Dejobbing	FJA
Job analysis	MPDQ
Job description	Occupation
Job specification	PAQ
	Position

QUESTIONS

1. Define the term job analysis and what are its objectives?
2. Explain the process of job analysis.
3. What the various methods of collecting job data?
4. Discuss the techniques of job analysis.
5. What are the various uses of job analysis?
6. Bring out the problems associated with job analysis.

ENDNOTES

1. "Customer Retention: If You're Angry at the Bank, They Have Specialists on Your Case", *Financial Services Marketing* (January-February 2000), pp. 1, 2, 35.
2. Edwin B. Flippo, *Personnel Management*, Sixth Edition, McGraw-Hill, New York, 1984, p. 114.
3. Dale Yoder, *Personnel Management &Industrial Relations*, Prentice-Hall of India, New Delhi, 1967, p. 280.
4. *Ibid.*
5. *Ibid.*
6. Edwin B. Flippo, op. cit., p. 114.
7. Michael J. Jucius, *Personnel Management,* Richard D. Irwin, Inc., Homewood, Illinois, 1975, p. 91.
8. Edwin B. Flippo, op. cit., p. 110.
9. Jones, Jean, J. and Decothis, Thomas, A., Job Analysis National Survey Findings, *Personnel Journal*, October, 1969, p. 805.
10. Edwin B. Flippo, op. cit., p. 114.
11. Edwin B. Flippo, op. cit., p. 114.
12. William P. Anthony, et al., *Strategic Human Resource Management*, Dryden Press, New York, 1993, p. 208.
13. Richard Henderson, *Compensation Management: Rewarding Performance,* NJ Prentice Hall, Upper Saddle River, 1994, pp. 139-150.
14. Luis R. Gomez-Mejia, David B. Balkin and Robert L. Cardy, *Managing Human Resources,* Third Edition, Pearson Education, Delhi, 2003, p. 65.
15. Gary Dessler, *Human Resource Management*, Pearson Education, Ninth Edition, Delhi, 2004, p. 63.
16. *Ibid.*, p. 64.

17. Luis R. Gomez-Mejia, David B. Balkin and Robert L. Cardy, op. cit., p. 66.
18. McCormick, E., and Jeannerette, R., "The Position Analysis Questionnaire", S. Gael (Ed.), *The Job Analysis Handbook for Business, Industry and Government*, 1988, John Wiley & Sons, New York: pp. 880-901.
19. Luis R. Gomez-Mejia, David B. Balkin and Robert L. Cardy, op. cit., p. 70.
20. Lloyd L. Byars and Leasile W. Rue, *Human Resource Management,* Irwin, 1997, p. 90.
21. Luis R. Gomez-Mejia, David B. Balkin and Robert L. Cardy, op. cit., p. 70.
22. J.C. Flanagan, "The Critical Incident Technique", *Psychological Bulletin*, 51, pp. 327-358.
23. Luis R. Gomez-Mejia, David B. Balkin and Robert L. Cardy, op. cit., p. 68.
24. Edwin B. Flippo, op. cit., p. 124.
25. *Ibid*., p. 125.
26. Gary Dessler, *Human Resource Management*, Pearson Education, Ninth Edition, Delhi, 2004, p. 82.
27. Gilbert Siegel, "Job Analysis in the TQM Environment", *Public Personnel Management*, 25, No. 4 (winter 1997), pp. 485-494.
28. Milan Moravec and Robert Tucker, "Job Descriptions for the 21st Century", *Personnel Journal* (June 1992), pp. 37-44.

Job Design

4

LEARNING OBJECTIVES

After studying this chapter, you should be able to:

1. Describe the concept of job design
2. Describe the factors which affect job design
3. Identify the techniques of job design

After job analysis the next logical step is job design. People spend a great deal of time on the job and it is important to design jobs so that individuals feel good about their work.[1] Job design involves conscious efforts to organise tasks, duties and responsibilities into a unit of work to achieve certain objectives.[2] A HR manager should have a keen interest in the design and specification of individual jobs within the organisation. The design of the job should be such, that it may motivate the employee to execute it effectively. Technological changes and excessive specialisation have made the jobs very boring. Until and unless, the jobs are properly designed, the objectives of the organisation may not be effectively accomplished. Jobs should be designed in a way to increase employee motivation and performance.

More specifically, job design that increases employee access, comfort and flexibility are likely to influence motivation and productivity positively.[3] For example, Amoco Corp. (now a part of British Petroleum) in Denver reported a 25 per cent decrease in product cycle time, a 75 per cent decrease in formal meeting time, an 80 per cent reduction in duplicated files, and a 44 per cent reduction in overall space costs after offices were redesigned to facilitate teamwork.[4] (Also see Exhibit 4.1)

Exhibit 4.1: Job Design at Volvo Plant at Sweden

Job design receives considerable attention worldwide. At the Volvo truck assembly plant in Sweden, work teams have a great deal of autonomy. For example, these teams choose their own supervisor, assign the work among themselves, set their own outputs within specified limits, and assumes responsibility for quality control. In Kalmar, Sweden, Volvo designed an auto plant for teams of fifteen to twenty-five employees; each team handles a specific major task. Employees also receive immediate feedback on hourly production rates, which are displayed on screen.

Source: H. Koontz and H.Weihrich, *Essentials of Management*, Tata McGraw-Hill, 2002, p. 234.

MEANING AND DEFINITION

Some definitions of job design are given below:

1. Job design is the process of organizing work into the tasks required to perform a specific job.[5]
2. Job design integrates work content (tasks, functions, relationships), the rewards (extrinsic and intrinsic), and the qualifications required (skills, knowledge, abilities) for each job in a way that meets the needs of employees and the organisations.[6]
3. Job design has been defined as the specification of the contents, methods and relationships of jobs in order to satisfy technological and organisational requirements as well as the social and personal requirements of the job holder.[7]

PRINCIPLES OF JOB DESIGN

The main principles of job design are following:

1. To influence skill variety, provide opportunities for people to do several tasks and combine tasks.
2. To influence task identity, combine tasks and form natural work units.
3. To influence task significance, form natural work units and inform people of the importance of their work.
4. To influence autonomy, give people responsibility for determining their own working systems.

5. To influence feedback, establish good relationships and open feedback channels.[8]

OBJECTIVES OF JOB DESIGN

The main objectives of job design are as follows:

1. To meet organisational requirements. For example, higher productivity, technical efficiency, etc.
2. To meet the needs of employees individually. Behavioural scientists have continually stressed the importance of designing jobs and systems of work in a manner that will satisfy psychological and sociological needs of people. One of the most commonly cited human relations problems in this area of job design is employee dissatisfaction with jobs that are repetitive, narrow, meaningless, and routine.[9]
3. To integrate/align the needs of individual employee with the organisational requirements.

The above said objectives highlight the importance of job design. A job should be well-designed otherwise there may be problems like lower productivity, absenteeism, complaints, resignations, turnover, boredom, insecurity and other related problems.

FACTORS AFFECTING JOB DESIGN

Among the many factors that will affect job design are: (1) the proven values of specialization and repetitive operations, (2) changing technology, (3) labour union policies, (4) abilities of present personnel, (5) available supply of potential employees, (6) the interaction requirements among the jobs within the system, and (7) psychological and social needs of human beings that can be met by the job.[10] Figure 4.1 presents a clear picture of these factors.

I. Environmental Factors

The main environmental factors that influence job design are as follows:

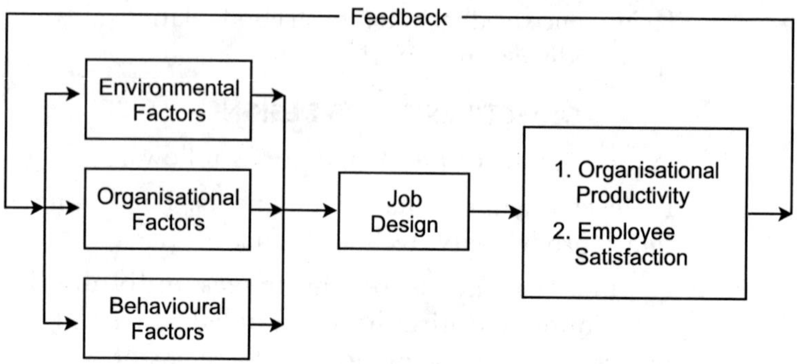

Fig. 4.1: Factors Affecting Job Design

Source: Adapted from *Human Resources and Personnel Management* by William B. Werther and Keith Davis, McGraw-Hill, New York, 1993, p. 147.

1. Availabilities and abilities of employees

There should be a proper match between efficiency consideration and availability and abilities of employees.

2. Expectations from the job

People have lot of expectations from a job and thus the jobs must be designed in order to meet employees' expectations, for example, social and cultural expectations. This includes rest breaks, religious beliefs, vacations, etc.

II. Organisational Factors

This includes factors like:

1. Work flow analysis

It seeks to ensure that each job in the organisation receives work as an input, adds value to that work and then passes it on to another worker.[11] During work flow analysis, sometimes few steps or even jobs are simplified or combined or even eliminated. Work is organised in a manner to meet the organisational production or service goals.

2. Organisation structure

Individual jobs must be properly fit in the overall organisation structure. For example, the autonomous work teams may do well in the decentralised organisation rather the centralised structure.

3. Business strategy

Overall corporate strategy also influences the job designing. For example, emphasis on highly specialised jobs involves more division of labour.

4. Organisational climate

It also influences job design. For example, groups may function well in an atmosphere that encourages participation, job enrichment and autonomous work, while they may not fit into an enterprise with an autocratic top-down approach to managerial leadership.[12]

5. Ergonomics

Ergonomics is science of adapting working conditions to employee safety and comfort needs.[13] In this a balance is sought between employee's physical abilities and job requirements.

6. Characteristics of task

Job design may require the assembly of a number of tasks into a job or a group of jobs. There may be only one main task for an individual to carry out. On the other hand, there may be a division of task functions among the team members. Further, in more complex and complicated jobs, employees may carry out a variety of related tasks.

7. Work practices

These are set ways to perform the work. Work practices may develop from traditional way of doing work. This limits the job design. Especially when such practices are a part of trade union-management relationship.

III. Behavioural Factors

This includes the following:

1. Employee needs

People having growth and development needs want to have jobs with greater responsibilities. Whereas, people having social needs want to work in groups/teams not individually.

2. Variety

Variety must be in jobs otherwise it's lack results in the boredom.

3. Feedback

Employees must get feedback regarding their job performance.

4. Autonomy

It refers to freedom to control one's activities. Jobs that give workers authority to make decisions will provide added responsibilities which tend to increase the employee's sense of recognition and self-esteem.[14]

5. Abilities

Individuals must perceive that they are utilising their abilities in doing the job.

TECHNIQUES OF JOB DESIGN

It refers to few options a manager has if he wants to change the makeup of employee's job or redesign it. Following are few approaches to job design:

1. Work simplification

In this, the work is broken down into simple and repetitive tasks that maximise efficiency. It utilises worker effectively to produce a larger amount of standardised product. For example, automobile assembly line which involves highly mechanical and repetitive tasks.

Work simplification is appropriate technique in a stable business environment but is less effective in a changing environment where there is great demand of custom-built products. Also, this approach often results in boredom, low satisfaction and turnover.

2. Job rotation

It refers to systematic movement of workers from one job to another without disrupting the flow of work. For example, on an auto assembly line; a worker whose job is installing carpets would be rotated periodically to a second workstation where she would install only seats in the car.[15] This technique relieves the employee from boredom, improves worker's skills and abilities, makes employee competent. However, job rotation may not have much impact on employee enthusiasm.

3. Job enlargement

It refers to the expansion of job content to include a wider variety. It expands duties of a job. In other words, additional same-level activities are assigned to workers. For example, instead of only sorting the incoming mail by department, a mail sorter's job could be enlarged to include physically delivering the mail; to the various departments.[16] The philosophy behind this approach is that enlarged jobs will be more intrinsically more satisfying to employees than highly specialised jobs. It is horizontal expansion of the job. Few research studies have shown that job enlargement results into reduced absenteeism and turnover, greater involvement of employees and motivate employees. However, according to Frederick Herzberg, job enlargement is simply "adding zero to zero".

4. Job enrichment

Job enrichment puts specialized tasks back together so that one person is responsible for producing a whole product or an entire service.[17] This approach tends to make jobs more interesting and to improve employee motivation (Fig. 4.2).

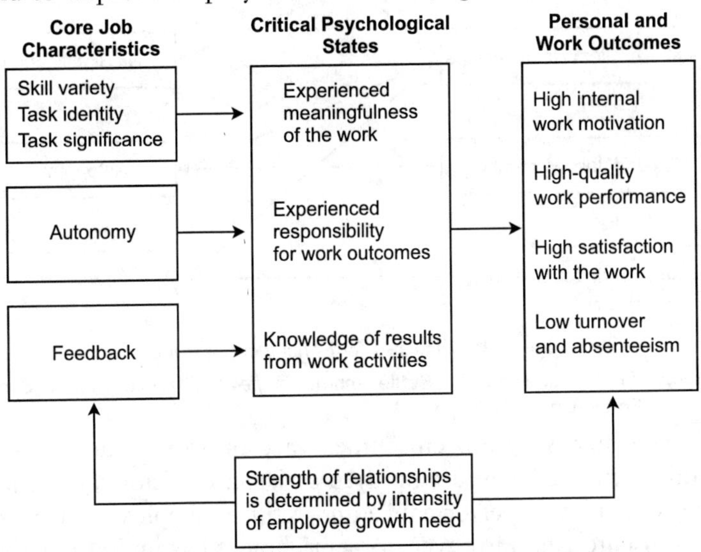

Fig. 4.2: Job Enrichment as a Technique of Job Design

Source: Gomez-Mejia et al., *Managing Human Resources,* Pearson Education, Delhi, 2003, p. 62.

Job enrichment refers to the vertical expansion of jobs. An enriched job organizes tasks so as to allow the worker to do a complete activity, increases the employee's freedom and independence, increases responsibility and provides feedback, so an individual will be able to assess and correct his or her own performance.[18] Job enrichment provides greater opportunities, autonomy and feedback to employees. But, the successful implementation of this approach to job design is limited by the production technology and employee's capabilities who produce the product or service. Figure 4.3 suggests few guidelines for management for enriching an employee's job. (Also see Exhibit 4.2).

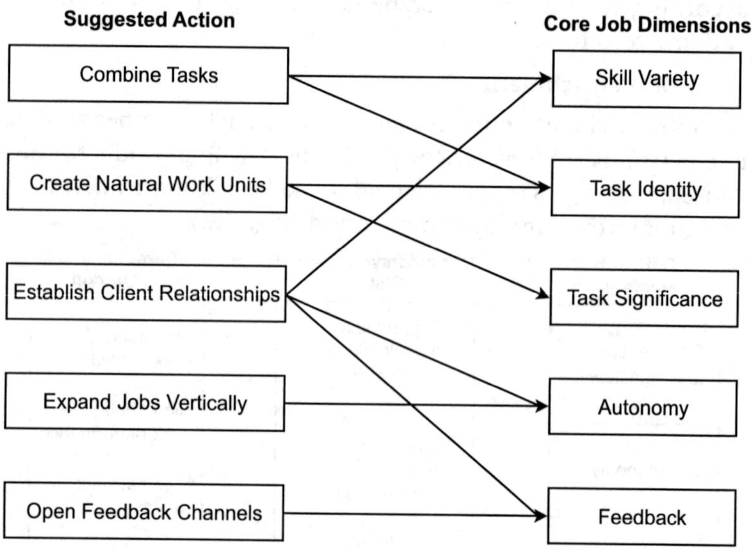

Fig. 4.3: Guidelines for Enrichment of a Job

Source: J.R. Hackman and J.L. Suttle, *Improving Life at Work*, Glenview, IL: Scott, Foresman, 1977, p. 138.

The merits of job enrichment are improved morale and productivity, increased employee satisfaction, motivation, job involvement and performance and reduced employee turnover and absenteeism. However, job enrichment has limitations too. It involves considerable time and investment. Workers show more interest in pay and job security rather than interesting jobs.

Moreover, some products are highly complex and require too many steps for one individual to produce them efficiently. Other products require the application of so many different skills that it is not feasible to train an employee in all of them. For example, it could take an employee a lifetime to master all the skills necessary to assemble an Airbus A380 aircraft.

Exhibit 4.2: Job Enrichment in Practice

To illustrate job enrichment, let's look at what management at Banc One in Chicago did with its international trade banking department. The department's chief product is commercial letters of credit—essentially a bank guarantee to stand behind huge import and export transactions. Prior to enriching jobs, the department's 300 employees processed document in an assembly line fashion, with errors creeping in at each handoff. Meanwhile, employees did little to hide the boredom they were experiencing from doing narrow and specialized tasks. Management enriched these jobs by making each clerk a trade expert who was able to handle a customer from start to finish. After 200 hours of training in finance and law, the clerks became full-service advisors who could turn around documents in a day while advising clients on such arcane matters as bank procedures in Turkey and U.S. munitions expert controls. And the results? Department productivity more than tripled, employee satisfaction soared and transactions volume rose more than 10 per cent a year.

Source: Stephen P. Robbins, *Organisational Behavior,* Pearson Education, Delhi, 2004, p. 474.

5. Self-managing teams/autonomous work teams

An autonomous or self-managing team is allocated an overall task. This technique shall focus on giving a team, rather than an individual, a whole and meaningful piece of work to do.[19] Work teams are responsible for a whole work process. Team members plan, execute and control the work processes together. Highly effective teams are composed of groups of committed individuals who trust each other; have a clear sense of purpose about their work; are effective communicators within and outside the team; make sure that everyone in the team is involved in decisions affecting the groups; and follow a process that helps them plan, make decisions and ensure the quality of their work.[20] (See Exhibit 4.3.)

Exhibit 4.3: Team-based Job Design

GM's Saturn division, located in Spring Hill, Tennessee emphasizes team-based job design. The process of assembling the Saturn car is accomplished by self-managed teams of 8 to 15 workers. Each team takes responsibility for managing itself. It interviews and hires new team members, manages its own budget and receives reports on the amount of waste it generates so that it can develop plans to utilize its materials more effectively.

Source: Geber, B., Saturn's Grand Experiment, *Training*, 1992, June, pp. 27-35.

For the success of a work team, managers should try to ensure that the following conditions are met: (1) individual members have the necessary task-relevant expertise to do their work; (2) the group is large enough to perform the work; (3) members possess interpersonal as well as task skills ; and (4) membership is moderately diverse in terms of talents and perspectives.[21]

6. High-performance job design

It concentrates on setting up working groups in environments where high levels of performance required. It starts from the principle of autonomous group working and develops an approach which enables groups to work effectively together in situations where the role of innovation is high.[22] Here, operational flexibility is important, therefore the need for employees to gain and apply new skills quickly with minimum supervision.[23] High performance work design requires the following steps:[24]

1. Management clearly defines what it needs in the form of new technology or methods of production and the results expected from its introduction.
2. Multi-skilling is encouraged—that is, job demarcation lines are eliminated as far as possible and encouragement and training are provided for employees to acquire new skills.
3. Equipment that can be used flexibly is selected and is laid out to allow freedom of movement and vision.
4. Self-managed teams or autonomous working groups are established each with around a dozen members and with full 'back-to-back' responsibility for

product assembly and testing, fault-finding and some maintenance.

5. Managers and team leaders adopt a supportive rather than an autocratic style.
6. Support systems are provided for kit-marshalling and material supply, which help the teams to function effectively as productive units.
7. Management sets goals and standards for success.
8. The new system is introduced with greater care by means of involvement and communication programmes.

Table 4.1: Job Design Approaches/Techniques

	Job Design Approach	Positive Outcome	Negative Outcome
1.	Work Simplification	Job is highly specialised, so that less trained and less paid employee can perform.	Over simplification results in boredom with attendant risks of errors and resignations.
2.	Job Rotation	Job's intrinsic reward potential is likely to increase. Organisation too stands to gain because of the versatility of its employees. Worker's self-image will grow. There is enhanced interdepartmental co-operation.	Jobs do not improve. Workers may feel rootless and alienated.
3.	Job Enlargement	Claims to have motivational impact.	Mere adding one zero to another zero-adding one more boring task to another. Likely to be resisted by employees.
4.	Job Enrichment	Increased motivation, reduced absenteeism, psychological needs of employees are met. Brings about empowered teams.	People may not like to accept new responsibilities. Union resistance adds to the problems. Job enrichment, if not accompanied by other job inputs, will fall in its goal.
5.	Autonomous Work Team	There is a greater involvement of employees in decision-making. Involvement brings in commitment.	There is a resistance from employees, unions and managers and supervisors.
6.	High Performance Work Design	Works in an environment of high rate of innovation and Operational Freedom.	May not work in large bureaucratic organisations.

Source: K. Aswathappa, *Human Resource and Personnel Management*, Tata McGraw Hill, New Delhi, 2003, pp. 107-108.

9. Thorough training is carried out on the basis of an assessment of training needs.
10. The payment system is specially designed with employee participation to fit their needs as well as those of management.
11. Payment may be related to team performance (team pay) but with skill-based pay for individuals.
12. In some cases, a 'peer performance review' process may be used which involves team members assessing one another's performance as well as the performance of the team as a whole.

Table 4.1 presents the positive and negative aspects of job design approaches/techniques.

KEY TERMS

Ergonomics	High performance work design
Job design	Self-managing teams
Job enlargement	Work flow analysis
Job enrichment	Work practices
Job rotation	Work simplification

QUESTIONS

1. Define the term job design and what are its objectives?
2. What are the factors affecting job design?
3. What the various approaches to job design?
4. Explain the following terms:
   (a) Job rotation
   (b) Job enrichment
   (c) Jon enlargement
   (d) High performance job design
   (e) Autonomous work groups.

ENDNOTES

1. Harold koontz and Heinz Weihrich, *Essentials of Management*, Fifth Edition, Tata McGraw-Hill, New Delhi, p. 233.

2. Barry Popplewell and Alan Wildsmith, *Becoming the Best,* 1998, p. 140.
3. E. Proper, "Surroundings Affect Worker Productivity", *Industry Week*, June 8, 1998, p. 14.
4. *Ibid.*
5. Luis R. Gomez-Mejia, David B. Balkin and Robert L. Cardy, *Managing Human Resources,* Third Edition, Pearson Education, Delhi, 2003, p. 62.
6. L. Mathis Robert and John H. Jackson, *Personnel—Contemporary Perspectives and Applications,* Third Edition, West Publishing Co., New York, 1982, p. 152.
7. L.E. Davis, The Design of Jobs, *Industrial Relations*, 1966, 6, pp. 20-32.
8. I.T. Robertson and M. Smith, *Motivation and Job Design,* IPM, London.
9. Edwin B. Flippo, *Personnel Management*, Sixth Edition, McGraw-Hill, New York, 1984, p. 106.
10. *Ibid.*
11. Luis R. Gomez-Mejia, David B. Balkin and Robert L. Cardy, op. cit., p. 63.
12. Harold Koontz and Heinz Weihrich, op. cit., p. 234.
13. Luis R. Gomez-Mejia, David B. Balkin and Robert L. Cardy, op. cit., p. 542.
14. William B. Werther and Keith Davis, *Human Resources and Personnel Management,* Fourth Edition, McGraw-Hill, New York, 1993, p. 148.
15. Luis R. Gomez-Mejia, David B. Balkin and Robert L. Cardy, op. cit., p. 63.
16. Stephen P. Robbins, *Organizational Behavior,* Tenth Edition, Pearson Education, Delhi, 2004, p. 473.
17. E. Lawler, *High Involvement Management*, Jossey-Bass, San Francisco, CA.
18. J.R. Hackman and G.R. Oldham, *Work Redesign,* Reading MA: Addison Wesley, 1980.
19. M.A. Campion and A.C. Higgs, "Design Work Teams to Increase Productivity and Satisfaction," *HR Magazine*, 1995, October, pp. 101-107.
20. S. Wellins Richard et al., *Empowered Teams,* Jossey-Bass Publishers, San Francisco, 1991, p. 22.
21. Stephen P. Robbins, op. cit., p. 475.

22. K. Aswathappa, *Human Resource and Personnel Management*, Tata McGraw-Hill, New Delhi, 2006, p. 107.

23. Michael Armstrong, *A Handbook of Human Resource Management Practice,* Third Edition, Kogan Page, London, 1988, p. 185.

24. D. Buchanan, "Job Enrichment is Dead: Long Live High Performance Work Design," *Personnel Management,* 1987, May, pp. 40-43.

Recruitment

5

LEARNING OBJECTIVES

After studying this chapter, you should be able to:

1. Understand the nature and importance of recruitment
2. Describe the factors which affect recruitment
3. Identify the sources of recruitment
4. Identify the techniques of recruitment

After completing the human resource planning and job analysis and job design the next logical step is the hiring of personnel in the organisation (Fig. 5.1). This involves recruitment and selection. Recruitment is discussed in this chapter. The next chapter deals with selection.

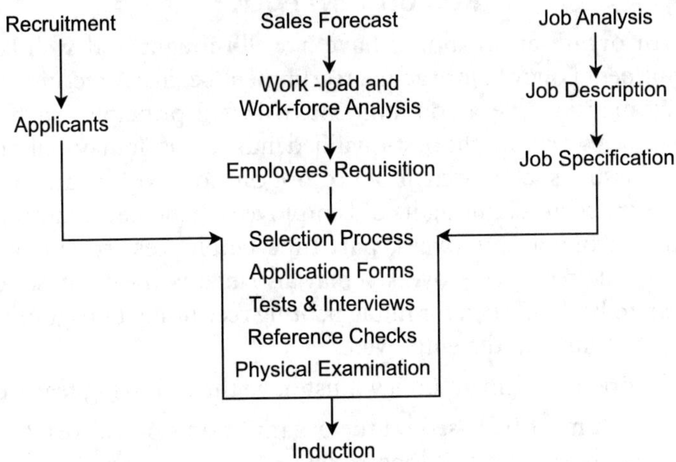

Fig. 5.1: Framework of Recruitment and Selection

Source: Adapted from Edwin B. Flippo, *Personnel Management,* Tata McGraw Hill, 1985, p. 148.

MEANING AND DEFINITION

Recruitment is the process by which a large number of prospective candidates are attracted by various methods to apply for the jobs. The formal definition of recruitment are as follows:

1. It is the process of searching for prospective employees and stimulating them to apply for jobs in the organisation.[1]
2. It is the process of generating a pool of qualified candidates for a particular job.[2]
3. It is the process to discover the sources of manpower to meet the requirements of the staffing schedule and to employ effective measures for attracting that manpower in adequate numbers to facilitate effective selection of an efficient working force.[3]

From the above definitions it is clear that the objectives of recruitment is to attract a large number of potential candidates for the jobs available. It is considered as a 'positive' concept. On the other hand, selection is often termed as 'negative' concept as it tends to eliminate applicants, leaving only the best to be appointed.

RECRUITMENT POLICY

An organisation should have a well-thought and well-laid recruitment policy before actual recruitment begins. A recruitment policy may involve a commitment to broad principles such as filling vacancies with the best-qualified individuals. It may embrace several issues such as extent of promotion from within, attitudes of enterprise in recruiting its old employees, handicaps, minority groups, women employees, part-time employees, friends and relatives of present employees. It may also involve the organisation system to be developed for implementing recruitment programme and procedures to the employed.[4]

A good recruitment policy must have the following features:

1. It must be based on the organisation's objectives, both short-term and long-terms.
2. Job analysis should take place well before recruitment.

3. It should clearly indicate the organisation's attitude toward employment of and reservations of women, physically handicapped, minorities, etc.
4. It should clearly lay down the long-term career plans for the workers.
5. It should clearly indicate the basis and extent of promotion in the organisation.
6. It should indicate the preferred sources of recruitment.

FACTORS AFFECTING RECRUITMENT

The factors affecting recruitment may be divided into two categories:

I. Internal Factors

This includes the following:

1. Organisation's growth and expansion plans
2. Organisation's human resource planning strategy
3. Recruitment policy of the organisation
4. Cost involved in recruiting employees
5. Organisation's size
6. Role of trade unions
7. Organisational culture
8. Company's image
9. Company's operations
10. Pay package of company
11. Quality of work life
12. Geographical spread of operations.

II. External Factors

This includes the following:

1. Socio-economic factors
2. Political and legal considerations like reservations of jobs for SC/ST/BC/PH, etc.
3. Supply and demand of specific skill in labour market
4. Employment rate

5. Technological factors
6. Employment exchanges.

SOURCES OF RECRUITMENT

Recruitment sources can be divided into two groups: (1) Internal sources and (2) External sources.

I. Internal Sources

This includes:

1. Current/present employees

Many companies adopt the policy of informing first the present employees about job opening before going for other sources. This result in either promotion or transfer within the organisation. However, it automatically creates another job opening that has to be filled.

2. Former employees

These are the persons who were once employees of the company, for example, laid-off, seasonal workers, etc. The company may decide to recruit these employees. These are safe hires as the employer already has experience with these people.

3. Referrals from current employees

Sometimes the companies may allow the current employees to recommend new recruits. This is a good source, as the current employee knows both the company and his acquaintances (for example, family member/friends) and hopefully would try to do please both. Studies have shown that employees who were hired through referrals from current employees tended to stay with the organisation longer and displayed greater loyalty and job satisfaction than employees who were recruited by other means.[5]

4. Previous-applicants

Although not truly an internal source, those who have previously applied for jobs can be contacted by mail, a quick and inexpensive way to fill an unexpected opening.[6]

Advantages of internal recruitment sources

1. It is less costly than the external recruiting.

2. It raises the morale of employees, as they are preferred than outsiders.
3. It promotes loyalty among the employees.
4. It provides a sense of job security and opportunities for advancement.
5. As the present employees are fully acquainted with the company so training can be reduced.
6. It gives a sense of recognition for employees.
7. As the current employees are tried and tested people so it's easy to rely upon them.
8. Internal recruiting has trade union support also.
9. It enhances company's social responsibility image.
10. The company is in a better position to evaluate the performance of present employees before considering them for promotions, thus reduces labour turnover, etc.
11. Internal recruiting helps retention.
12. It motivates the current employees to prepare themselves for higher posts.

Disadvantages of internal recruitment sources

1. Creativity may be hindered by the lack of new talents.
2. It limits the choice to few employees only.
3. It leads to inbreeding and discourages new blood from entering into company.
4. Sometimes it may be difficult to find the required person from within the company.
5. Here, likes and dislikes of the management also play their role. So, great chances of biasness.
6. As promotions are seniority basis, so meritorious people may go unconsidered.
7. During the period of expansion and growth requiring large people, internal sources may not be adequate.

II. External Sources

Although companies fill the positions from within as it is easy and economical but over the years, companies have gone for the external sources. Need arises may be due to expansion, growth, diversification, vacant lower level positions, etc. external sources lie outside the company. These usually include:

1. Advertisement

It is the most frequently used method to attract candidates. Companies advertise in newspapers, magazines, trade journals, etc. An advertisement should be well-thought out. The main objectives of an advertisement should be based on the concept of AIDA, i.e.

(1) Attract attention of readers
(2) Generate interest in the vacancy
(3) Arouse desire for the job
(4) Generate action.

A company may take help of an advertising agency on the choice of media (TV, press, etc.) and its cost. Local newspaper can be a good source of blue-collar workers, clerical employees and lower-level administrative employees.[7] According to *Advertisement Tactics and Strategy in Personnel Recruitment*, three points need to be borne in mind before an advertisement is inserted. First, to visualize the type of applicant one is trying to recruit. Second, to write out a list of the advantages a company offers, in other words, why the reader should work for the company. Third, to decide where to run the advertisement, not only in which area but in which newspaper having a local, state or nation-wide circulation.[8]

2. Employment exchanges

As per the provisions of the Employment Exchanges (Compulsory Notification of Vacancies) Act, 1959, a number of employment exchanges have been set up all over India. The main functions of employment exchange are registration of job-seekers and their suitable placement. They maintain separate records for non-graduates, graduates and postgraduates. Whenever employers have vacancies in their organisations', they will intimate the exchange and in return, exchange will forward names of suitable candidates to employers.

3. Campus recruitment

Many companies make special efforts to establish and maintain constructive relationships with professional colleges and universities (e.g. IITs, IIMs, TISS, etc.) in order to get qualified personnel. These companies send their representatives to interview the candidates at the campuses. The short-listed candidates may be further interviewed at the company's premises later on. However, this technique is very expensive.

4. Consultants/private agencies

There are consulting agencies that act mediator between the firm and the prospective candidates, for example, ABC Consultants, Human Resource Consultants, etc. (see Exhibit 5.1). Organisations rely on these agencies for recruiting executive and managerial personnel. These agencies will bring together the employees and job-seekers for which they will charge fees either from the employers or the job-seeker or sometimes from both. It costs money, but it can save a lot of time and transfer.

Exhibit 5.1: Process of Recruitment and Mobilization at Creative Enterprise—Manpower Consultants

Employing company has to provide us detailed job description, qualification, experience and candidate specification and other information with the principal's special knowledge relating to the position to be filled, condition of employment, number of employees required for each classification and approximate date on which the employees are required in order to enable us to carry out service. We will conduct the search, release the advertisement if required with the consent of the principal and pre-screening of candidates in connection with the selection and requirements of Indian nationals for the employing company. All advertisement will be undertaken by us only with the principal's prior written approval.

We will screen application and resumes received. The competence of each person being considered for employment shall be evaluated solely on the basis of the specific requirements of the particular job to be filled. Those candidates whose application and resume indicate that they possess the minimum qualification for the position to be filled will be interviewed by us. During the interview we will evaluate the candidates on the basis of job specification, collect personal data, like the complete history, qualification, experience, areas he worked, present drawing salary, expected salary, availability, etc. and short listed resumes will be forwarded to the employing company. Subsequently, interview with the short listed candidates would be arranged as per the schedule of the principlas. After the final interview, the offer of employment shall in all cases be made by us to the candidates only after we have received employing their visas and complete other procedures for the mobilization as per the schedule of the employing company.

Source: www.hrnext.com

5. Labour contractors

Some firms employ contractors to recruit casual workers. This is a commonly used method when the work is of temporary nature.

6. Unsolicited applicants

Sometimes the job-seekers send their applications in the office of company without any invitation from the company. Whenever there is vacancy in the company, recruiter can consider the unsolicited applications.

7. Leasing

This is commonly used to meet short-term urgent requirements of employees, leasing employees by the hour/day. In this case, the company escapes from the liabilities of making payments for pension, insurance, etc.

8. Data banks

Company's HR department can collect the bio-data of candidates from different sources like employment exchange, campuses, etc. and store/save in the computer. Whenever need arises, it will be a ready source of recruitment.

9. Competitors

Generally organisations attract the suitable candidates from their competitors in the industry. They may be offered higher pay package or more benefits, etc. This is very common in today's competitive era. For instance, the pilots from Air India and Indian are leaving for Jet Airways, Kingfisher, Air Deccan, etc.

10. Internet recruitment

This uses internet to advertise vacancies and enable e-mail communications to take place between employers and candidates. On-line ads are cheaper and produce fast results. Moreover, the reach of the internet has expanded dramatically so companies can connect with the people all over the world who are looking for jobs.[9] Initially, internet was used mainly for IT jobs but now it is increasingly being used for professional and managerial jobs.

11. Walk-in interviews

In the busy organisations candidates are advised to attend directly the walk-in interviews on the prescribed time and date. No prior applications are required. This is very economic in nature.

Advantages of external sources

1. Organisation will have a right type of candidate with required qualifications in the right number.
2. New talent and skill entered into the organisation.
3. As the employees are selected from a pool of candidates so best selection is made.
4. It is easy to compliance with reservation policy.
5. Fresh candidates may bring good changes in the organisation. Old but not productive work practices may be erased gradually.

Disadvantages of external sources

1. It reduces the morale of insiders because outsiders are preferred.
2. It may deny career advancement schemes.
3. In some cases, outsiders may require initial training, which is quite expensive.
4. Outsiders need more time to adjust into new environment.
5. Sometimes lack of proper recruiting time results later on in faulty selection of employees.
6. It is costly.

METHODS/TECHNIQUES OF RECRUITMENT

Various methods of recruitment can be divided into three categories:

I. Direct Methods

1. Sending recruiters to:

(a) Educational and professional institutes
(b) Conventions and seminars
(c) Fairs or desired centers.

2. Recruiting at the factory gate.

II. Indirect Methods

1. Advertising in/or:
   (a) Newspapers
   (b) Trade journals
   (c) Technical magazines and brochures
   (d) Radio and TV
   (e) Internet
   (f) Professional journals.

III. Third Party Methods

1. Public/state employment agencies
2. Private employment agencies
3. Placement cell of professional colleges and campuses where complete bio-data and other particulars are available
4. Employment referrals
5. Trade unions
6. Casual labour or applicant at the gate
7. Unsolicited applications
8. Data banks
9. Recruiting agencies
10. Leasing.

EVALUATION OF RECRUITMENT PROGRAMME

There should be a periodical assessment and judgement of sources for recruiting (manpower supply). This will explain the degree of success in obtaining competent personnel. For each major category of jobs, present personnel can be evaluated in terms of job success. If a correlation is discovered between successful personnel and particular labour sources, those sources should be further developed with money and effort.[10] For evaluation, the organisation may adopt criteria such as the applicant/hiring ratio, cost per applicant, performance appraisals, tenure, grievances, disciplinary action, etc. First of all, the organisation should identify how an applicant was attracted towards the company. Question like "How you came to know about this job vacancy?" After that, it should be checked that whether any one method has attracted consistently better applicants. Finally, use all this information in order to improve the recruiting process.

RECRUITMENT PROCESS

Figure 5.2 shows the recruitment process in general.

LIMITATIONS OF RECRUITMENT

Few constraints in the way of good recruitment are as follows:

1. Unattractive jobs

It would be difficult for recruiters to attract people towards a job which is considered as boring, lacking promotion potential, hazardous, etc.

2. Trade unions

At some times, powerful trade unions emphasise on recruitment from trade union members only.

3. Image

If a firm does not enjoy goodwill in the market or not socially responsible, least number of candidates would be interested in joining it.

4. Paucity of desired expertise

If the desired experts may not be available or may be available to a limited extent, this creates a problem for the organisation.

5. Location

If a firm is located in an area where there is a shortage of manpower supply then it may not be easy to get the required number of candidates.

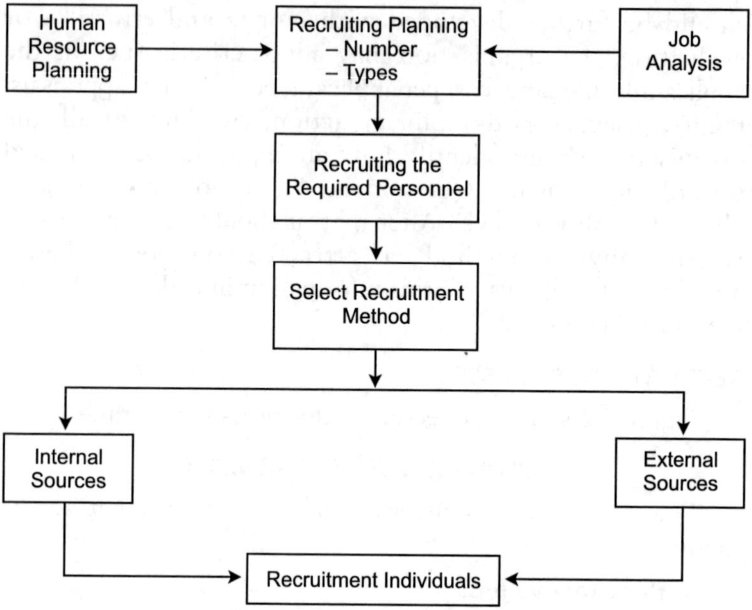

Fig. 5.2: The Recruitment Process

6. Immobility

Labour is not so mobile as other production factors. For example, married women hesitate to take jobs at distant places, etc.

KEY TERMS

Campus recruiting
Consultants
Employment exchanges
Internet recruiting
Leasing
Recruitment
Recruitment policy
Walk-in interview
Unsolicited applicants

QUESTIONS

1. Define the term recruitment and bring out its importance.
2. Write a note on recruitment policy of an organisation.
3. What the various factors affecting recruitment?

4. What the various sources of recruitment?
5. Bring out the techniques of recruitment.
6. Explain the limitations of recruitment.

ENDNOTES

1. Edwin B. Flippo, *Personnel Management*, Sixth Edition, McGraw-Hill, New York, 1984, p. 141.
2. Luis R. Gomez-Mejia, David B. Balkin and Robert L. Cardy, *Managing Human Resources,* Third Edition, Pearson Education, Delhi, 2003, p. 167.
3. Dale Yoder, *Personnel Management &Industrial Relations*, Prentice-Hall of India, New Delhi, 1967.
4. D. Yoder, H.G. Heneman, J.G. Turnbull and C.H. Stone, *Handbook of Personnel Management and Labour Relations*, McGraw-Hill, New York, 1968, pp. 7.2-7.5.
5. S.L. Rynes, "Recruitment, Job Choice and Post Hire Consequences: A Call for New Research Directions", in M.D. Dunnette and L.M. Hough (Eds.) *Handbook of Industrial and Organizational Psychology* (2nd Ed.), 1991, Vol. 2, pp. 399-444, Palo Alto, CA: Consulting Psychologists.
6. L. Mathis Robert and John H. Jackson, *Personnel—Contemporary Perspectives and Applications,* Third Edition, West Publishing, 1982, p. 180.
7. Pell, Arthur, *Recruiting and Selecting Personnel,* Regents, New York, 1969, p. 16.
8. National Advertising Service, *Advertising Tactics and Strategy in Personnel Recruitment*, Cleveland, Ohio, 1966, pp. 4-9.
9. K. Komando, "Job Hunt Made Easier by Variety of Online Sites," *Arizona Republic*, 1999, April 26, E2.
10. Edwin B. Flippo, op. cit., p. 146.

Selection

6

LEARNING OBJECTIVES

After studying this chapter, you should be able to:

1. Understand the nature and importance of selection in organisations
2. Describe the selection process
3. Identify the constraints in the effective selection
4. Describe the importance of preliminary interview

Once a pool of candidates has been developed from recruiting effort, the next step in the employment process is determining qualified candidates. This chapter will discuss the various stages in a selection procedure.

MEANING AND DEFINITION

1. Selection is the process by which all candidates are divided into two groups, viz. those selected and those rejected.[1]
2. It is the process of differentiating between applicants in order to identify (and hire) those with a greater likelihood of success in a job.[2]
3. It is the process of screening job applicants to ensure that the most appropriate candidates are hired.[3]

From the above definitions, it is clear that selection is the process of choosing from a pool of candidates, the most suitable person for the current position or for future positions. Generally, any selection decision can result in four possible outcomes. Two of those outcomes would indicate correct decisions and two would indicate errors (Fig. 6.1).

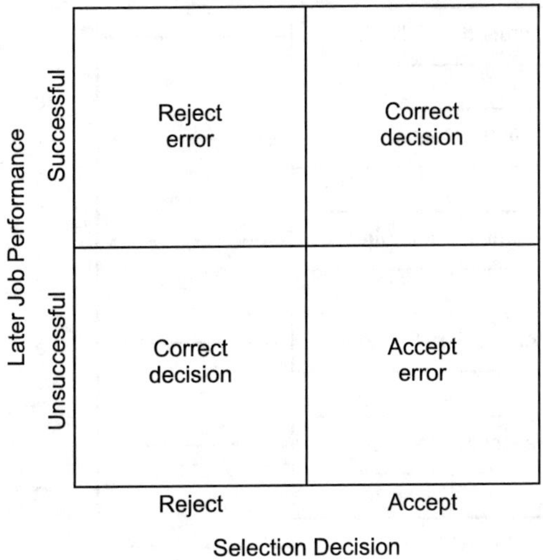

Fig. 6.1: Selection Decision Outcomes

Source: S.P. Robbings and D.A. Decenzo, *Fundamentals of Management*, Pearson Education, 2002, Delhi, p. 191.

As shown in Figure 6.1, a decision is correct (1) when the applicant was predicted to be successful (was accepted) and later proved to be successful on the job or (2) when the applicant was predicted to be unsuccessful (was rejected) and, if hired, would not have been able to do the job. In the former case, we have successfully accepted and in the latter case, we have successfully rejected. Problems occur, however, when we reject candidates who, if hired, would have performed successfully on the job (called reject errors) or accept those who subsequently perform poorly (accept errors). These problems, are, unfortunately, far from insignificant.[4] Earlier, reject errors only meant that costs of selection were increased. But nowadays, the selection technique that result in reject errors can open the organisation towards charges of discrimination.

SELECTION PROCEDURE/PROCESS

Selection is a long process commencing from the initial contact with the applicants and ending with the contract of employment. All the stages between first and last step seems to be successive hurdles or barriers for candidates. Qualified candidates will go

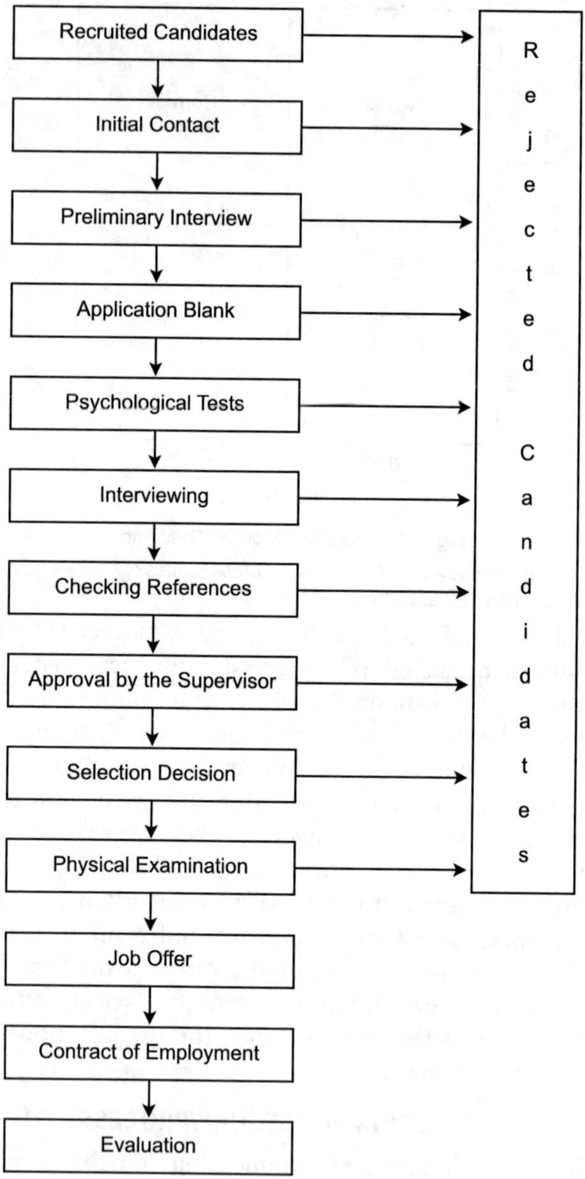

Fig. 6.2: The Selection Process

on to next hurdle, while the unqualified are eliminated. Figure 6.2 shows a model selection process.

I. Initial Contact/Reception of Applicants

Initial contact with the candidates is usually made through their applications for the jobs in the company. Almost every organisation maintains a proper record of applications received in their employment office.

II. Initial/Preliminary Interview or Screening

This is an introductory interview, which is quite short and just aims at elimination of the obviously unqualified. This is generally done to weed out those who do not possess the minimum requirements laid down for the vacancies. However, care should be taken that this weeding out process does not lead to elimination of desirable candidates.

In this preliminary interview, on one hand, the applicants are provided with the necessary information regarding the nature of jobs in the organisation. On the other hand, necessary information is elicited from the applicants regarding their education, experience, desired salary, reasons for leaving their current jobs, time required to join the job, job interest, etc. If the candidate suits to the organisation's requirements then will be taken into consideration for further selection phases otherwise he or she would be eliminated at this stage itself.

III. Application Blank/Form

This is one of the most common device for getting factual information. This is a universally accepted tool for gathering relevant information from the applicant which may be of vital importance to the management for making proper selection. Although the application blanks may differ from organisation to organisation but still there is high degree of similarity among the application forms of various organisations. Following are the main classes of information usually sought through the application blank:

1. Biographical data

This includes name, father's name, age, sex, nationality, marital status, height, weight, number of dependents and identification marks.

2. Education

This includes the courses and subjects studied and grades secured. The common practice in India is to start from 10th/Matric level onwards. Organisation look at class division (First/Second/Third class) and percentage of marks obtained.

3. Experience

This includes the previous work experience of the applicant. It shows the years of experience, nature of duties and responsibilities involved in the previous job.

4. Personal items

This includes extra-curricular activities (NSS/NCC/NSO), hobbies, association memberships, etc.

5. Salary and other benefits

This includes present and expected salary, perks, other fringe benefits, etc.

6. References

This is a common practice everywhere. This includes the letters of recommendations from the previous employers, departmental head and teachers. Care should be taken not to ask embarrassing questions or questions that can be easily misinterpreted. Some firms are now attempting to analyse the relationship between data items on application and the extent of job success. This kind of application blanks are known as weighted application blanks.

IV. Psychological Tests

These are the most carefully designed instruments. Tests provide a systematic criteria/base for selecting the candidates. Test designed to measure mental alertness, special aptitude, achievement, physical dexterity, etc. are used by an increasing number of organisations as an aid in the selection of prospective candidates.[5] Tests seek to eliminate the possibility that the prejudice of the interviewer or supervisor instead of potential ability, will govern selection decisions.[6] As psychological testing is a comprehensive and complex subject, it will be discussed in detail in the next chapter.

V. Interviewing

Interviewing is probably the oldest method of selection. If given an option of a single tool for selection, perhaps every organisation will choose interviewing. A substantial amount of subjectivity and therefore, unreliability, is to be expected from interviewing when used as a tool of evaluation.[7] Despite its subjectivity the interview is useful and can be improved in accuracy. The use of structured formats with the same or similar questions used for all applicants for a particular job will increase reliability.[8] Interview will also be discussed at greater length in the next chapter along with psychological tests.

VI. Checking References

Checking references and investigating background information is the most common in selection procedures. It is economical, less time consuming and requires minimum efforts. Opinions of previous employers, departmental heads, university/college professors are generally used in getting a clear picture of candidate's potential performance in a particular job. For checking references, organisation may seek letters of references or sometimes telephone references or through mail or occasionally personal visits.

VII. Approval by the Supervisor

This selection device is of great practical significance. Once a candidate has successfully cleared the earlier barriers, next is to handover that candidate to the concerned supervisor for acceptance or rejection. Although this third interview may involve some amount of overlapping but still it is very important for at least two reasons. First, the organisation relationships often require that the supervisor be given the right to pass upon personnel, otherwise he or she cannot be held accountable for their performance.[9] This maintains the principle of authority and responsibility. Secondly, the qualities that are generally appraised in an interview are highly intangible such as personality, ability to get along with others, etc. In such matters, it is helpful to have an appraisal by both the staff employment interviewer and the supervisor, who is better acquainted with the actual job conditions and the type of personnel at present in the department.[10]

VIII. Selection Decision

Once a candidate has passed the preceding steps successfully one by one, now the critical decision is of finally picking the candidate. The final decision has to be made from the pool of individuals who pass the tests, interview and reference checks.[11]

IX. Physical Examination

Generally, organisations require that a candidate goes through a physical examination before he or she can be finally accepted for the job. There are some jobs which require unusual strength, stamina or tolerance of hard working conditions. Thus, only a physical examination can reveal whether a candidate possess those qualities or not. It is in the interest of both the organisation as well as the candidate. For instance, in case of a textile company, a candidate having breathing problem will not be physically fit to do the job. Thus, it would be costly for the organisation if it selects that candidate, as it has to again recruit new persons. Moreover, candidate will loose health as well as the job. Physical examination also helps the organisation to prevent communicable diseases from entering the organisation. Also it safeguards the interest of the hiring company against payment of claims under compensation law. Generally, a physical test includes:

1. Measurement of weight, height, etc.
2. Quick examination of eyes, ears, throat, etc.
3. Quick examination of respiratory system
4. Checking of lungs and chest
5. Check up of blood pressure
6. Test of urine, blood, etc. in the lab
7. Bronchial problems leading to nervousness, tuberculosis, etc.

X. Job Offer

Job offer is made through appointment letter to those candidates who have passed all the earlier barriers. It means a person has successfully cleared all written tests, interviews, approved by supervisors, stands good in various inquiries, and is medically declared fit. After all this, appointment letter is formally given to the candidate. This will indicate the time and place of reporting. Usually, a sufficient time is provided for reporting. If the candidate was already in job, he should bring relieving certificate from the previous organisation.

XI. Contract of Employment

Once an organisation made a job offer and the candidate accepts the offer, then there is need to prepare and execute a contract of employment. Generally, this includes the following items:

(i) Job title
(ii) Duties in detail
(iii) Date when continuous employment starts
(iv) Remuneration and method of payment
(v) Working hours, overtime, lunch and tea break, etc.
(vi) Details of holidays
(vii) Sickness rules
(viii) Length of notice due to and from employee
(ix) Grievance handling system
(x) Disciplinary procedure
(xi) Work rules
(xii) Conditions of termination of employment
(xiii) Terms of union memberships
(xiv) Employer's right to vary terms and conditions of contract subject to proper notification being given.

Proper care should be taken while drafting the contracts. Generally, organisations take the help of law firms/agencies for drafting and finalising the contracts.

XII. Evaluation of Selection Procedure

Finally, there should be an assessment of the selection process of organisation. Success of a good selection process was the availability of competence, qualified and committed persons in the organisation. Organisations must conduct a period audit by people who work independently of the HR department.

BARRIERS TO EFFECTIVE SELECTION

These includes the following:

1. Pressure to hire

There is a pressure upon selectors from friends, politicians, family, peers, etc. to hire particular applicants.

2. Fairness

This demands no discrimination on the basis of religion, caste, gender or race. But in practice, women are discriminated against male members in certain jobs. People from urban areas have upper hand against rural area applicants.

3. Perception

It refers to our ability to understand others. All persons perceive the world differently. Selection demands an individual or group of people to assess and compare the respective competencies of others, with the aim of choosing the right persons for the jobs. But our limited perceptual ability is obviously a stumbling block to the objective and rational selection of people.[12]

4. Reliability

It refers to degree of consistency. Sometimes, even a reliable selection test fails to accurately predict job performance.

5. Validity

It refers to the extent to which a selection test measures what it intends to measure. It just raises the possibility of success but sometimes it does not predict success accurately. (Reliability and validity are covered in detail in next chapter.)

KEY TERMS

Accept error	Reject error
Job offer	Reliability

Perception | Selection
Preliminary interview | Validity

QUESTIONS

1. What do you mean by selection?
2. Discuss in detail the selection process.
3. What is application blank and give its contents?
4. What are the barriers to effective selection?
5. Differentiate between recruitment and selection.

ENDNOTES

1. Dale Yoder, *Personnel Management &Industrial Relations*, Prentice-Hall of India, New Delhi, 1967, p. 327.
2. Thomas H. Stone, *Understanding Personality,* CBS College Publishing, 1989, p. 173.
3. S.P. Robbins and D.A. Decenzo, *Fundamentals of Management,* Pearson Education, Delhi, 2002, p. 190.
4. *Ibid.*, p. 191.
5. See National Industrial Conference Board, Inc., "The Use of Tests in Employment and Promotion", *Studies in Personnel Polices*, p. 14, New York.
6. G. Strauss and L.R. Sayles, *Personnel,* Prentice-Hall of India, New Delhi, 1976, p. 420.
7. Edwin B. Flippo, *Personnel Management*, Sixth Edition, McGraw-Hill, New York, 1984, p. 155.
8. E.C. Mayfield, "The Selection Interview: A Revaluation of Published Research", *Personnel Psychology*, Vol. 17, No. 3, Autumn, 1964, pp. 239-260.
9. Edwin B. Flippo, op. cit., p. 160.
10. *Ibid.*
11. R. Wayne Mondy and Robert M. Noe III, *Personnel—The Management of Human Resources,* Allyn and Bacon, 1981, p. 174.
12. K. Aswathappa, *Human Resource and Personnel Management*, Tata McGraw-Hill, New Delhi, 2006, p. 172.

Psychological Tests and Interviews

7

LEARNING OBJECTIVES

After studying this chapter, you should be able to:

1. Explain the significance of psychological tests and interviews
2. Explain the administration of selection tests
3. Describe the types of employment tests
4. Describe the types of employment interviews
5. Understand the principles of psychological tests
6. Understand the principles of employment interviews

Psychological tests and interviews are important selection devices. The present chapter is devoted to these two important tools in the selection process. First, psychological tests are discussed.

It was Hugo Munsterberg who provides psychological testing a prominent place in the human resource management. Munsterberg identified his role as helping to find employees best suited to a job and determining under what psychological conditions greatest output per person could be achieved.[1] Today, psychological testing is a big business in workplaces. A test of a particular ability does not measure that particular ability alone but also a class or group of abilities. For example, in a test of numerical ability the candidate has not only to grasp the relation between various data presented and to deduce something new to reach an answer but also to be able to read and comprehend the question. All tests, therefore, are first psychological and then tests of specific abilities.[2]

An employment test is an instrument designed to measure selected psychological factors.[3] These factors include capacity for learning, personality, specific attitudes and temperament, etc.

PRINCIPLES OF PSYCHOLOGICAL TESTING

The important principles of psychological testing are the following:

1. Job analysis basis

Since the purpose of testing is to predict future success in a job situation, the beginning point of analysis is obviously the job. [4] Psychological tests should be selected on the basis of job analysis. The tests should be designed in order to measure those requirements which have been suggested under job specifications.

2. Standardisation

Standardisation refers to the consistency or uniformity of the conditions and procedures for administering a psychological test.[5] In order to make test results comparable, tests should be standardised.

3. Objectivity

This means equality of opportunities for those taking the test. The scoring procedure should be free of subjective judgements on the part of the scorer. A test should not discriminate against sex, caste, creed, etc.

4. Reliability

Reliability refers to the degree of consistency of results obtained.[6] In other words, it means stability of response on a test. A test is reliable if it yields the same result even if a person is tested for the second or third time provided the test and situation remains the same. A slight variation in test scores when a test is retaken at a later time is common, however, if the fluctuation is great then the test is not reliable one. There are three methods to determine the reliability of a test. These are the following:

(i) *Test-retest (repetition) method*

This is the simplest method of determining reliability of a test. In this, a test is administered twice to the same group of people and correlating the two sets of scores. In other words, a test is given and repeated on the same group and the correlation computed between the first and second set of scores. Closer the correlation/reliability coefficient, more reliable the test is considered to be. In choosing a test for employee selection, the reliability coefficient ideally should exceed +.80, although in practice a value of approximately +.70 is considered acceptable.[7]

This method suffers from few limitations. First, the time gap between the two tests is an important factor. For example, if the test is repeated immediately, many candidates will recall their first answers and spend their time on new material, thus tending to increase their scores. On the other hand, if the time interval between the tests is long (e.g. six months or more) and if the candidates were young children, growth changes will affect retest scores. Secondly, it is also very uneconomical to ask employees to find time from their busy schedules to take the test twice.

(ii) *Alternate/Parallel/Equivalent-Form method*

This method also uses a test-retest approach, but instead of using the same test for the second time, an alternate/similar form of the test is administered. However, it is costly and difficult to develop two separate and equivalent tests.

(iii) *Split-halves method*

In this method, the test is divided into two equivalent halves and the correlation found for these halves-tests. Generally, there is odd-even split. This is less time-consuming as only one administration of the test is required.

5. Validity

Validity refers to the extent to which a test measures what it is designed to measure. There may be three types of validity. These are given below:

(i) *Criterion-related validity*

This is concerned with the relationship between test scores and the subsequent job performance. If a person scores high on test, he also does well on the job and vice-versa. There are two approaches to establish criterion-related validity. These are as follows:

(a) Predictive validity

An approach to establishing criterion-related validity in which a new test is administered to all job applicants and all applicants are hired, regardless of test scores. Later, when a measure of job performance can be obtained, test scores are correlated with job performance to see how well the test predicted job success.[8] Generally, management is unwilling to use this approach as some of the people hired will turn out to be poor workers.

(b) Concurrent validity

A way to establish criterion-related validity that involves administering a test to employees on the job and correlating their scores with job performance data.[9] This is popular with management.

(ii) *Rational validity*

This is the type of validity that relates to the nature, properties and content of a test, independent of its relationship to job performance measures.[10] There are two approaches to establish the rational validity of a test. These are given below:

(a) Content validity

This means how well the contents/items of the test, as a sample, represent all the situations that could have been included.

(b) Construct validity

It refers to the extent the test measures the psychological characteristics such as intelligence, motivation, emotional stability, etc.

(iii) *Face validity*

Face validity is not a statistical measure but a subjective expression of how well the test items seem to be related to the job in question.[11]

6. Test norms

In order to interpret the results of a test, a point of comparison must be established. This is necessary so that the performance of one person can be compared with the performance of others. This is accomplished by means of the test norms, the distribution of scores of a large group of people similar in nature to the job applicants being tested.[12] The most widely used psychological tests have sets of norms for men and women, for different age groups, for various racial and ethnic groups and for levels of education.[13]

TYPES OF TESTS

The main types of tests used in selection can be classified into five categories which are given below:

1. Intelligence tests

Intelligence tests are defined as the capacity for abstract thinking and reasoning.[14] Intelligence tests seek to measure the general level of intelligence of the applicant. For example, Raven's Progressive Matrices measures general intelligence. Intelligence is a highly complex concept and generally there is difficulty in deciding about what constitutes intelligence.

2. Aptitude tests

These tests are designed to measure specific abilities like mechanical aptitude, numerical aptitude, clerical aptitude and dexterity. These are job-specific tests that are used to predict the potential an individual has to perform tasks within a job. These are also known as potential ability tests.

3. Personality tests

Personality refers to the dynamic organisation within the individual of those psychophysical systems that determine his unique adjustments to his environment.[15] Personality tests attempts to measure the basic characteristics of an individual. These tests measure emotional stability, extroversion/introversion, agreeableness, conscientiousness (hard working and reliable), openness to experience, integrity, self-confidence, etc. For example, Thematic Appreciation Test (TAT), Bell Adjustment Inventory, etc.

4. Interest tests

These tests attempt to measure interests and preferences of people. These are mainly used in career counselling. These tests assess a person's field of interest and identify the kind of work that will suit him. In a sense, interest tests make likes and dislikes of people. Examples here are Strong's Vocational Interest Blank and the Occupational Interest Survey.

5. Achievement tests

These tests measure applicant's abilities that have already been acquainted by training or experience. For example, a typing test, in this, it's easy to assess how many words in a minute a typist can type and compare it with the standard required for the job. These tests are also known as attainment tests and proficiency tests. Examples are Stanford Binet Scales and Millar Analogies Test.

ADMINISTRATION OF PSYCHOLOGICAL TESTS

Psychological tests can be administered in two ways:

1. Group tests

These tests can be administered to a large number of people at the same time. For example it can be given to 10, 100 or 1000 applicants simultaneously. The only constraint is the availability of space and number of computerised testing stations for testing large candidates.

2. Individual tests

These tests are administered to one person at a time. These are less frequently used, as these are costly than group tests.

CRITERIA FOR THE USE OF TESTS IN A SELECTION PROCESS

The six criteria for the use of psychological tests are given below:[16]

1. Everyone responsible for the application of tests including evaluation, interpretation and feedback should be trained.
2. Potential test users should satisfy themselves that it is appropriate to use tests at all before incorporating tests into decision-making processes.
3. Users must satisfy themselves that any tests they decide to use actively measure factors which are directly relevant to the employment situation.

4. Users must satisfy themselves that all tests they use should have been rigorously developed and that claims about their reliability, validity and effectiveness are supported by statistical evidence.
5. Care must be taken to provide equality of opportunity among all individuals required to take tests.
6. The results of single tests should not be used as the sole basis for decision-making. This is particularly relevant with regard to personality tests.

INTERVIEWING

An interview refers to conversation with a purpose. It is a widely used selection technique. A study of 852 employers found that 99% used interviews for employee selection.[17] Although application blank and selection tests produce evidence of candidate but interview is required to further supplement this data with more detailed information about personal characteristics and experience which can be obtained in a face-to-face meeting. An interview is a selection procedure designed to predict future job performance on the basis of applicant's oral responses to oral inquires.[18] The main aim of the selection interview is to assess information about a candidate which will enable a valid prediction of his future job performance.

The interview makes three unique contributions to the selection process. First, it is the only way to see an applicant in action—how he looks, his manner, his bearing. Second, it is the only way to witness how he interacts and how he responds, his way of thinking, the effects of his personality on another. Third, it is perhaps the best way to get at the 'will do' features of a performance-motivation, initiative, stability, perseverance, work habits and judgements. The so-called 'can do' aspect can be examined by application, tests and reference checks. An important by-product, unique to the interview, is the opportunity it affords to the management to identify with the applicant a factor for a new employee's ultimate success.[19]

TYPES OF INTERVIEWS

Interviews can be classified as follows:

I. According to the Purpose of the Interview

Interviews serve several purposes in the organisations. These can be broadly classified as follows:

1. Appraisal interview

An appraisal interview is a discussion, following the performance appraisal, in which supervisor and employee discuss the employee's rating and possible remedial action.[20]

2. Exit interview

This is conducted when an employee leaves the organisation. The aim of the exit interview is to elect information about the job, supervisor or other related matters. Information obtained through exit interview may give the employer some insight into what's wrong or right about the organisation (see Exhibit 7.1).

Exhibit 7.1: Exit Interview must for Bank Official Opting to Quit: SC

The monetary importance attached to a bank officer's job does not give him liberty to just walk away from the service to seek voluntary retirement to escape charges of serious misconduct as an officer of a financial institute like bank cannot be relieved without an exit interview before opting to quit, the Supreme Court has held.

"Voluntary retirement from the bank's service is not automatic. It is preceded by an exit interview," ruled a Bench of Mr. Justice H.K. Sema and Mr. Justice P.K. Balasubramanyan in a judgement on the bank officers' service conditions.

The court said the specimen of exit interview form was prescribed in a 1993 memorandum on the service conditions of bank officers. It prescribed detailed criteria to be followed in the exit interview before granting the request for voluntary retirement.

"The format of the exit interview is, therefore, not an empty formality...reasons for leaving the bank's service, date of interaction or interview held, name of the interviewing authority, his designation have to be clearly specified," the court said.

It said same importance was attached to the exit interview that was given to the other eligibility criterion to become a bank officer, including educational qualification, date of promotion to the officer grade, details of the branches he had served and the last five postings in such branches.

The ruling was laid down by the apex court while allowing an appeal of the Bank of India management against the Andhra Pradesh High Court order that had set aside dismissal of its grade-II officer Mohammed Nizamuddin, found guilty of remaining absent for three years without sanction of leave, claiming false LTC of Rs. 39,780 and misappropriating a loan of Rs. 80,000 taken from the bank's Secundrabed branch.

When the bank initiated disciplinary action against him after an official inquiry in which he refused to participate despite repeated notices, he sent in his resignation. But when the bank took a decision to dismiss him after finding him guilty, he first challenged it unsuccessfully before the bank's appellate authority and later filed a writ petition in the high court.

The high court held that dismissal from the service in his case was too harsh a punishment given by the bank authorities.

But the apex court did not agree with the high court's finding and termed its judgement "unsustainable in the law".

"The gravity of the misconduct must necessarily be measured in terms of its nature," the court said, pointing out that a middle management officer of grade-II, which was responsible post in a bank, absenting for three years was undoubtedly detrimental to the public interest and there could not be a more grave misconduct than this.

But when an inquiry was conducted against him, he simply had chosen to take a stand that he had resigned from the service and did not prefer to participate in the inquiry proceedings. "This conduct is also unbecoming of a responsible officer of a bank," the court ruled.

Source: *The Tribune*, 25th September, 2006

3. Selection/employment interview

Here the interviews are used as a key selection device. The candidates are interviewed regarding their appropriateness to the organisation.

4. Grievance interview

The general purpose of a grievance interview is resolution of the controversy to the satisfaction of both the employee and the company.[21]

II. According to the Structure/Pattern

1. Structured or Directive interview

In this type of interview, a set sequence of questions is followed. These are well planned to a higher degree of precision and accuracy. The questions and acceptable responses are specified in advance and responses are related for appropriateness of content.[22] For example, McMurray's patterned interview. There are certain benefits associated with structured interviews. As all applicants are asked same set of questions, thus these are more reliable and valid. Standardizing the administration of the interview also increases consistency across candidates, enhances job relatedness, reduces overall subjectivity and may enhance the ability to withstand legal challenge.[23]

2. Unstructured or non-directive interview

Opposite to structured interview, in an unstructured interview there is no set format of questions followed. In this, the format and questions to be asked are left to the discretion of the interviewer. No advance planning is required. The main weakness of unstructured interview is that it lacks consistency in assessing candidates.

III. According to the Contents of Interview

1. Situational interview

In this the interviewer asks the candidate what his or her behaviour would be in a given situation.[24] The interview questions are not designed to inquire about general work experience or personal characteristics and abilities but, rather, about the specific behaviours needed for successful performance of the job in question.[25]

2. Behavioural interview

These interviews ask interviewees to describe how they reacted to actual situations in the past.[26]

3. Job-related interview

In this interview, a number of job-related questions are asked that just focus on relevant past job-related behaviours.

4. Stress interview

The aim of this interview is to identify sensitive candidates and those with low or high stress tolerance. The interviewee is made uncomfortable by asking a number of rude questions. The interviewer adopts a hostile approach and deliberately frustrates and embarrasses the candidate. This is generally for the jobs where emotional balance is required.

IV. According to the Administration of Interview

1. One-to-one interview

In this, two people meet alone and one interviews the other by seeking oral responses to oral inquires.[27] Most of the interviews are one-to-one.

2. Sequential interview

In this, several persons interview the candidate, in sequence before a final decision is made. In an unstructured sequential interview, each interviewer may ask different questions and form an independent opinion, whereas in a structured sequential interview, each interviewer rates the candidate on a standard evaluation form.[28]

3. Panel interview

In this a panel (or group) of interviewers ask questions to the candidate. The panel members may ask questions in random or turn wise on the concerned topic.

4. Mass interview

In this, a panel interviews several candidates simultaneously. The panel poses a problem and then sits back and watches to see which candidate takes the lead in formulating an answer.[29]

SOME PRINCIPLES OF INTERVIEWING

The main principles of good interviewing can be classified into the following sequence of functions that occur within the interview are:

1. Preparation,
2. Setting,
3. Conduct of interview,
4. Close, and
5. Evaluation.[30]

1. Preparation

The interviewer should do considerable amount of planning required for interviews well in advance. This may include the following:

(i) *Determining the main objectives of the interview*

First of all, the objectives of the interview should be clearly spelled out. Objectives of appraisal interview will be different from grievance interview.

(ii) *Determining the method*

At this stage, the method to accomplish interviewing objective should be decided. For example, whether there is a need of stress interview or structured interview or unstructured interview, etc. to fill the objectives.

(iii) *Inform yourself regarding the applicant*

The interviewer should acquaint himself with the knowledge of the candidate. For example, in an employment interview, the interviewer can study the application blank.

2. Setting

This involves two kinds of settings, these are:

(i) *Physical setting*

The physical setting of the interview should be such that privacy is maintained as well as it is comfortable. An individual who is sitting in a comfortable padded chair has a tendency to relax and talk more freely thus providing more and truer information for the interviewer to evaluate.[31]

(ii) *Mental setting*

This refers to the rapport and relax atmosphere. At least initially, interviewer should try to establish atmosphere of ease. First build up a good rapport with the interviewee and gradually come to the main points of interview.

3. Conduct of the interview

This is the stage of action where desired information is obtained and facts are provided to the interviewee, if he desires. Here, the main principles are:

(i) The interviewer should possess and demonstrate a basic liking and respect for people.

(ii) Questions should be asked in way that interviewee is encouraged to answer.

(iii) Listen with full attention.

4. Close

Closing the interview is equally important as the beginning. To open, conduct and close the interview smoothly is an art. The main principles here are:

(i) At the end of the interview, the interviewer should make some overt sign to indicate the end such as lay down a pen, stand up, push the chair back, say thanks, etc.

(ii) The interviewee should be informed of some type of action.

5. Evaluation

When the interviewee leaves the room, the interviewer should immediately note down the strength and weaknesses of the candidate. Finally, the interviewer should also do self- evaluation. Interviewing is largely an art, the application of which can be improved by practice.

LIMITATIONS OF INTERVIEW

1. First impression

Interviewers tend to jump to conclusion within a few minutes of the interview. As per a researcher in 85% of the cases, the interviewers make up their minds before the actual interview begins, based on the first impression from the candidate's personal appearance or from the application forms.

2. Halo effect

This refers to the phenomenon of generalising from one characteristic or trait to the entire person in a positive or negative direction. For example, candidate's fluency in English, his foreign return status, physical appearance, etc.

3. Contrast/candidate-order effect

Candidates are not only evaluated on an absolute basis or on their merit alone, but are also judged relative to the other candidates interviewed during the same period. In other words, it means an error of judgement on the part of interviewer due to interviewing one or more very good or very bad candidates just before the interview in question.[32]

4. Pressure to hire

Pressure to hire also affects the interview process. In one study, researchers told one group of managers to assume they were behind in their recruiting quota. They told a second group they were ahead of their quota. Those 'behind' evaluated the same recruits much more highly than did those 'ahead'.[33]

5. Interviewers' prejudices

Interviewers' personal likes and dislikes (regarding gender, race, etc.) affect their judgement. For example, female interviewers' may be reluctant to consider men for teaching or nursing jobs. On the other hand, male interviewers' may hesitate to hire women in traditional male jobs. In an organisation even when female managers exhibited the same career-advancing behaviours as male managers, they still earned less money and were offered fewer career-progressing transfer opportunities.[34]

6. Prior information

The interviewers have prior information about applicant, for example, through application blanks, psychological test results, etc. The nature of that prior information can predispose an interviewer to have favourable or unfavourable attitude toward an applicant before he or she even shows up for the interview.[35]

7. Stereotyping

This type of error arises when the interviewers have already formed some associations between a particular trait, origin and particular type of personality. For example, the interviewer may form the opinion that people from metro cities are more competitive and competent.

8. Projection

This type of error arises when an interviewer expects his own values, qualities and skills in the candidate. So, he may select a candidate who just resembles him in appearance, manner, thoughts, age and background.

9. Leniency

This error refers to tendency to give high scores. Generally, it is associated with lack of confidence and interest in the rating.

10. Non-verbal behaviour

Applicant's non-verbal behaviour also has a great impact on his or her rating. In a study, 52 HR specialists watched videotaped job interviews in which applicants' verbal content was identical, but their non-verbal behaviour differed markedly.[36]

KEY TERMS

Achievement tests	Objectivity
Aptitude tests	Personality tests
Exit interviews	Projection
Halo effect	Reliability
Intelligence tests	Standardisation
Interest tests	Stereotyping
Interviews	Validity

QUESTIONS

1. Define psychological tests and discuss their importance.
2. What are the various types of validation?
3. Describe the various types of employment tests.
4. What are the various types of interviews?
5. Describe the principles of interviewing.
6. Discuss the limitations of interviewing.

ENDNOTES

1. S. George Claude Jr., *The History of Management Thought,* Prentice Hall, Inc., Englewood Cliffs, N.J., 1968, p. 103.
2. A. Monappa and M. Saiyadin, *Personnel Management*, Tata McGraw-Hill, New Delhi, 1979, p. 114.

3. Edwin B. Flippo, *Personnel Management*, Sixth Edition, McGraw-Hill, New York, 1984, p. 165.
4. *Ibid.*, p. 166.
5. D. Schultz and S.E. Schultz, *Psychology and Work Today,* Pearson Education, Delhi, 2004, p. 99.
6. Edwin B. Flippo, op. cit., p. 166.
7. D. Schultz and S.E. Schultz, op. cit., p. 101.
8. *Ibid.*, p. 102.
9. *Ibid.*
10. *Ibid.*
11. *Ibid.*, p. 103.
12. *Ibid.*, p. 100.
13. *Ibid.*, p. 101.
14. J. Toplis, V. Dulewicz and C. Fletcher, *Psychological Testing,* 1991, IPM, London.
15. G.W. Allport, *Personality: A Psychological Interpretation,* New York: Holt, Rinchart and Winston, 1937, p. 48.
16. IPD, *Key Facts on Psychological Testing,* 1997, London.
17. L. Ulrich and D. Trumbo, "The Selection Interview Since 1949", *Psychological Bulletin,* 1965, 63, pp. 100-116.
18. Michael McDaniel et al., " The Validity of Employment Interviews: A Comprehensive Review and Meta-Analysis", *Journal of Applied Psychology,* 1994, 79, No. 4, p. 599.
19. Richard Calhoon, *Managing the Personnel,* 1964, p. 151.
20. Gary Dessler, *Human Resource Management*, Pearson Education, Ninth Edition, Delhi, 2004, p. 161.
21. Edwin B. Flippo, op. cit., p. 157.
22. Michael McDaniel et al., op. cit., p. 602.
23. L.G. Williamson et al., "Employment Interview on Trial: Linking Interview Structure with Litigation Outcomes", *Journal of Applied Psychology,* 1996, 82, No. 6, p. 900.
24. *Ibid.*, p. 601.
25. D. Schultz and S.E. Schultz, op. cit., p. 86.
26. Michael McDaniel et al., op. cit., p. 602.
27. Gary Dessler, op. cit., p. 166.
28. *Ibid.*
29. *Ibid.*, p. 167.

30. Edwin B. Flippo, op. cit., p. 157.
31. *Ibid.*
32. Gary Dessler, op. cit., p.170.
33. R.E. Carlson, "Effects of Applicant Sample on Ratings of Valid Information in an Employment Settings", *Journal of Applied Psychology*, 1967, 20, pp. 259-280.
34. C. Marlowe, S. Schneider and C. Nelson, "Gender and Attractiveness Biases in Hiring Decisions: Are More Experienced Managers Less Biased?" *Journal of Applied Psychology*, 1996, 81, No. 1, pp. 11-21.
35. D. Schultz and S.E. Schultz, op. cit., p. 87.
36. T.V. McGovern and H.E. Tinsley, "Interviewer Evaluations of Interviewees' Nonverbal Behaviour", *Journal of Vocational Behaviour*, 1978, 13, pp. 163-171.

Placement and Induction 8

LEARNING OBJECTIVES

After studying this chapter, you should be able to:

1. Understand the nature and purpose of induction in organisations
2. Describe the different steps in the induction process
3. Understand the problems associated with induction

Once a candidate has been selected then the final stage in the procurement is to be concluded with the placement of the individual on the new job and introducing him or her to the job and the organisation. Placement refers to the determination of the job to which an accepted candidate is to be assigned and his assignment to that job. It is matching of what the supervisor has reason to think he can do which the job demands (job requirements), it is a matching of what he deserves, companionship with others, promotional possibilities, etc.[1] Generally candidates are hired for a specific position in a company. In case the number of candidates hired for the same position is large, then there may arise the problem of placement, i.e. who should be placed under which supervisor. In these cases placement decision is made by assigning the candidate to the position where he or she is considered to be best qualified. Every care should be taken for introducing candidates to the job and organisation through effective induction arrangements as discussed in the present chapter.

MEANING AND DEFINITION

Induction or orientation is concerned with the introduction of a new employee to the organisation. In other words, induction is the process of receiving and welcoming employees when they first join a company and giving them the basic information they need to settle down quickly and happily and start work.[2] Induction constitutes a significant part of fusion process "which is simultaneous operation of the socializing process by which the organisation seeks to make an agent of the individual for the achievement of organisational objectives and of the personalizing process by which the individual seeks to make an agency of the organisation for the achievement of his personal objectives."[3]

Although during the process of recruitment and selection, the interviewer imparts sufficient information regarding the history, policies and products of the organisation that develops confidence and interest in the worker but through formal induction the organisation ensures the new employee is imparted all necessary information that will make him or her more confident, interested and a capable hand. In as much as various firms report that over half of their voluntary resignations occur within the first six months, proper orientation can do much to reduce this problem and its accompanying costs.[4]

OBJECTIVES OF INDUCTION

1. To smooth the earlier stages where everything is strange and unfamiliar to new employee.
2. To acquaint the newcomer with the requirements of the job.
3. To explain to employee the terms and conditions of the job.
4. To establish a favourable attitude regarding the company in the mind of employee.
5. To bring about integration between the personal goals and organisational goals.
6. To provide information to the employee regarding organisation's policies and procedure.
7. To get effective output from the employee.
8. To develop enthusiasm for the organisation in the mind of newcomer so that he or she is more likely to stay.

9. To reduce the employees' chances of leaving organisation quickly.
10. To acquaint the new employee with his immediate supervisor and fellow workers with whom he has to work.
11. To promote the feeling of belongingness to the organisation.

IMPORTANCE/BENEFITS OF INDUCTION PROGRAMME

Induction is important because of the following:

1. Turnover among the new employee is higher than the other workers. Employees are far more likely to resign during their first months after joining the organisation.[5] Thus, the organisations should induct an employee properly.
2. An organisation always needs committed persons. The first step in achieving commitment is to present the organisation as one that is worth working for and to ensure that this first impression is reinforced during the first weeks of employment.[6]
3. New employees are the great learners and organisation should help them in this direction. Although, the length of the learning curve and rates of learning vary, but it is important to provide for it to take place in a planned and systematic manner from the first day to maximize individual contributions as quickly as possible.[7]
4. For most people social aspects of the job are very important such as relationship with fellow workers, etc. New employees are likely to settle in more quickly and enjoy working for the organisation if the process of socialization takes place smoothly.[8]
5. With the help of induction programmes, organisation can easily inform the new employees regarding what is expected from them in terms of behavioural norms, values and attitudes.

INDUCTION PROCEDURE

As such there is no model induction procedure. Every organisation has its own induction procedure according to its needs. Generally, the following steps are undertaken:

1. Properly receive the new employee. This first step just ensures that new employee receives warm welcome. Following checklist for proper reception is recommended:[9]

   (i) Ensure that the person whom the starter first meets (i.e. the receptionist, personnel assistant or supervisor) knows of their pending arrival and what to do next.

   (ii) Set a reporting time, which will avoid the risk of the starter turning up before the reception or office staff arrives.

   (iii) Train reception staff in the need for friendly and efficient helpfulness towards new starters.

   (iv) If the new starter has to go to another location, immediately after reporting, provide a guide.

   (v) Avoid keeping the new starter waiting.

2. Now, complete the administrative work. This includes informing the employee regarding probationary period, vacations, leaves, etc.

3. Next, conduct the departmental orientation. This includes introduction to the department, departmental functions, etc. New starters will be concerned about who they are going to work for (immediate manager or team leader), who they are going to work with, what work they are going to do on their first day and the geographical layout of their place of work/location of entrances, exits, lavatories, rest rooms and the canteens.[10] Wherever possible, department induction should be conducted by immediate supervisor.

4. Finally, conduct a follow-up interview after few weeks later. This interview, conducted by either the supervisor or a personnel specialist, is concerned with (1) employee satisfaction with the job and organisation, and (2) supervisor satisfaction with the employee.[11] If there is any dissatisfaction it may be cleared by discussions and explanations.

CONTENTS OF INDUCTION

These include information regarding:

1. Organisation's history, core values, mission and philosophy
2. Organisation's products/services
3. Department's location
4. Personnel policies and procedures
5. Conditions of services like holidays, hours, leave, medical leave, etc.
6. Remuneration and other benefits
7. Health and safety measures
8. Career advancement schemes
9. Trade unions and memberships
10. Grievance handling system.

METHODS OF PROVIDING INFORMATION

Generally, the following methods are used for providing information to the new employee:

1. Lectures
2. Motion pictures
3. Slide shows
4. Printed material
5. Trips to the department and the plant
6. Notice boards
7. Models of finished products
8. Charts and drawing.

PROBLEMS ASSOCIATED WITH INDUCTION

The main barriers in the successful conduct of induction programme of an organisation are the following:

1. The supervisor who is in charge with the job of induction is not well trained or he is too bossy.
2. New employee is overloaded with the forms to fill.

3. New employee is overwhelmed with so much information in a short time.
4. New employee is thrown into action so soon.
5. New employee may develop wrong perception because of short time spent on each job.
6. There is difficulty for employee to find the balance between broad orientation by HR department and narrow orientation by his own department.
7. New employee may be asked to perform challenging tasks initially where chances of failure are high that will discourage job involvement, interest and commitment.

Few indicators of wrong induction are less productivity, more accidents, low morale, more absenteeism, request for transfers and quits.

KEY TERMS

Induction	Placement
Orientation	Socialising process
Personalising process	

QUESTIONS

1. Define placement and what is its significance?
2. What do you mean by induction and describe its objectives?
3. Describe the steps of a formal induction procedure.
4. What are the benefits and problems associated with induction?

ENDNOTES

1. Paul Pigors and Charles A. Myers, *Personnel Administration: A Point of View and a Method*, McGraw-Hill, Kogakusha Ltd, Tokyo, 1973, p. 285.
2. Michael Armstrong, *A Handbook of Human Resource Management Practice,* Ninth Edition, Kogan Page, London, 2005, p. 453.
3. E.W. Bakke, *The Fusion Process,* New Heaven, Conn: Yale University Labour and Management Centre, 1955, p. 5.
4. Edwin B. Flippo, *Personnel Management*, Sixth Edition, McGraw-Hill, New York, 1984, p. 161.

5. A. Fowler, *Induction,* IPD, 1996, London.
6. Michael Armstrong, op. cit., p. 454.
7. *Ibid.*, p. 455.
8. *Ibid.*
9. A. Fowler, op. cit.
10. Michael Armstrong, op. cit., p. 457.
11. Edwin B. Flippo, op. cit., p. 162.

Training and Development

9

LEARNING OBJECTIVES

After studying this chapter, you should be able to:

1. Understand the nature and importance of training and development
2. Describe the training and development process
3. Describe the various training and development methods

After the recruitment, selection and induction of an employee, the next human resource management function is to provide the employee training and development facilities. No person is fully fit at the time of procurement some training is always essential. In today's era of competition, organisations view training and development (T&D) programmes as an investment in the employee, not as an expense. Organisations want their people must have the best skills and full knowledge. In fact, no organisation has a choice whether to give training or not, the only choice is that of method of imparting training.

MEANING AND DEFINITION

1. Training is the act of increasing the knowledge and skill of an employee for doing a particular job.[1]
2. Training refers to the methods used to give new or present employees the skills they need to perform their jobs.[2]
3. Training refers to any process by which the aptitudes, skills and abilities of employees to perform specific jobs are increased.[3]

RELATED TERMS

Learning and Training

Learning is the process by which a person acquires new knowledge, skills and capabilities. Whereas training is use of systematic and planned instruction and development activities to promote learning.[4]

Education and Training

If the training is concerned with increased skill in doing a particular job, education is generally concerned with increased general knowledge and overall understanding. The relationship between education and training is that of from general to specific (Table 9.1).

Table 9.1: Difference between Training and Education

Training	Education
Application	Theoretical orientation
Job experience	Classroom learning
Specific tasks	General concepts
Narrow perspective	Broad perspective

Source: K. Aswathappa, *Human Resource and Personnel Management,* Tata McGraw-Hill, New Delhi, 2006, p. 94.

Training and Development

Training focuses on providing employees with specific skills or helping them correct deficiencies in their performance.[5] In other words, training is used to correct the skill deficit. In contrast to it, development is an effort to provide employees with the abilities the organisation will need in the future.[6] Table 9.2 makes this difference more clear.

Table 9.2: Difference between Training and Development

	Training	Development
Focus	Current job	Current and future jobs
Scope	Individual employees	Work group or organisation
Time Frame	Immediate	Long term
Goal	Fix current skill deficit	Prepare for future work

Source: Gomex-Mejia et. al., *Managing Human Resources,* Pearson Education, Delhi, 2003, p. 260.

PURPOSE OF TRAINING

Training is essential in organisations because of the following reasons:

1. To increase employees' performance on their current assignment.
2. To prevent industrial accidents. Through training workers know the right way of doing the job and how to handle the machines. Thus it increases safety measures taken by workers and reducing the chances of accidents.
3. To prevent manpower obsolescence. Due to technological changes and competition, workers are required to update and well-equip themselves with the latest ways of job performance. So, training helps them in learning the new methods.
4. To increase employee morale. A well-trained employee will take interest in his work and derives satisfaction from his job. This raises his morale to perform well in future.
5. To reduce wastage. An untrained person will waste the costlier raw material, damage machines and even cause accidents. With the help of training, workers come to know what is the right way of using the material, what is the right way of operating and handling the machine, etc.
6. A trained person needs less supervision as compared to an untrained person. A trained person can take routine decisions by himself and is most disciplined. Training helps to make employee independent and more responsible towards the job.
7. To enhance employee's adjustment with the latest changes at work place. For instance, technological developments require new approach towards work. It is only through training that a worker can easily learn new work techniques. A little bit of computer training is required these days in almost every field like banks, railways, etc. to adjust to new ways of doing work.

8. To reduce absenteeism and turnover. A trained worker takes full interest in his job thus derives job satisfaction. A satisfied worker will be regular and thinks less to quit.
9. To fill the vacancies when need arises. An organisation by imparting training makes a ready pool of trained candidates available with it. Whenever there is vacancy at higher level so it will take less time and effort to promote a trained person.
10. Lastly, training is also essential for the overall growth of workers. Management development programmes seem to give participants a wider awareness, an enlarged skill and enlightened altruistic philosophy and make enhanced personal growth possible.[7] Also, with the help of training, employees acquire knowledge and skills, this increases their market value and earning power.

THE TRAINING PROCESS

Generally, training programs consist of six steps. These are the following:

I. Assessment of Organisational Objectives

First of all, in an organisation, there should be a proper assessment of objectives. Employers today have to adopt to technological changes, improve product and service quality and boost productivity to stay competitive.[8]

II. Assessment of Training Needs

Before an organisation takes decision regarding training of its workers and allocates huge resources for it, organisations have to assess the training needs of its employees. In this regard, a trainer has said, "we sit down with management and help them identify strategic goals and objectives and the skills and knowledge needed to achieve them. Then we work together to identify whether our staff has the skills and knowledge and when they do not that's when we discuss training needs."[9]

Training need analysis step is crucial for many reasons. For example, employees' performance may be down because the work standards are not clear to them, due to faulty selection, due to lack of motivation, poor job design, less supervision or personal problem. In these cases, the problem may be solved just by proper job design, offering incentives to motivate, improving supervision, etc. Where the deficiency in performance is because of lack of knowledge or skill, there training is essentially required.

The two main ways to identify training needs are task analysis and performance analysis. Task analysis is a detailed study of a job to identify the specific skill required and it is especially suitable for determining the needs of employees who are new to their jobs.[10] Whereas, performance analysis is the process of verifying that there is performance deficiency and determining if such deficiency should be corrected through training or through some other means (like transferring the employee).[11] Apart from task and performance analysis supplementary methods can be used to identify training needs such as supervisors' reports, personnel records, management requests, observations, test of job knowledge and questionnaire surveys.[12]

III. Establish the Training Objectives

Once it is clear that training is the solution of performance deficiency then the training objectives are set. In other words, once training needs are assessed, then the objectives of training are established. These objectives will specify what a trainee should accomplish after the successful completion of a training programme. For example, to type 60 words per minute without difficulty and 2 to 3 errors per page, to program a single website in half a day, etc.

IV. Designing the Training Programme

Once it is decided that there is a need to train employees and what they should learn, now this is the time to design the training programme. This refers to deciding about the contents of the training programme, i.e. deciding about trainers, methods and techniques of training.

Regarding trainers, these are usually recommended by the HR department. Most of the professional organisations have a centralised database of their employees, by regular evaluation of the skills required they just inform the regional heads to send their employees for training. For example, Indian Airline's (now known as 'Indian') training programmes are conducted at Hyderabad. Trainers can be HR department's staff, consultants, supervisors, university faculty members, etc. Selection of trainers is linked with selection of training methods and techniques. Generally, training is divided into two broad categories, on-the-job training (OJT) and off-the-job training. These methods are discussed in detail in the next section of this chapter.

V. Implementation of Training Programme

Once a training programme has been designed now there is need to implement it. This involves finding a suitable place for the conduct of training, schedule the whole training programme in such a way that it does not disrupt the smooth functioning of organisation, keep record about the performance of trainees during the training period and monitor trainees progress side by side.

VI. Evaluation of Training Programme

After the completion of the training programme, the organisation evaluates the programme to see the effectiveness of training efforts. This is done to check whether the training programme accomplish specific training objectives or not. Also, the conduct of training programme is costly; this includes needs assessment costs, salaries of the training department staff, purchase of equipment (computers, video, handouts), programme development cost, evaluation costs, trainer's costs, rental facilities and trainees wage during the training period.[13] Thus it is important to assess the costs and benefits associated with the training programme, in order to convince the top management that the benefits outplay costs.

What to Measure

While evaluating training programme the experts should collect data on the following categories:

1. Reaction of trainees

Reaction of trainees towards the training programme i.e., what they felt about the training.

Fig. 9.1: Training process

Level	Evaluation type (what is measured)	Evaluation description and characteristics	Examples of evaluation tools and methods	Relevance and practicability
1.	Reaction	• **reaction evaluation** is how the **delegates felt** about the training or learning experience	• e.g., 'happy sheets', feedback forms • also verbal reaction, post-training surveys or questionnaires	• quick and very easy to obtain • not expensive to gather or to analyse
2.	Learning	• **learning evaluation** is the measurement of the **increase in knowledge**—before and after	• typical assessments or tests before and after the training • interview or observation can also be used	• relatively simple to set up; clear-cut for quantifiable skills • less easy for complex learning
3.	Behaviour	• **behaviour evaluation** is the extent of **applied learning** back on the job—implementation	• observation and interview over time are required to assess change, relevance of change, and sustainability of change	• measurement of behaviour change typically requires cooperation and skill of line-managers
4.	Results	• **results evaluation** is the **effect on the business or environment** by the trainee	• measures are already in place via normal management systems and reporting—the challenge is to relate to the trainee	• individually not difficult; unlike whole organisation • process must attribute clear accountabilities

Source: www.businessballs.com

2. Learning

Whether the trainees learn the desired principles and skills.

3. Behaviour

Whether the trainees' on the job behaviour improved.

4. Results

The results of the training programme are compared against the set objectives (Fig. 9.1).

How to Evaluate

There are several methods of evaluation. One is the use of experimental and control group. Both these groups are randomly selected, one group receive training (experimental group) and other does not receive training (control group). Few indicators of success are identified (e.g. words typed per minute with 2-3 errors) and measures are taken from both the groups. A training programme is considered successful if the experimental group shows better performance than the control group. Another way to evaluate training programme is to take interviewees of trainees regarding

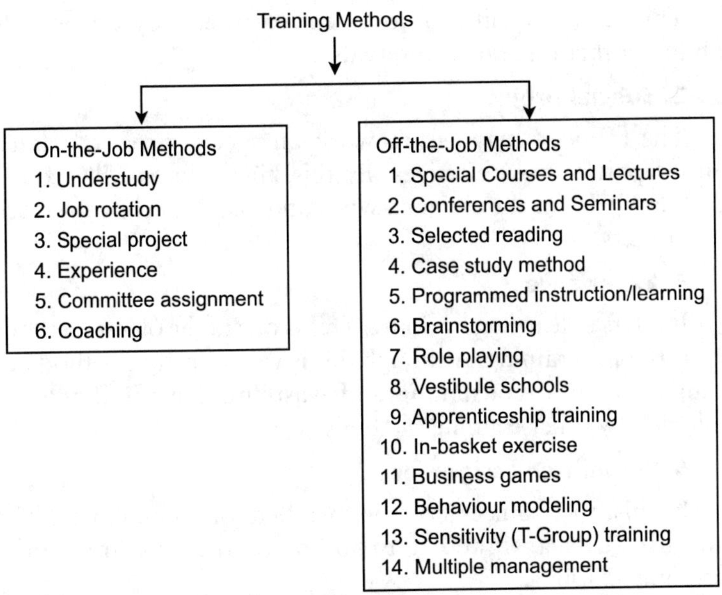

Fig. 9.2: The Training Methods

programme's worth or send them to fill questionnaire to know their opinion.

TRAINING AND DEVELOPMENT (T&D) METHODS

There are several T&D methods available. The use of a particular method depends which method accomplishes the training needs and objectives. Training methods can be classified into two categories:

I. On-the-Job Methods

This refers to the methods of training in which a person learns a job by actually doing/performing it. A person works on a job and learns and develops expertise at the same time.

1. Understudy

In this the employee is trained by his or her supervisor. The trainee is attached with his or her senior and called understudy or assistant. For example, a future manager might spend few months as assistant to the present manager.

2. Job rotation

This refers to shifting/movement of an employee from one job to another on regular intervals.

3. Special projects

The trainees' may ask to work on special projects related with departmental objectives. By this, the trainees will acquire the knowledge of the assigned work and also learn how to work with others.

4. Experience

It refers to learning by doing. This is one of the oldest methods of on-the-job training. Although this is very effective method but it also very time-consuming and wasteful. Thus it should be followed by other training methods.

5. Committee assignment

In this, the trainees become members of a committee. The committee is assigned a problem to discuss and make recommendations.

6. Coaching

In this, the supervisor or the superior acts as a guide and instructor of the trainee. This involves extensive demonstration and continuous critical evaluation and correction.

II. Off-the-Job Methods

These methods require trainees to leave their workplace and concentrate their entire time towards the training objectives. These days off-the-job training methods have become popular due to limitations of the on-the-job training methods such as facilities and environment, lack of group discussion and full participation among the trainees from different disciplines, etc. In the off-the-job methods, the development of trainees is the primary task rest everything is secondary. Following are the main off-the-job training methods:

1. Special courses and lectures

These are the most traditional and even famous today, method of developing personnel. Special courses and lectures are either designed by the company itself or by the management/professional schools. Companies then sponsor their trainees to attend these courses or lectures. These are the quick and most simple ways to provide knowledge to a large group of trainees.

2. Conferences and seminars

In this, the participants are required to pool their thoughts, ideas, viewpoints, suggestions and recommendations. By attending conferences and seminars, trainees try to look at a problem from different angles as the participants are normally from different fields and sectors.

3. Selected reading

This is the self-improvement training technique. The persons acquire knowledge and awareness by reading various trade journals and magazines. Most of the companies have their own libraries. The employees become the members of the professional associations to keep abreast of latest developments in their respective fields.

4. Case study method

This technique was developed by Harvard Business School, U.S.A. It is used as a supplement to lecture method. A case is a written record of a real business situation/problem faced by a company. The case is provided to the trainees for discussion and analysis. Identification and diagnose of the problem is the aim in case study method. Alternate courses of action are suggested from participants.

5. Programmed instruction/learning

This is step-by-step self-learning method where the medium may be a textbook, computer or the internet. This is a systematic method for teaching job skills involving presenting questions or facts, allowing the person to respond and giving the learner immediate feedback on the accuracy of his or her answers.[14]

6. Brainstorming

This is creativity-training technique, it helps people to solve problems in a new and different way. In this technique, the trainees are given the opportunity to generate ideas openly and without any fear of judgement. Criticism of any idea is not allowed so as to reduce inhibiting forces. Once a lot of ideas are generated then they are evaluated for their cost and feasibility.

7. Role-playing

In this method, the trainees are assigned a role, which they have to play in an artificially created situation. For example, a trainee is asked to play the role of a trade union leader and another trainee is required to perform the role of a HR manager. This technique results in better understanding of each other's situation by putting foot in other's shoes.

8. Vestibule schools

Large organisations frequently provide what are described as vestibule schools a preliminary to actual shop experience. As far as possible, shop conditions are duplicated, but instruction, not output is major objective.[15] A vestibule school is operated as a specialised endeavor by the personnel department. This training is required when the amount of training that has to be done exceeds the capacity of the line supervisor; a portion of training is evolved from the line and assigned to staff through a vestibule school.[16] The advantage of a vestibule school is specialisation.

9. Apprenticeship training

This training approach began in the Middle Ages when those who wanted to learn trade skill bound themselves to a master craftsman and worked under his guidance. Apprenticeship training is a structured process by which people become skilled workers through a combination of classroom instruction and on-the-job training.[17]

10. In-basket exercise

In this technique, the trainees are provided background information on a simulated firm and its products, and key personnel. After this, the trainees are provided with in-basket of memos, letters, reports, requests and other documents related with the firm. The trainee must make sense out of this mass of paperwork and prepare memos, make notes and delegate tasks within a limited time period.[18] In-basket exercise helps to develop the following ablities:[19]

(i) Situational judgement in being able to recall details, establish priorities, interrelate items and determine need for more information;

(ii) Social sensitivity in exhibiting courtesy in written notes, scheduling meetings with involved personnel and explaining reasons for actions taken; and

(iii) Willingness to make a decision and take action.

11. Business games

Business games involve teams of trainees. The teams discuss and analyse the problem and arrive at decisions. Generally, issues related with inventories, sales, R&D, production process, etc. are taken up for consideration.

12. Behaviour modeling

This is structured approach to teach specific supervisory skill. This is based on the social learning theory in which the trainee is provided with a specific model of behaviour and is informed in advance of the consequences of engaging in that type of behaviour.[20] Generally this approach involves the following steps:[21]

1. A conceptual presentation is made in the proper handling of particular problem. Each key action step is identified and emphasised.
2. A video tape of the effective handling of the problem is presented. Each key action step is performed.
3. A behavioural rehearsal period is then undertaken. Although, this may look like role-playing, the trainee is not free to select a response. Rather, he or she rehearses the behaviour presented in the first two steps.
4. During and after the rehearsal period, the trainee is given feedback on performance and is positively reinforced when demonstrating the behavioural model.
5. Finally, the trainee is encouraged to try the behaviour out on the job and to report back for discussion the results of that tryout.

13. Sensitivity (T-group) training

In this type of training, a small group of trainees consisting of 10 to 12 persons is formed which meets in an unstructured situation. There is no set agenda or schedule or plan. The main objectives are more openness with each other, increased listening skills, trust, support, tolerance and concern for others. The trainers serve a catalytic role. The group meets in isolation without any formal agenda. There is great focus on inter-personal behaviour. And, the trainer provides honest but supportive feedback to members on how they interacted with one another.

14. Multiple management

This technique of training was first introduced by McCormick, President of McCormick & co. of Baltimore in 1932. He gave the idea of establishing a junior board of directors. Authority is given to the junior board members to discuss any problem that could be discuss in senior board and give recommendations to the senior board. Innovative and productive ideas became available for senior board.

EXECUTIVE/MANAGEMENT DEVELOPMENT

More and more organisations give increased attention to executive development, at all levels, from supervisory through middle management levels to the top.[22] In other words, management development is any attempt to improve current or future management performance by imparting knowledge, changing attitudes or increasing skills.[23]

Objective of Management Development

1. To train and develop the managers to meet the technological and social change.
2. To ensure a ready pool of competent people at all levels to meet organisational needs at all times.
3. To prepare the junior managers for future replacements.
4. To prevent managerial obsolescence by inculcating new concepts in their areas.
5. To promote a high morale among employees.

KEY TERMS

Apprenticeship training	Learning
Behaviour modeling	Management development
Brainstorming	Multiple management
Business games	Programmed instructions
Case study method	Role-playing
Coaching	Sensitivity training
Committee assignment	Training
Development	Understudy
Education	Vestibule schools
In-basket training	

QUESTIONS

1. Define training and development and discuss their significance.
2. Describe the training and development process.
3. Bring out the purpose of training in organisations.
4. What are the various methods of training and development?

5. Write short notes on the following:
   (a) Case study method
   (b) Sensitivity training
   (c) Brainstorming
   (d) Business games
   (e) Role-playing
   (f) Executive development
   (g) Behaviour modeling

ENDNOTES

1. Edwin B. Flippo, *Personnel Management,* McGraw-Hill, Kogakusha Ltd, Tokyo, 1976, p. 209.
2. Gary Dessler, *Human Resource Management*, Pearson Education, Ninth Edition, Delhi, 2004, p. 187.
3. Michael J. Jucius, *Personnel Management,* Richard D. Irwin, Inc., Homewood, Illinois, 1975, p. 225.
4. Michael Armstrong, *A Handbook of Human Resource Management Practice,* Ninth Edition, Kogan Page, London, 2005, p. 549.
5. W. Fitzgerald, "Training versus Development", *Training and Development*, 1992, 46, pp. 81-84.
6. Luis R. Gomez-Mejia, David B. Balkin and Robert L. Cardy, *Managing Human Resources,* Third Edition, Pearson Education, Delhi, 2003, p. 260.
7. E.L. Wiener and D.A. Attwood, "Training for Vigilance, Combined Cueing and Knowledge of Results", *Journal of Applied Psychology*, 52, 8, 1968, pp. 474-479.
8. Carolyn Wiley, "Training for the 90s: How Leading Companies Focus on Quality Improvement, Technological Change and Customer Service", *Employee Relations Today,* Spring, 1993, p. 80.
9. Cheristine Ellis and Sarah Gale, "A Seat at Table", *Training,* March 2001, pp. 90-96.
10. Gary Dessler, op. cit., p. 190.
11. *Ibid.*
12. B.A. Bass and J.A. Vaughan, " Assessing Training Needs", in Craig Schneier and Richard Beatty, *Personnel Administration Today*, Reading MA: Addison-Wesley, 1978, p. 311.
13. J.H. Bernardin and J.E.A. Russell, *Human Resource Management—An Experimental Approach*, McGraw-Hill, New York, p. 315.

14. Gary Dessler, op. cit., p. 195.
15. D.C. Sharma and R.C. Sharma, *Personnel Management &Industrial Relations*, First Edition, S.J. Publications, Meerut, p. 161.
16. Edwin B. Flippo, *Personnel Management*, Sixth Edition, McGraw-Hill, New York, 1984, p. 201.
17. Gary Dessler, op. cit., p. 193.
18. Edwin B. Flippo, op. cit., p. 206.
19. *Ibid.*
20. A. Bandura, *Social Learning Theory*, Prentice-Hall, Englewood Cliffs, N.J., 1977.
21. J.I. Porras and B. Anderson, "Improving Managerial Effectiveness Through Modeling-Based Training", *Organisational Dynamics*, Vol. 9, No. 4, 1981 Spring, p. 64.
22. Michael J. Jucius, op. cit., p. 243.
23. Gary Dessler, op. cit., p. 204.

Performance Appraisal

10

LEARNING OBJECTIVES

After studying this chapter, you should be able to:

1. Understand the concept of performance appraisal and its usefulness
2. Describe the performance appraisal process
3. Identify the various methods of performance appraisal
4. Describe the 360-degree feedback method

Though with the help of training and development programmes, employees acquire new knowledge and skills and hence, become more capable and competent, but there is need to systematically appraise them and provide them information regarding their performance. This enables employees to know how they are performing in comparison with set standards.

MEANING AND DEFINITION

1. Performance appraisal is the periodic, formal evaluation of employee performance for the purpose of making career decisions.[1]
2. Performance appraisal is a formal, structured system of measuring and evaluating an employee's job related behaviours and outcomes to discover how and why the employee is presently performing on the job and how the employee can perform more effectively in the future so that the employee, organisation and society all benefit.[2]
3. Performance appraisal involves the identification, measurement and management of human performance in organisation.[3]

In the above definition identification refers to determine what areas of job the manager should be examining when measuring performance. Measurement is the centerpiece of the appraisal system. It is checking and making judgements of how 'good' or 'bad' employee performance was. Finally, management means the performance appraisal should be future-oriented, means that managers should provide their employees feedback and guide them to higher levels of performance in future.

USES OF PERFORMANCE APPRAISAL

Performance appraisal serves several purposes of the organisations. The main uses of performance appraisal are as follows:

1. Administrative use

Performance appraisals are used administratively whenever they are the basis for the personnel decisions like promotions, transfers, demotions, terminations and rewards.

2. Developmental use

Performance appraisal helps to identify the need and areas for further training and development of the employees.

3. Compensation use

Performance appraisal provides a rational basis for constructing a system of rewards, benefits or bonus.

4. Feedback use

It provides feedback to the employees and informs them where they can improve their performance.

5. Reduce grievances

With the help of proper feedback, the employees receive information about their performance thus reduces the grievances among the employees.

6. Improvement in supervision

A systematic performance appraisal system in organisation makes supervisor always aware and alert about their subordinate performance, as they have to fill the rating forms periodically.

7. Database

Performance appraisal documents and records protect the employer from the charges of discrimination, biasness and favouritisim. These documents may be needed for legal defense.

8. Effectiveness of earlier stages

Performance appraisal acts as mean of evaluating the effectiveness of recruitment, selection, placement and induction systems in an organisation.

9. Career planning

Performance appraisal records provide a systematic and rational base for management in the career planning of its employees.

10. Motivation

Fair performance appraisal systems help in the assessment and recognition of performance levels of employees. This motivates employees to improve their performance.

The above said uses of performance appraisal highlight its importance in any organisation. All workers are appraised on their work/job performance in some manner or the other, the choice lies in the method of performance appraisal an organisation adopts.

PROCESS OF PERFORMANCE APPRAISAL

The logical sequence of steps in a performance appraisal process are the following:

1. Set the objectives of performance appraisal

Generally, a performance appraisal serves three purposes:

(a) **Administrative**—for the use of personnel decisions like promotions, transfers, pay increase, etc.

(b) **Research**—for validating selection instruments.

(c) **Developmental**—to identify the training needs of employees.

So, objectives of performance appraisal are set depending upon the needs of the organisation.

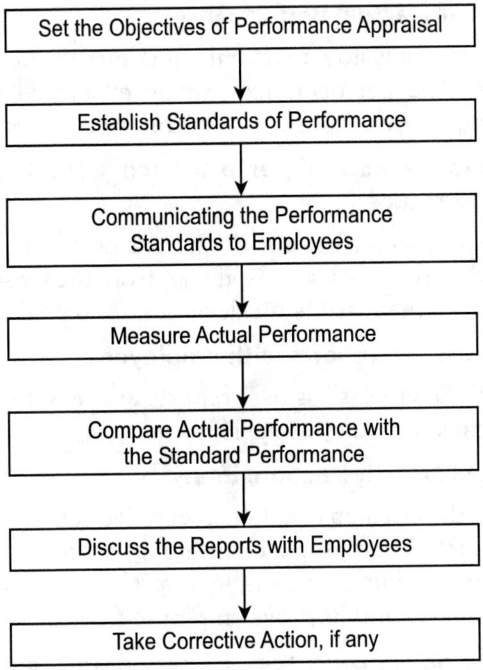

Fig. 10.1: The Performance Appraisal Process

2. Establish standards of performance

The next step is of setting the standards of employee performance. These standards act as a base, yardstick or benchmark for evaluating the performance. The set standards will inform the employee that what is expected from him or her on the job.

3. Communicating the performance standards to employees

The next logical step is to communicate the set standards to the employees. Inform the employees what is desired from them on the job. It is important that they understand what is expected from them or is there any confusion or misunderstanding. If needed, clarify the standards.

4. Measure actual performance

The next step is now to actually measure the performance of employees. The performance can be measured by personal observation, written reports, ratings by supervisors, etc.

5. Compare actual performance with the standard performance

Next step is to compare the actual performance with the standard set earlier. Deviations, if any, from the set standards are noted. Identify the reasons for deviations and analyse it.

6. Discuss the reports with employees

Now discuss the assessment reports with employees. Provide them feedback how they are performing.

7. Take corrective action, if any

Finally, the last step is to take corrective action if need arises. This may include advising, counselling, warning, motivating, coaching, and training, etc. employees. These are useful ways to correct the defect and improve employee's performance.

METHODS OR TECHNIQUES OF PERFORMANCE APPRAISAL

Searching for an ideal and suitable performance appraisal method is same as searching for the Holy Grail. Figure 10.2 summarises the main methods of performance appraisal.

I. Casual, Unsystematic and Often Haphazard Appraisal Methods

This is an old performance appraisal approach, which is very common among all organisations. In this approach, more emphasis is placed on the evaluation of the employee's worth as a person. But this approach does not evaluate all performances in the same manner. Moreover, there is a greater scope for human bias and prejudice.

II. Traditional Methods

1. Ranking

This is one of the simplest and oldest method of performance appraisal. In this method one person is compared with all other employees for the purpose of placing them in a simple rank order

Performance Appraisal Methods

I. Casual, Unsystematic and Often Haphazard Appraisal Methods

II. Traditional Methods

1. Ranking
2. Paired-comparison
3. Person-to-person-comparison
4. Grading
5. Forced-distribution
6. Graphic rating scales
7. Check lists
8. Forced-choice distribution
9. Critical incidents
10. Field review
11. Confidential report
12. Free essay
13. Behaviourally Anchored Rating Scales (BARS)

III. Modern Methods

1. Management by objectives
2. 360-degree feedback
3. Psychological appraisals
4. Assessment centre
5. Human Resource Accounting (HRA)

Fig. 10.2: Methods of Performance Appraisal

of worth. All the employees are place in order of their relative worth. This method separates the efficient from the inefficient but it suffers from following defects:[4]

(i) It does not appear to be desirable to compare one person with another because different persons have different traits and qualities.

(ii) It simply tells us who is better than the other but it does not indicate how much better he is than the other.

(iii) This method may be used only in case of small organisations. If a company employs a large number of employees then it may not be possible to rank all of them in order of their worth.

(iv) This system is based on snap judgement and does not have any systematic procedure to determine the relative worth of an employee.

2. Paired-comparison

This method was developed to overcome the defects of ranking method. This method compares the performance of each worker with that of every other worker in the group or section. At one time, comparisons are made between two people and a decision is made about which of the pair is superior. Suppose there are four employees in a firm. Employee A's performance is compared with B's and a judgement is made regarding who is better performer. Then A is compared with C and D in the same manner. Similarly the approach is used for other personnel. Following formula is used for determining total number of comparisons:

$$\text{Total number of comparisons} = \frac{N(N-1)}{2}$$

where N = number of personnel to be compared. As discussed in the earlier example, four employees mean a total of six decisions.

3. Person-to-person comparison

In this method, certain factors like initiative, faithfulness, leadership, dependability, creativity, etc. are selected for the purpose of analysis. After this, a scale is designed for each factor. Now, instead of defining varying degrees of each factor like leadership, dependability, etc. particular employees are used to represent these degrees. For each factor the most efficient and least efficient person are selected. These two persons represent the two ends of the scale. Then an average person is selected to represent the medium point. After this, two points are marked one above and one below the average. So, in this way a scale of five points is ascertained. Thus, in this way, a scale of persons for each factor is created. Now, instead of comparing whole people to whole people, personnel are compared to key persons, one factor at a time. The main limitation of this method is that the preparation of scales for each factor is largely complicated and difficult.

4. Grading

In this method certain categories of worth are established well in advance. For example, categories can be clearly defined as extraordinary, satisfactory, average, unsatisfactory, worst, etc. After this, employee performance can be compared with these grades and the person is allocated the suitable grade, i.e. the grade that best represents his or her performance.

5. Forced-distribution

This is the modification of the grading system. In this system, certain percentages are established for each grade. A standard distribution looks like the following:

Best/Superior	10%
Good	20%
Average	40%
Bad	20%
Poor	10%

So, in this system, the rater cannot relax and judge them all in same category. Here, the rater has judged in this way that 10 per cent of the total personnel must go into the top grade, 20 per cent must go into the second grade and so on. The main disadvantage of this technique is that it compels/forces the rater to do something or use predetermined rating categories that might not fairly represent that particular group of employees.

6. Graphic rating scales

This approach is similar to person-to-person comparison but the difference is that the degrees on the factor scales are represented by definitions rather than by key people. These are the most commonly used methods of performance appraisal. The rater is asked to rate the employees on the basis of certain factors on a scale. Generally two types of factors are considered, these are: (i) job-related characteristics such as dependability, cooperation, judgement, attendance, initiative and (ii) contributions such as quality and quantity of work. The rater evaluates the performance on the basis of these traits on a continuous scale. The advantages of the graphic rating scale are that they are easy to construct and use and also they attempt to reduce the personal bias.

7. Checklists

This method is used to reduce the burden on the evaluator. Instead of evaluating employee performance the rater merely reports it. A checklist is prepared in which several questions in relation to a particular job are included. The rater has to simply mark the tick against the column of yes or no. The questions may be weighted but the rater is not aware of the specific values attached to different questions. The main disadvantage of the checklist system is that it is difficult to assemble and weigh a number of statements (in question forms) about a person's contribution and characteristics. Moreover, each department needs separate checklist due to difference in the nature of duties and responsibilities of different work.

8. Forced-choice distribution

The main objective of this method is to reduce or eliminate the possibility of rater bias by forcing the rater to do choice between descriptive statements of seemingly equal worth. The rater has to select one statement out of the pair that best describes an employee or is least applicable to that employee. The statements within each pair designed to appear equally positive or equally negative. For example, the rater may be asked to select one statement out of the following pair that best describes the worker:

(i) He is reliable

(ii) He is agreeable.

Then, the rater may be asked to choose one statement out of the following pair that least describes the worker:

(i) He is uncooperative

(ii) He is not interested in doing well.

One statement out of each pair is correct in identifying the better performance and this scoring key is kept secret and not known to the rater. It is difficult for the rater to distinguish the items that represent desirable or undesirable characteristics, thus, the chances of deliberately assigning favourable or unfavourable ratings are reduced very much.

9. Critical incidents

Critical incidents refer to certain key acts of behaviour that make the difference between success and failure on a job. The supervisor keeps the record of positive and negative acts/events of a subordinate's work-related behaviour. All these acts are critical incidents. After a fixed time interval like six months or so, the supervisor and subordinate meet together to discuss the latter's performance on the basis of the critical incidents. For example, incidents in a purchasing agent's job might be the following:[5]

(i) Treated a salesperson in a markedly discourteous manner

(ii) Rejected a bid that was excessively overpriced

(iii) Persuaded a local vendor to stock an important item

(iv) Failed to return an important phone call.

The main advantage of this method is that by keeping systematic record helps in backing up personnel decisions when challenged by the trade union, workers, courts, etc. as these are hard evidence.

10. Field review

In this method, the evaluator, usually HR specialist, asks/interviews supervisors questions about their subordinates. The evaluator gets the opinions of the supervisor regarding subordinate's work progress, performance, strengths, weakness, etc. and record it and kept it for future reference.

11. Confidential report

This is one of the traditional and most common method of performance appraisal in most of the government organisations. An annual confidential report (ACR) of each subordinate is prepared by the immediate supervisor. This is descriptive in nature and usually prepared at the end of every year. An ACR highlights the strengths, weaknesses, performance, character, ability, etc. of the subordinate. The main disadvantage of this method is that it involves a lot of subjectivity. Also, no feedback is provided to the employee being appraised. So, its credibility is low. Least emphasis on developing the employee, only thing is to evaluate the employee.

12. Free essay method

In this method, the evaluator, usually supervisor, writes a report about employees' performance. The supervisor considers the following factors about an employee while preparing the essay:

(i) Job knowledge
(ii) Relations with co-workers and superiors
(iii) Attitudes and perceptions
(iv) Understanding of organisational plans and policies
(v) Training and development needs
(vi) Strengths and weaknesses.

This is a non-quantitative technique of performance appraisal. However, the disadvantage of this method is that it is highly subjective. Essay writing is an art, which everyone cannot do.

13. Behaviourally anchored rating scales (BARS)

It attempts to evaluate job performance in terms of key/specific behaviours that are important to success or failure on the job. The critical-incident approach has been merged with the graphic rating concept to produce behaviourally anchored rating scales.[6] In this method, the evaluator rates the critical employee behaviours. There are two types of scales: (i) Behaviour Expectation Scales (BES), where anchors are illustrations that help the rater to define as superior, average or below average the behaviour of the employee, and (ii) Behaviour Observation Scales

(BOS), where the rater reports the frequency with which the employee engages in the behaviour specified in the anchor.[7]

(i) *Behaviour Expectation Scales (BES)*

Following are the steps in the development of a BES system:

(a) Identification of critical incidents

Firstly, the jobholders or supervisors or other knowledgeable persons (means who knows the job) are asked to study the job and describe specific examples (critical incidents) of effective and ineffective performance.

(b) Identify the performance dimensions

Now, cluster the critical incidents into a smaller set (5 to 5) performance dimensions and also define each dimension such as conscientiousness, adaptability, promptness, etc.

(c) Reallocate the incidents/anchors

All the organisational critical incidents/anchors are listed in random order. Now ask another group of people who also know the job to reallocate them to specific dimension. Incidents/anchors for which there is less than 75 per cent agreement are not taken for further consideration.

(d) Scale the incidents/anchors

The retained anchors/incidents under each dimension are ranked in order of desirability and a scale is formed. The net result is a rating scale that has examples of behaviour anchoring for each degree[8] (Fig. 10.3).

Although this approach to performance appraisal is quite complex, costly and time-consuming but it also has certain distinct advantages. BARS are based on the job analysis and involvement of those people who know the job and its requirements better than everyone. Secondly, there is separate checking of critical behaviours by second group of evaluators; this enhances the quality in setting clear standards of behaviour. Thirdly, the critical incidents are also easier to provide/explain the ratings to appraisees and help well if challenged by agencies and courts. Fourthly, BARS approach is relatively consistent and reliable in different raters' appraisals of the same person.

Area of Performance	Far Excels Job Requirements	Exceeds Job Requirements	Meets Job Requirements	Needs Improvement	Does Not Meet Minimum Requirements
Quality of work	Leaps tall buildings in a single bound	Leaps tall buildings with running start	Can leap over houses, if prodded	Often stumbles into buildings	Is often knocked down by buildings
Promptness	Is faster than a speeding bullet	Is as fast as a speeding bullet	Would you believe a slow bullet?	Misfires frequently	Wounds self when handling a gun
Initiative	Is stronger than a locomotive	Is stronger than bull elephant	Almost as strong as a bull	Shoots the bull	Smells like a bull
Adaptability	Walks on water	Strong swimmer	A good water treader	Favorite haunt is the water cooler	Passes water in emergencies
Communication	Talks with God	Talks with the angels	Talks to self	Argues with self	Losses most of these arguments

Fig. 10.3: Behaviourally Anchored Rating Scale (BARS)

Source: D. Schultz and S.E. Schultz, *Psychology and Work Today*, Pearson Education, Delhi, 2002, p. 152.

(ii) Behaviour Observation Scales (BOS)

In this method, the evaluators rate the subordinates on the basis of frequency of the critical incidents. In other words, appraisers note the frequency of critical employee behaviours as they are observed to occur over a given period of time and rate subordinates according to that. Development of a BOS is the same as for the BES and both evaluate employees in terms of critical incidents. However, the difference between the two is that in case of BOS frequency of critical incident is noted and becomes a base for rating.

III. Modern Methods

These methods are the improvements over the traditional methods. They attempt to remove the defects of the earlier methods. These methods are the following:

1. Management by objectives (MBO)

There is one thing common in all the traditional methods of performance appraisal that the superior sits in the chair of a judge for his or her employees' performance. He evaluates and gives his or her judgement. However, this philosophy of performance appraisal has attracted a lot of criticism. To overcome this problem, a new concept of performance appraisal known by management of objectives (MBO) was given by Peter F. Drucker in 1954.

MBO refers to joint setting of specific measurable goals and periodical review of the progress made. MBO tends to emphasise a participative but joint determination of objectives followed by a participative but joint evaluation of success in periodic appraisal interviews.[9] The major steps involved in a MBO programme are the following:

(i) Establish the objectives/goals

The first step is the meeting of superior and subordinates with the aim to reach on agreement upon the key goals to be achieved by the subordinate. It's better if there is limited number of goals.

(ii) Performance Reviews

The second step is to compare each employee's actual and targeted performance. Each employee's achievement is compared with the agreed goals.

(iii) Provide the feedback

Finally, the superior discusses with the subordinate his progress towards the earlier set goals. The atmosphere of the discussion is of mutual respect and supportive. Here, the superior does not sit in the capacity of judge and evaluates and passes judgement. Here, the approach is two persons working on joint problems with joint goals.

However, there are few limitations of this method. Firstly, problem comes in the individual goal setting. As all the activities in an organisation are interdependent and interrelated, thus, clear-cut setting of individual objectives is a complex task. Secondly, this is a time-consuming process. Lot of time is taken in meeting, joint setting of objectives, measuring progress and conveying to employee. Thirdly, it is not applicable to all jobs in a firm. There comes difficulty in applying this approach to non-managerial positions such as assembly-line work where there is very little or no flexibility to set performance standards as these are already determined. Fourthly, setting objectives with the subordinate sometimes turns into a tug-of-war with you pushing with higher quotas and the subordinate pushing for lower ones.[10] Lastly, in MBO, comparative assessment of so many employees in an organisation is very difficult task to do. Here, different people set different goals to achieve so comparison is practically impossible to do unlike the traditional methods where all employees are rated on common factors.

2. 360-degree feedback

This method of performance appraisal is also known as multi-source assessment or multi-rater feedback. 360-degree feedback can be defined as the systematic collection and feedback of performance data on an individual or group derived from a number of the stakeholders on their performance.[11] The stakeholders are immediate supervisors, peers, team members, customers (internal and external) and self (Fig. 10.4).

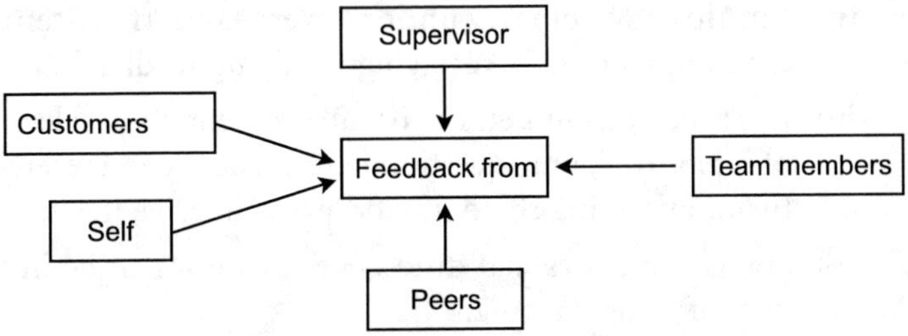

Fig. 10.4: A 360-degree Feedback Model

The main objectives of 360-degree appraisal method is that each employee gets his performance report/feedback from all angles in an organisation (i.e. supervisor, peers, customers, etc.) and this makes him understand how effective he or she is as an employee, team member, co-worker, etc. This provides an employee a broader perspective about his or her performance. This method of performance appraisal is mostly concentrated on the senior level employees for example, managers, directors, senior executives, etc. The main advantages of this method are the following:[12]

(i) Individual gets a broader perspective of how they are perceived by others.

(ii) Increased awareness of and relevance of competencies.

(iii) Increased awareness by senior management that they too have development needs.

(iv) More reliable feedback to senior managers about their performance.

(v) Gaining acceptance of the principle of multiple stakeholders as a measure of performance.

(vi) Encouraging more open feedback—new insights.

(vii) Reinforcing the desired competencies of the business.

(viii) Provides a clear picture to senior management of individual's real worth.

The main drawbacks of this system are the following:

(i) It is difficult to receive and organise feedback from different sources.

(ii) Employees remain under stress and threatening environment while receiving or giving feedback.

(iii) It is time-consuming. Lot of time is spent upon selection of raters, designing questionnaires, sending and receiving them, analysing the data and providing feedback.

(iv) Sometimes, personal differences or biases come in the way of honest rating.

Development and Implementation of 360-degree Feedback

The main steps involved are the following:[13]

1. Define objectives—spell out clearly what 360 degree feedback is expected to achieve.
2. Decide on recipients—who will be at the receiving end of feedback.
3. Decide on who will give the feedback—means supervisor, peers, customers, etc. the stakeholders in the performance.
4. Decide on the areas of work and behaviour on which feedback will be given.
5. Decide on the method of collecting the data—questionnaire, etc.
6. Decide on data analysis and presentation—develop or purchase software.
7. Plan implementation programme—it is desirable to pilot the process, preferably at the top level or with all the managers in a function or department.
8. Analyse outcome of pilot scheme.
9. Plan and implement full programme—this should include briefing, communicating, training and support from HR and, possibly, the external consultants.
10. Monitor and evaluate—this process can cause anxiety and stress or produce little practical gain in terms of development and improved performance for a lot of effort.

3. Psychological appraisals

Psychological appraisals are conducted to assess the future potential of the employees. In this method, the past and actual performance is not assessed. The focus is on the future potential. Big organisations generally employ full-time industrial psychologists for the purpose. Usually, the appraisals consist of psychological tests, in-department interviews and discussions with the immediate supervisors. The areas covered about an employee are his or her emotional stability, reasoning abilities, sociability, intellectual abilities, ability to foresee the future and analytical abilities. The psychologist prepares his report on the above said characteristics of employees. The report may suggest or predict the employee's future performance. This will help in taking decisions regarding employee's career planning and development, training, placement, etc.

4. Assessment center

This is a widely used technique of selecting and appraising the candidates. Earlier, it was called situational testing. It was developed by the German army in 1920s to select officer candidates of higher quality. Generally, an assessment center involves 6 to 12 candidates at a time. These candidates will be evaluated with the help of a series of exercises over next several days (1 to 3 days). These tests do not assess actual job behaviour but a variety of activities that are likely to encounter on the job. The candidates or managers participate in simulated job tasks such as in-basket tests, role-playing, leaderless group discussion, computer simulations, group problem solving, management or business games, interviewing, etc. The raters, who are the trained observers, record the observations of participants and, later on, discuss these observations and finally give their decision regarding the performance of each participant.

5. Human resource accounting (HRA)

According to American Accounting Association, "HRA is the process of identifying and measuring data about human resources and communicating this information to interested parties". HRA aims to quantify the economic value of people to the organisation in order to provide input for managerial and financial decisions.[14]

HRA evaluates the cost and contributions of human resources to the organisation. Cost of human resources refers to all expenses incurred on human resource planning, recruitment, selection, induction, placement, training and development, salaries, benefits, etc. Contribution refers to revenue from employee services to the organisation. It provides information about the values of human capital to the organisation. It facilitates the effective and efficient management of human resources by providing information about utility of cost reduction and budgeting control.

PROBLEMS ASSOCIATED WITH PERFORMANCE APPRAISAL

Certain barriers work against the effectiveness of the appraisal system. Most employers still depend on graphic-type rating scales to appraise performance but these scales are especially susceptible to several problems: unclear standards, halo effect, central tendency, leniency or strictness and bias.[15]

1. Unclear standards

In some rating scales, the traits and degrees of merit are ambiguous. For example, different raters have different definitions of terms 'good', 'bad', 'fair', 'creativity', 'dependability', etc.

2. Halo effect/error

This occurs when the rater is influenced by ratee's specific qualities (good or bad) and he evaluates the entire performance accordingly.

3. Central tendency

This problem occurs when the rater evaluates all employees the same way, generally, rating them all average.

4. Leniency or strictness

This problem occurs when the rater has a tendency to rate all the employees either high or low on a scale.

5. Bias

Personal characteristics like age, sex, caste, etc. can affect the supervisor's rating of subordinates.

6. Psychological blocks

There are certain psychological barriers due to which the raters do no tend to become impartial or objective in evaluating their subordinates. For example, considering appraisal as extra burden, supervisor's feeling of insecurity, disliking resentment by subordinates, disliking conveying poor performance to subordinates, etc.

7. Faulty assumptions

There are some faulty assumptions of both the parties—superior and the subordinates, about the appraisal system, because of which it does not work properly. These are the following:

(i) The assumption that managers naturally wish to make fair and accurate appraisal of subordinates is not practical.

(ii) Another faulty assumption is that managers take a particular appraisal system as perfect and feel that once they have launched a programme that would continue forever.

(iii) Managers sometimes assume that personal opinion is better than appraisal and they find little use of systematic appraisal and review procedures.

(iv) Managers' assumptions that employees want to know frankly where they stand and what their supervisors think about them are not valid. Infact, subordinates resist to be appraised.

KEY TERMS

ACR
Assessment center method
BARS
Critical incidents
Human resource accounting
MBO
Performance appraisal
Psychological appraisals
Psychological blocks
360-degree feedback

QUESTIONS

1. What is performance appraisal? What are its objectives?
2. Explain the performance appraisal process in detail.
3. Describe the traditional methods of performance appraisal.
4. What are the modern methods of performance appraisal?

5. What are the constraints in effective performance appraisal system?

ENDNOTES

1. D. Schultz and S.E. Schultz, *Psychology and Work Today,* Pearson Education, Delhi, 2004, p. 127.
2. R.S. Schuler, *Personnel and Human Resource Management,* West Publishing, New York, 1981, p. 221.
3. S.J. Carroll and C.E. Schneir, *Performance Appraisal and Review Systems: The Identification, Measurement, Development of Performance in Organisations,* 1982, Glenview, IL: Scott, Foresman.
4. D.C. Sharma and R.C. Sharma, *Personnel Management &Industrial Relations*, First Edition, S.J. Publications, Meerut, p. 191.
5. Richard D. Scott, "Taking Subjectivity Out of Performance Appraisal", *Personnel*, Vol. 50, No. 4, July-August, 1973, pp. 45-49.
6. Edwin B. Flippo, *Personnel Management*, Sixth Edition, McGraw-Hill, New York, 1984, p. 234.
7. *Ibid.*
8. *Ibid.*
9. *Ibid.*, p. 241.
10. Gary Dessler, *Human Resource Management*, Pearson Education, 9th edition, Delhi, 2004, p. 252.
11. P. Ward, "A 360 Degree Turn for the Better", *People Management*, 1995, February, pp. 20-22.
12. Michael Armstrong, *A Handbook of Human Resource Management Practice,* Ninth Edition, Kogan Page, London, 2005, p. 519.
13. *Ibid.*, p. 518.
14. S. Sackmann, E. Flamholz and M. Bullen, "Human Asset Accounting", *Journal of Accounting Literature*, 1989, 5, pp. 235-64.
15. Gary Dessler, op. cit., p. 253.
16. D.C. Sharma and R.C. Sharma, op. cit., p. 196.

Career Planning and Development

11

LEARNING OBJECTIVES

After studying this chapter, you should be able to:

1. Understand the nature of career planning and development
2. Describe the career development programme
3. Describe the life cycle of a career

Once an employee is hired, trained, and appraised, it seems like that the development function comes to an end. However, neither organisation's requirements nor individual's abilities are ever constant. So, in an organisation's comprehensive employee development programme, people's long-term career planning and development programme should be taken side by side.

MEANING AND DEFINITION

A career can be defined as a sequence of separate but related work activities that provides continuity, order and meaning in a person's life.[1] Earlier, organisations did not give importance to an individual's career development. It is ironic that what is most precious to the individual insofar as work is concerned, that is, the career, is given the least attention by the organisation.[2] An organisation should give opportunities to its employees to grow and develop. This will ensure that your workforce keeps pace with the demands of the ever-changing business environment. Moreover, once you make these kinds of investments, you will be able to grow a loyal workforce for your organisation.

Career planning and development is a deliberate process through which a person becomes aware of personal career-related attributes and lifelong series of stages that contribute to his or her career fulfillment.[3] Career planning and development is not a one-shot training programme. It has longer time frame and wider focus. It is an ongoing organised and formalized effort that recognizes people as a vital organisational resource.[4]

In contrast to traditional views, nowadays, many organisations view career development as a way of preventing job burnout, improving the quantity of employees' work lives and meeting affirmative action goals[5] (see Table 11.1). This changed emphasis has largely resulted from a combination of competitive pressures (such as downsizing and technological changes) and workers demand for more opportunities for growth and skill development.[6]

Table 11.1: The Traditional Versus Carrier Development Focus

HR Activity	Traditional Focus	Career Development Focus
Human resource planning	Analyzes jobs, skills, tasks—present and future. Projects needs. Uses statistical data.	Adds information about individual interests, preferences, and the like to data.
Training and development	Provides opportunities for learning skills, information, and attitudes related to job.	Provides career path information. Add individual growth orientation.
Performance appraisal	Rating and/or rewards.	Adds development plans and individual goal setting.
Recruiting and placement	Matching organisation's needs with qualified individuals.	Matches individual and jobs based on a number of variables including employees' career interests.
Compensation and benefits	Rewards for time, productivity, talent, and so on.	Adds non-job-related activities to be rewarded, such as United Way leadership positions.

Source: G. Dessler, *Human Resource Management*, Pearson Education, Delhi, 2004, p. 274.

CAREER PLANNING AND DEVELOPMENT—WHOSE RESPONSIBILITY?

The employer and the employee are equally responsible for career planning and development.

Employee responsibility

In today's competitive world of business, employees must take active role in career planning and implementing their own personal development. Employees should be responsible to update their skills, abilities and knowledge. Some organisations provide employee empowerment approach to development where employees can create their own developmental programmes (see Exhibit 11.1). However, giving employees total responsibility for managing their own careers can create problem in today's flatter organisations, where opportunities to move through the hierarchy are far fewer than in traditional bureaucratic organisations.[7]

Exhibit 11.1: Employees Responsibility of their Careers

When 29-year-old Vicky Michener discovered that she is one of the youngest employees at consulting firm of Management Systems International, she spotted an opportunity. Michener knew that most of her co-workers had significant experience she could learn from, but the company had no mechanism that allowed experienced workers to share their knowledge with less experienced workers. What to do? Michener developed a plan for a mentorship programme through which junior employees could acquire knowledge from the senior employees. Her supervisor and the company president responded enthusiastically to her plan and at the same time of this writing are working to implement it. Here's how the plan works: Each junior worker receives feedback and direction from a main advisor as well as from additional resource people. This way, junior employees can receive both general direction and specific, quick feedback as needed. For example, mentors might provide useful suggestions on steps needed for the worker to achieve his or her goals, and can provide feedback immediately after the worker completes a project.

Source: Luis R. Gomez—Mejia, David B. Balkin and Robert L. Cardy, *Managing Human Resources,* 3rd Edition, Pearson Education, Delhi, 2003, p. 296.

The primary responsibility of an employee's career development lies on the employee himself or herself. Following are few suggestions for the employees in this regard:

1. Set your own mission statement—what you want to achieve in job and life?
2. Identify your strengths and weaknesses.
3. Take full responsibility for your own growth and development.
4. Manage your image inside and outside the organisation. Show your achievements.
5. Always update yourself with current knowledge, skills and abilities.
6. Build your own network by attending conferences, seminars and social gatherings.
7. Try to be a team member. Provide solutions and do not point out the problems.
8. Hope for the best but be prepared for the worst. Always have different options available with you. Develop contingency plans for yourself, in case of worse situations like lay-offs, retrenchment, downsizing, M&A's, closure, etc.

Organisation's Responsibility

An organisation and its managers can play a very influential role in a person's career development. A manager should provide developmental assignments to an employee and also provide him constructive and timely performance feedback. The employer can provide career-oriented training and development opportunities, offer career management programmes and establish career-oriented performance appraisal and job-posting policies.[8] The essence of a progressive career development programme is built on providing support for employees to continually add to their skills, abilities and knowledge and for this the logical sequence of steps includes:[9]

1. Clearly communicating the organisation's goals and future strategies to its people so that they know what is the target of organisation and how they can themselves develop to achieve this.
2. Creating growth opportunities, provide employees good opportunities for new, interesting and challenging tasks.

3. Offering financial assistance—may be in the form of tuition reimbursement so that they keep current knowledge.
4. Providing the time for each employee to learn-such as paid time off from work for off-the-job training and development.

For instance, a college or university or UGC supports a teacher/lecturer in his career development such as providing him paid study leave to go for higher degree like Ph.D, financial support for research projects, payment for attending conferences and seminars nationally as well as internationally, refresher courses, etc.

In addition to the above-said steps, an employer can take many other steps like the following:

1. Realistic job previews

Providing realistic job previews before actually hiring a person is very important. Realistic job previews can help prospective employees more accurately gauge whether the job is indeed for them and particularly whether a job's demands are a good fit with a candidate's skills and interests.[10] This is especially important for a fresh candidate whose confidence is yet to build up. By providing interesting and challenging job to a fresh candidate an employer can prevent reality shock. Reality shock is considered as phenomenon that occurs when the new employee's high job expectations meet/confront with reality of a boring, uninteresting and unchallenging job.

2. Career-oriented appraisals

In this the supervisor or manager is so trained that not only he appraises the employee performance but also aligns that performance with the feasible career path and finds out where training and development is required.

3. Planned job rotation

This refers to well-planned movement of an employee from one position to another so as to enhance his or her role with the organisation.

4. Mentoring

A mentor is an older and respected manager or professional who counsels and listens for feelings as well as facts and stimulates people through ideas and information.[11] Mentoring is a developmentally oriented relationship between senior and junior colleagues or peers that involves advising, role modeling, sharing contacts and giving general support.[12] Mentoring can be voluntary and informal or involuntary and formal. Informal mentoring is generally more effective than mentoring done solely as a formal responsibility.[13]

5. Job-posting

This refers to the announcement of job openings in the company either posting on bulletin board, or in a company's newsletter. Job-posting system have the advantage of reinforcing the notion that the organisation promotes from within.[14]

6. Coaching

It refers to meetings and discussion between a manager and his or her employee regarding the latter's career development. Coaching involves setting of conducive environment, actively listen to employee, ask questions and provide useful feedback.

CAREER ANCHORS

Research has shown that certain attitudes formed early in life to guide many people through out their careers.[15] These attitudinal syndromes serve to 'anchor' an individual to one or a few related types of career. Having knowledge of these anchors helps in career planning and development. Five identified anchors were:

1. Managerial competence

The fundamental characteristics of the individuals anchored by overriding interest in management include a capacity to take responsibility, ability to influence and control others, and skills in problem-solving. People who wish to be effective managers should possess competence like interpersonal, intergroup, emotional and analytical.

2. Technical-functional competence

Their primary interest is in the performance of functional work. They want to be expert in their field.

3. Security

They are more attached to a specific organisation and area than to their work.

4. Creativity

They have an overriding interest in developing or creating something new. They become entrepreneurs and want to be identified with their product or service.

5. Autonomy-independence

They have an overriding interest in freedom and independence. They prefer their own working time. For example, consultants, freelance writers, etc. A HR manager must have knowledge of these basic drives and needs of employees while planning for their career development.

CAREER DEVELOPMENT PROGRAMME

A well-designed career development programme has the following three stages:

1. Career need assessment

This refers to assisting employers in assessing their own personal career needs. Often employees are uncertain as to which type of work will suit them. So, a HR manager should help them in this decision-making process. A number of evaluation instruments are available that help a person in determining his or her main interests and basic aptitudes. For example, Strong's Vocational Interest Blank. This helps individuals to do their own career planning.

2. Career opportunities

As employees have definite career needs, so it is obligatory upon an organisation to chart out specific career paths through the organisation. Employees want to know what types of job are now and will be available in the near future. What type of duties are to be performed whether any training and development is required or not and what jobs lead to other jobs in the organisation.

3. Need-opportunity alignment

After the employees have assessed their career needs and have become aware of organisational career opportunities, rest is the alignment of need and opportunities. Now, a HR manager should select suitable development technique, for example, special assignment, planned position rotation, coaching, mentoring, etc. Few developmental techniques have been discussed earlier in this chapter.

LIFE CYCLE OF A CAREER

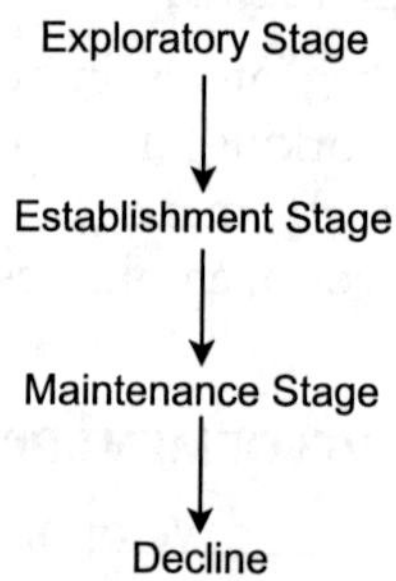

Fig. 11.1: Career Development Cycle

A career can be viewed as made up of various stages (Fig. 11.1), these are the following:

1. Exploratory stage

This is the stage when a fresh employee enters the organisation. Organisation should understand its responsibility towards the newcomer and try to prevent the reality shock by making the job challenging and interesting. Research has shown that more challenging the job in the first year of service, the more effective and successful the employee will be 5 or 10 years later.[16] Apart from initial training, other approach includes 'sink or swim' means full-time training with no job responsibility and work while training.

2. Establishment stage

At this stage, the employee has chosen some specific direction. For a successful career development programme an organisation is required to feedback the progress information to employee. For example, first performance appraisal, first promotion, first completed project/assignment, first foreign trip all are extremely important occasions in a young person's career.

3. Maintenance stage

This is the stage when an employee attempts to retain what he or she has established in the career. In today's competitive and dynamic business environment, this requires continued learning and updating in order to maintain their continuity with the organisation. This is the stage where an employee faces mid-career crisis. In some cases, people try to switch over to an entirely different job. For example, an employee leaves the factory job for teaching profession.

4. Decline

This is the stage of retirement. Although it shocks everyone but it is almost inevitable. Organisation should ensure a smooth retirement event.

KEY TERMS

Career	Coaching
Career anchors	Job-posting
Career development cycle	Mentoring
Career planning and development	Realistic job previews
Career-oriented appraisal	Reality shock

QUESTIONS

1. Describe career planning and development and give its significance.
2. How an employer can play an influential role in an employee's career development?
3. Describe the career anchors.
4. Describe a career development programme.
5. What are the various stages in the life cycle of a career?

ENDNOTES

1. Edwin B. Flippo, *Personnel Management*, Sixth Edition, McGraw-Hill, New York, 1984, p. 248.

2. J. Leach, "The Nation and Nature of Careers", *The Personnel Administrator*, 1977, Vol. 22, No. 7, September, p. 50.
3. Gary Dessler, *Human Resource Management*, Pearson Education, Ninth Edition, Delhi, 2004, p. 274.
4. Z.B. Leibowitz, "Designing Career Development Systems: Principles and Practices", *Human Resource Planning*, 1987, Vol. 10, pp. 195-207.
5. T. Gutteridge and F. Otte, "Organisational Career Development: What's Going On Out There?" *Training and Development*, 1983, Vol. 37, pp. 22-26.
6. J.E.A. Russell, "Career Development Intervention in Organisation's", *Journal of Vocational Behaviour*, 1991, Vol. 38, pp. 237-287.
7. Luis R. Gomez–Mejia, David B. Balkin and Robert L. Cardy, *Managing Human Resources,* Third Edition, Pearson Education, Delhi, 2003, p. 296.
8. Gary Dessler, op. cit., p. 275.
9. Stephen P. Robbins, *Organisational Behavior,* Tenth Edition, Pearson Education, Delhi, 2004, p. 497.
10. Gary Dessler, op. cit., p. 275.
11. Edwin B. Flippo, op. cit., p. 261.
12. Luis R. Gomez–Mejia, David B. Balkin and Robert L. Cardy, op. cit., p. 309.
13. R.A. Noe, "An Investigation of the Determinants of Successful Assigned Mentoring Relationships", *Personnel Psychology*, 1988, Vol. 41, pp. 457-479.
14. T. Gutteridge, "Organisational Career Development Systems: The State of the Practice", in D.T. Hall et al., *Career Development in Organisation's*, 1986, San Francisco: Jossey Bass, pp. 50-94.
15. Edgar H. Schein, "How Career Anchors' Hold Executives to their Career Paths", *Personnel*, 1975, May–June, Vol. 52, No. 3, pp. 11-24.
16. D.E. Berlw and D.T. Hall, "The Socialization of Managers: Effects of Expectations on Performance", *Administrative Science Quarterly*, 1966, June, Vol. 11, No. 2, p. 222.

Promotions, Transfers, Demotions and Separations

12

LEARNING OBJECTIVES

After studying this chapter, you should be able to:

1. Describe the purposes, policy and types of promotion
2. Describe the purposes, policy and types of transfers
3. Describe the principles of demotion policy
4. Understand the costs and benefits associated with separations
5. State the types of separations

By promotions, transfers, demotions and separations, an organisation makes adjustments in its workforce size in order to meet the changing business situations. Changes may be due to change in the organisation structure, demands of product or service, employment rate, methods or techniques, etc. All this necessitates workforce readjustment according to new situation.

PROMOTION

Promotion refers to advancement to position of increased responsibility. In other words, promotion is the advancement of an employee to a better job—better in terms of greater responsibility, more prestige or status, greater skill and specially, increased rate of pay or salary.[1] From these definitions, it is clear that promotion involves the following ingredients:

1. Improves job, status and prestige

2. More responsibility
3. Increase in pay and perks.

PURPOSES OF PROMOTIONS

The main purposes of promotion in organisations are the following:

1. To recognise and reward the efforts of an employee.
2. To attract and retain the competent personnel.
3. To inculcate enthusiasm in employees to acquire knowledge, skills and jobs in the organisation.
4. To develop a competitive spirit in the workforce.
5. To motivate employee for higher productivity.
6. To develop a ready internal pool of competent personnel within the organisation who can take the higher level of challenging jobs.
7. To promote a sense of belongingness in the employees.
8. To boost the morale in the workforce.
9. To increase an employee's effectiveness.
10. To place a worker in a position where he or she is more valuable to the organisation.
11. To fill up vacancies from within the organisation.
12. To reduce discontent and labour unrest.
13. To promote interest in training and development programmes.
14. To increase job satisfaction.

PRINCIPLES OF A PROMOTION POLICY

Promotion is a very critical subject in case of human resource management. It should be handled very carefully. It may prove to be a source of satisfaction, if handled well or it may attract lot of criticism from employees in case of mishandling. It's a duty of a HR manager to design a sound promotion policy in organisation and also ensures its full implementation. A sound promotion policy means a policy, which is fair, impartial and enjoy consistency. It should outline the following matters clearly:

1. It should state management's intention regarding filling of vacancies from within the organisation (i.e. by promotions) or recruit from outside or from both. Mostly, the superior/higher vacancies in an organisation are filled through external recruitment while the lower level vacancies are filled by promotions.
2. Once it is decided that these positions will be filled up by promotions, the next is the decision regarding the basis of promotion. Management should state clearly the base of promotion, i.e. whether seniority is considered or merit or both. Seniority means the length of service and is counted from the date of his or her appointment in the organisation. Merit refers to a person's qualifications and his or her competence. There always remains a great controversy with regard to the question whether promotions should be based on seniority or merit or both. Each base has its own advantages/merits and disadvantages/demerits.

SENIORITY BASED PROMOTION

Seniority is the oldest and widely used basis of promotion especially in government owned organisations, unionised industrial establishments and educational institutes.

Advantages

It has the following advantages:

1. It is easy to measure the length of service and judge the seniority.
2. It brings objectivity in distinguishing among personnel so less scope for subjectivity or favouritism.
3. It is simple to understand and easy to administer.
4. Trade unions provide full support to this system.
5. This ensures a more experienced person takes higher position first.
6. It creates a sense of security.
7. It helps to reward loyal workers.
8. Less scope of grievances and conflicts.

9. Employees are willing to work under an older and experienced person.
10. It is economical.
11. It reduces labour turnover, as employees will not be willing to lose their seniority in case of quitting.

Disadvantages

1. Employees with longest service need not necessarily be the more competent.
2. Young, ambitious and able persons with little service may get frustrated and leave the organisation.
3. Seniority fails to differentiate between efficient and inefficient workers.
4. It kills the enthusiasm to do better as everyone will promote as his or her turn comes.
5. It acts as a hurdle in attracting capable persons.
6. It is not a valid assumption that employees learn more with length of service. Up to a certain age employees learn and beyond that learning capabilities may diminish.

MERIT BASED PROMOTION

When the promotion is given to an employee on the basis of his qualification, ability, competence or performance ignoring of his or her seniority in the organisation, then the promotion is known on the basis of merit. It is just like a reward or incentive for hard work, dedication and excellent performance. Management favour promotions on the basis of merit.

Advantages

Its advantages are as follows:

1. It encourages, recognises and rewards extra knowledge, competence and efficiency of employees.
2. It motivates the competent persons to work hard.
3. It helps to retain the capable persons.
4. It increases the productivity.

5. It increases the efficiency and profitability of the organisation.
6. It encourages employees to keep on learning, adding knowledge and skills, enhances their personal growth also.
7. It results in maximum utilisation of employees.

Disadvantages

1. Accurate measurement of merit is highly difficult.
2. Scope for subjectivity and favouritism.
3. Trade unions distrust management's integrity in judging merit.
4. Loyal senior persons are not rewarded.
5. Feeling of discontent among senior employees.

So, whether it is seniority or merit as the basis for promotion, each has its own merits and demerits. Managements mostly prefer merit base for promotions as it increases the productivity and profitability of organisation. Moreover, it rewards those who deserve it. But trade unions prefer seniority as the sole basis for promotion in order to protect the interests of their workers.

A combination of both seniority and merit can be considered as the basis for promotion. The best option is to find a mid-way, i.e. blend of these two systems should be used. In other words, a balance should be struck between the two and a new basis of promotion should be developed which will satisfy all the concerned parties. A sound promotion policy should ensure that whenever there are two employees of equal seniority, then ability or competence should be the deciding factor in a promotion. And, on the other hand, where two persons of almost equal competence are available, then seniority should be the deciding factor.

3. A promotion policy should provide a well-defined and clear-cut promotion chart. This chart will display the various ladders of promotion within an organisation. This chart helps management in clearing all doubts, which the employees may have.

4. A promotion policy should use the job analysis information. Job analysis information helps in knowing the basic requirements for job in terms of competency. Employees should know what job demands are.
5. A promotion policy should make a provision for use of performance appraisal reports. It will indicate whether employee can match the job requirements or not. Whether there is a need for any training and development programme.
6. A promotion policy should be discussed with the trade union in the organisation and agreement should be signed showing trade unions acceptance to the policy.
7. A promotion policy should not aim at forcing promotions on reluctant employees.
8. In case the promotions are to be given on the basis of merit, then it should be displayed openly at prominent places so that interested persons can apply. This is known as job-posting or bid system.
9. A sound promotion policy should indicate clearly whether to promote employees against vacancies or non-vacancies. When the employees are promoted after a minimum period of service even when there was no vacancy at high level it is called promotion on non-vacancy basis. For example, a lecturer after certain years of teaching experience will become senior lecturer then reader and then professor. These are the time-bound promotions.
10. A sound promotion policy should not make provision of frequent promotions. This is neither good for employer nor for employee. For employer, frequent promotions means higher salary, perks, etc. For employee, frequent promotions will keep on changing their nature of assignments and this will prevent stability and peace in their mind.
11. Finally, a promotion policy should be communicated to the workforce. To have a sound promotion policy and not communicated openly will only create

suspicions. Policy should be communicated in the form of manuals, in the standing orders, or in the form of agreements required with the trade union.

TYPES OF PROMOTION

Promotions may be of following types:

1. Horizontal promotion

This type of promotion includes an increase in responsibilities, pay and a change in designation. However, the employee doesn't shift the job classification. For example, a production worker shifted to HR department to develop new skills. Another example can be that enrich the job and provide training to enhance the opportunity for assuming more responsibility.[2]

2. Vertical promotion

In this type of promotion, an employee is moved to higher level in the hierarchy. This involves increase in pay, status and responsibilities.

3. Dry promotion

This type of promotion involves increase in responsibilities and status without any increase in pay.

TRANSFERS

A transfer refers to a movement of an employee from one job to another with no change in salary, status and responsibilities. In other words, a transfer is a change in job where the new job is substantially equal to the old in terms of pay, status and responsibilities. The main objective of transfer is to make adjustment in the work, place and the employee. Employees seek transfers for many reasons, including personal enrichment, more interesting jobs, greater convenience, better hours, location of work and so on—or to jobs offering greater advancement possibilities.[3] On the other hand, employers may transfer a worker to vacate a position where he or she is no longer needed, or more generally to find a better fit for the employee within the firm.[4]

PURPOSES OF TRANSFERS

The main purposes behind the transfers in any organisation are the following:

1. To meet the organisational requirements—Transfer may be due to changes in the volume of production, change in technology, changes in product mix, market fluctuations, production schedules, etc. Because of these factors there may be surplus labour in one department or plant and there may be shortage of labour in another department or plant. So, employees are transfered in order to stabilise the situation.
2. To meet employees request—Employee also make request for transfer because to work under a friendly boss, to work on interesting jobs where advancement chances are bright, to work in the branch nearest to their home town, to work on a job of flexible working hours, etc. A young female employee may ask for transfer, as she wants to join her husband.
3. To utilise employee's service properly—An employee may be transfered to another place where the management can utilise his or her capacities better.
4. To increase the productivity of an individual. Transfer from one job to another breaks the monotony associated with the earlier job.
5. To correct the faulty initial placement of an employee.
6. To suit the health and age of an employee.
7. To correct the incompatibilities between the employee and boss or between one employee and his or her colleague.
8. To penalise an employee so he or she may be transferred to remote branch or near a village or in border area.
9. To maintain a tenure system. An employee holds a certain job for a fixed tenure then he or she is made to move to next place.

PRINCIPLES OF A TRANSFER POLICY

Every organisation should have a clear, unambiguous and sound transfer policy. It must be based on the following principles:

1. It should clearly indicate the types and circumstances under which a transfer will be made.

2. It should state the frequency of transfers and minimum time period between the transfers.
3. It should tell who will be responsible for initiating and approving the transfers.
4. It should indicate the criteria or the basis of transfer and follow it strictly.
5. It should point out the effect of transfer on the pay and seniority of the transferred employee.
6. It should indicate whether this transfer is temporary or permanent.
7. It should make a provision for timely communicating the transfer decision.
8. It should specify the area of the organisation over which the transfers can be made.

TYPES OF TRANSFERS

There are various types of transfers such as (1) those designed to enhance training and development, (2) those making possible adjustment to varying volumes of work within the firm, and (3) those designed to remedy a problem of poor placement.[5] Specifically, transfers can be of following types:

1. Production transfers

These are transfers made from one department or plant to the other department or plant where there are labour surplus or shortage. It is not desirable that in one part of the organisation there is condition of surplus labour or lay-offs and in another part of the organisation there is need/requirement of labour. So, production transfer helps to stabilise the employment in the organisation.

2. Replacement transfers

These are similar to production transfers as these are also intended to avoid lay-offs, especially of senior employees. A new employee may be replaced by a senior employee to avoid laying-off senior employee.

3. Remedial transfers

Transfers made to remedy the situation are known as remedial transfers. These take place if the initial placement of the employee has been faulty, or the employee cannot get along with his supervisor or with other workers in the department. Then his or her transfer to a more appropriate job or under a more agreeable supervisor might result in better performance.

4. Versatility transfers

These are made to make an employee more competent and versatile by shifting him from one job to another. In this way, an employee learns more skills and gets varied and broader job experience. These also help the employee for future advancement.

5. Shift transfers

When the industrial establishments are operating on more than one shift then shift transfers are made. An employee is shifted from one shift to another on the same work. These transfers are made on rotation basis.

DEMOTIONS

Demotion is just the opposite of promotion. It means shifting an employee to a lower level where responsibilities and wages are less. Demotion can be defined as the assignment of an individual to a job of lower rank and pay usually involving lower level of difficulty and responsibility.[6]

REASONS FOR DEMOTIONS

The main causes for demoting an employee from his or her present position are the following:

1. Employees when got promoted on the basis of seniority and past performance may prove to be incompetent in doing the higher-level job. They find it difficult to meet the performance standards. So, such employees may be demoted back to the lower level job where their capabilities, aptitude and knowledge suit with the requirements of the job.
2. Demotions may result from adverse business conditions such as closure of certain departments or plants,

withdrawal of some products, reduction in quality of production. Also, organisation may start downsizing. In such situations, new or junior employees may be laid-off or retrenched and senior employees may be demoted.

3. Changes in technology, techniques and methods result in the demand of new and higher level skills. Present employees if do not acquire new skills, knowledge and abilities through training, etc. may be demoted to lower level jobs where they are suitable.
4. Demotions also result from a disciplinary action. However, it is rarely used in the organisations.

PRINCIPLES OF DEMOTION POLICY

Demotion is a painful action. Not only it reduces an employee's authority, morale, interest, job satisfaction, pay, status in the organisation, it also affects badly his image and status in the society. A demotion policy should be based upon sound principles like the following:

1. Clearly specify the list of circumstances under which an employee will be demoted.
2. Indicate the authority responsible to initiate a demotion.
3. Indicate the nature of demotion, i.e. whether it is permanent or temporary.
4. Indicate the jobs from and to which demotions will be made.
5. Indicate the criteria for demotion, i.e. whether length of service or merit or both, for example, in case of need, a junior person will be demoted first or person whose performance is poor will be demoted first.
6. Demotion policy should be clearly communicated to employees well in advance.
7. Indicate clearly the competent authority, which will investigate any alleged violation of demotion principles.
8. In case violation is discovered, there should be a consistent and equitable application of penalty.

9. There should be a provision for review.

SEPARATIONS

Separation refers to termination of the employment. It means termination of an employee's association or membership in an organisation. An employee separation occurs when an employee ceases to be a member of an organisation.[7] Separations are painful to both employer and employee. For an employer, it may damage his organisation's reputation in industry or in society and restrict its ability to attract talented employees in future. For an employee, depending upon the type of separation, it may result in loss of money, job and status. So, the unpleasant task of separation should be handled carefully in an organisation.

COSTS AND BENEFITS ASSOCIATED WITH SEPARATIONS

There are certain costs and benefits associated with the separation, these are the following:

Costs

The costs of employee separation depend on whether managers intend to eliminate the position or to replace the departing employee. By eliminating positions, the company can reduce costs in the long run.[8] This is the main reason why companies' across the globe have downsized their workforce. In September 2006 Intel, the world's largest chip-maker announced its plan to slash 10,500 jobs by the middle of 2007. Even when the positions are eliminated separation costs may be considerable. Apart from monetary loss (for example incentives offered) a company loses the talented people and morale of the remaining workforce also goes down.

In the case of replacement of employee, separation costs include costs associated with recruitment, selection, training and development and also the compensation in the form of pay and benefits. For example, companies provide severance or separation pay for laid-off employees. This has to be given as per law whether or not they will be replaced.

Other costs include costs associated with the administration of separation itself, for example, conduct of exit interview.

Recently, Supreme Court has made exit interview compulsory for bank officials opting to quit. Another is cost on outplacement assistance. Outplacement is an HR programme created to help separated employees' deal with the emotional stress of job loss and provide assistance in finding a new job.[9] It includes counselling and provides training for new skills required on new job.

Benefits

Mostly separations are considered in a negative sense, however, there are certain benefits also associated with it. A certain level of employee separation is a good and necessary part of doing business and the benefits of employee separation to the organisation include the following: labour costs are reduced, poor performers are replaced, innovation is increased and opportunities for greater diversity are enhanced.[10] There are benefits for employees too, such as they escape from working in uninteresting and unpleasant situations. Other benefits are as follows:

1. Reduced labour cost

By reducing the size of workforce, an organisation reduces its total labour costs. Although compensation has to be paid in case of lay-offs and retrenchment but in long-run salary saving results from such decision outperform the separation pay.

2. Replacement of poor performers

In case a poor performer leaves the company or is terminated as per company rules, organisation gets opportunity to hire good performers in future.

3. Increased innovation and creativity

Newly hired people are great source of new thoughts and ideas for the organisation.

4. Opportunity for greater diversity

After selection, an organisation can hire workforce from different backgrounds and cultures. This especially helps MNCs having work teams comprising people of different countries.

TYPES OF SEPARATIONS

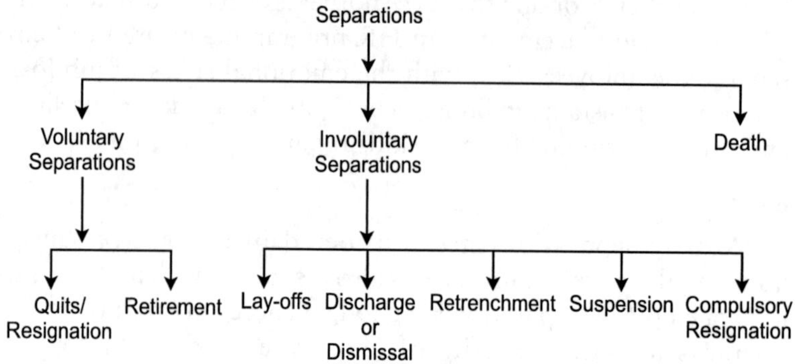

Fig. 12.1: Types of Separations

I. Voluntary Separations

Separations, which are initiated by the employee, are known as voluntary separations. This separation occurs when an employee decides, for personal or professional reasons, to end the relationship with the employer.[11] Voluntary separations can be following types:

1. Quits/resignations

An employee resigns or quits due to several reasons such as ill health, physical disabilities, availability of attractive alternative jobs, maladjustment in the organisation, and dissatisfaction with the job. A female employee may quit due to marriage, as she has to join her husband in other place. Also, female employees resign to avoid work-family conflict.

2. Retirements

Similar to quit, retirements are also initiated by the employee. Usually employees postpone their retirement until they reach the age of retirement. However, these days many employees are opting for VRS (also called Golden Handshake Scheme) offered by the companies both in public and private sectors. As the decision depends solely upon the employee so trade union cannot object this separation. Unlike quits, retirement results in employee receiving retirement benefits such as lump sum payment, pension benefits and other social security benefits. These benefits make the retirement decision financially attractive for employee and reduce surplus labour for management. VRS are good alternative to lay-offs, as they seem to be gentle and thus protect company image.

II. Involuntary Separations

It refers to a separation, which occurs when management decides to terminate its relationship with an employee due to (1) economic necessity or (2) a poor fit between the employee and the orgnisation.[12] Involuntary separations are painful decisions that should taken very carefully as per company's employment policy and according to laws. Following are the types of voluntary separation:

1. Lay-offs

Lay-offs means temporarily putting aside the workers. The reason may be due to the change in companies' business environment, global competition, reductions in product demand, changing technologies that reduce the need for workers and mergers and acquisitions are the primary factors behind most layoff.[13]

According to Section 2(kkk) of the Industrial Disputes Act, 1947, lay-offs means the failure, refusal or inability of an employer to give employment to a worker whose name is borne on the muster rolls of his industrial establishment and who has not been retrenched. The reasons of lay-off may be the following:

1. Shortage of coal, power or raw material
2. Accumulation of stocks
3. Breakdown of machinery
4. Natural calamity
5. Any other connected reason.

Lay-offs result in immediate unemployment although temporary in nature. Lay-offs affect the morale of the remaining workforce. As the employer initiates lay-offs, employees have to be paid compensation for the period of lay-off. According to section 25 of Industrial Disputes Act, 1947, a workman is entitled to lay-off compensation at the rate equal to fifty per cent of the total of the basic wage and dearness allowance for the period of his or her lay-off except for weekly holidays, which may intervene. Compensation can normally be claimed for not more than forty-five days during any period of twelve months.

Lay-off hurt the image of the company. It is a decision, which has powerful impact. Companies may face difficulty in future to attract talented people; its value of share may go down in the market as the investors might think that lay-off is a signal of serious trouble inside the company. Thus, management should be ready for such consequences. It should be careful in designing the basis for lay-off, i.e. whether merit or seniority. Merit means people who are not performing well they will be laid-off first. But for this performance appraisal will be necessary in order to determine who is efficient and who is not performing as per standards. However, trade unions may show resistance to this procedure of lay-off. So, usually companies adopt seniority basis, means, junior employees will be first laid-off.

In today's era of restructuring, business process reengineering, lay-offs are common these days. For example, world's largest chipmaker, Intel, announced its plan to lay-off 10,500 employees worldwide, including a significant number of the company's 3,000 strong team in India. This is one of the huge lay-off plan. This restructuring plan is expected to generate saving in costs and operating expenses of approximately $ 2 billion—$ 3 billion annually. According to Intel, these actions, while difficult, are essential to Intel in becoming a more agile and efficient company in future.

2. Discharge or dismissal

Dismissal takes place when the employer terminates the services of the employee. Discharge also means termination from services of an employee, but not necessarily as a punitive measure.[14] Dismissal may be the result of either poor performance of employee or the failure of employee to fit in the organisation. The main causes of discharges are:

(i) Misconduct like theft or dishonesty
(ii) Incapability
(iii) Carelessness, negligence and violation of rules

(iv) Lack of co-operation

(v) Frequent absences without leave

(vi) Wrong attitude

(vii) Failure to have required qualification at the time of employment.

Dismissal or discharge is a painful and hard decision and it may result in grievances. Management should make sure that they had followed the company's well-established discipline procedure. Dismissal should be justified and should not arise from unfair discrimination or personal prejudice of the supervisor. Generally, the discipline procedure allows employee the opportunity to correct their behaviour before the serious punishment.

3. Retrenchment

It refers to termination of the services of an employee by the employer because of economic reasons. This includes rationalisation in organisation, installation of new machines that replaces the labour, etc. Termination of services of employee as punishment given by way of disciplinary action, retirement either voluntary or on reaching the age of superannuation or continued ill-health does not constitute retrenchment.

Like lay-off, under Industrial Disputes Act, 1947, an employee is entitled to retrenchment compensation equivalent to fifteen days average pay for every completed year of continued service. Further, the Industrial Disputes Act specifies the procedure to be followed while taking the decision of retrenchment. Under the Act, the principle of retrenchment should be, "first come, last go" or "last come, first go". In case of vacancies, in future, retrenched workers should be given preference over other persons.

4. Suspension

Suspension means prohibiting an employee from attending work, stopping him from performing the duties assigned to him and withholding the remuneration payable to him.[15] Although it is not the termination of services of an employee but in some cases it may eventually lead to termination. Suspension of an employee may be as a matter of punishment for a specified period or the employee is kept away from the work pending enquiring into his alleged misconduct so that he or she cannot temper with the evidence or misuses power of the chair. During suspension, the employee receives a subsistence allowance.

5. Compulsory/forced resignation

In some cases, an employer may advise/ask the employee to resign or otherwise face action. This decision may be taken by the employer to avoid termination of services of employee. In unavoidable situations, compulsory resignation is beneficial for both parties. For employee, his or her career (resume) is saved from hard action like discharge or dismissal and for employer, it protects company's image and is economical also.

However, in case of disciplinary action, it will be better in long run to follow the due process of enquiry rather than to shorten the process and accept forced resignation. The employee may later go to the trade union or court and assert that the resignation was obtained from him under duress.

III. Death

Another reason for separation may be the death of the workman. In case the death of workman results from injury caused by an accident, which must have arisen out of and in the course of employment, then the employer provides compensation as per the provisions of the Workmen's Compensation Act, 1923. As per the Act, the amount of compensation payable to his or her dependents shall be an amount equal to fifty per cent of the monthly wages of the deceased workman multiplied by the relevant factor or Rs. 80,000, whichever is more. Relevant factors are provided in the Schedule IV of the act according to the age of workman. Also, there is a provision for payment of funeral expenses, which is equal to Rs. 2,500. Most of the organisations also have a policy of offering employment to the spouse/child/or other dependent of employee.

KEY TERMS

Demotion	Remedial transfers
Discharge	Replacement transfers
Dismissal	Retirement

Dry promotion	Retrenchment
Horizontal promotion	Separations
Lay-off	Shift transfers
Promotion	Vertical promotion
Production transfers	VRS

QUESTIONS

1. What is promotion? Explain the purposes of promotion?
2. What are the principles of a promotion policy?
3. Describe the different types of promotion.
4. What is transfer and discuss the various types of transfer?
5. What are the causes of demotion?
6. What are the costs and benefits associated with separations?
7. What are the types of separations?

ENDNOTES

1. Paul Pigors and Charles A. Myers, *Personnel Administration: A Point of View and a Method*, McGraw-Hill, Kogakusha Ltd, Tokyo, 1973, p. 308.
2. Edwin B. Flippo, *Personnel Management*, Sixth Edition, McGraw-Hill, New York, 1984, p. 266.
3. Richard Chanick, "Career Growth for Baby Boomers", *Personnel Journal*, 1991, Vol. 71, pp. 40-46.
4. Gary Dessler, *Human Resource Management*, Pearson Education, Ninth Edition, Delhi, 2004, p. 279.
5. Edwin B. Flippo, op. cit., p. 266.
6. Dale S. Beach, *Personnel—The Management of People at Work*, Macmillan, New York, 1975, p. 362.
7. D. Polsky, "Changing Consequences of Job Separations in the United States", *Industrial and Labour Realtions Review*, 1999, Vol. 52, pp. 565-580.
8. Luis R. Gomez-Mejia, David B. Balkin and Robert L. Cardy, *Managing Human Resources,* Third Edition, Pearson Education, Delhi, 2003, p. 200.

9. D.H. Sweet, "Outplacement" in W. Cascio (Ed.), *Human Resource Planning, Employment and Placement*, 1989, Washington DC: Bureau of National Affairs.
10. Luis R. Gomez-Mejia, David B. Balkin and Robert L. Cardy, op. cit., p. 202.
11. *Ibid.*, p. 203.
12. *Ibid.*, p. 205.
13. D. Richards, "Petrochemical Manufactures Lay Off Thousand", *Chemical Market Reporter,* 1999, p. 540.
14. C.S. Venkataratnam and B.K. Srivastava, *Personnel Management and Human Resources,* Tata McGraw–Hill, 1995, New Delhi, p. 94.
15. *Ibid.*

Job Evaluation

13

LEARNING OBJECTIVES

After studying this chapter, you should be able to:

1. Understand the nature and importance of job evaluation
2. Describe the principles of job evaluation
3. Describe the process of job evaluation
4. Describe the various methods of job evaluation

The process of establishing a consistent and systematic relationship among compensation rates for all jobs within the organisation is known as job evaluation. Job evaluation is conducted in order to have equity in compensation. It is the systematic appraisal of each job in the organisation to determine its comparative value.

MEANING AND DEFINITION

Job evaluation is an attempt to determine and compare demands, which the normal performance of a particular job makes on normal workers without taking into account the individual abilities or performance of the workers concerned.[1] The aim of job evaluation is to determine systematically a job's relative worth. It is a formal and systematic comparison of jobs to determine the worth of one job relative to another and eventually results in a wage or salary hierarchy.[2]

IMPORTANCE OF JOB EVALUATION

Growing size and complexity of organisations and societal requirements for justification of pay differentials demands a systematic as well as defensible approach to determine the relative worth of jobs. This led to the increase in adoption of job evaluation in all organisations. Other advantages of job evaluation are following:

1. It helps in establishing a consistent wage structure in the organisation. It helps in obtaining internal and external consistency in wage and salaries. Internal consistency is referred to concept of relative wages within the firm whereas external consistency means the desired relativity of an organisation's wage structure to that of industry and economy.
2. It helps to establish harmonious and good industrial relations on the issues of wages. Job evaluation is a systematic process so it brings uniformity in wage rates thus it prevents industrial disputes due to wages.
3. It is a standard and factual basis for determining the relative worth of all jobs in an organisation.
4. It helps to raise the morale of employee. Fair and justifiable wage payment plans and their well administration has a great impact on the workforce. Employees feel happy and satisfied from their jobs and their morale increases thus resulting in great output.
5. It also helps to settle the wage rates of new jobs in the organisation.
6. It is a logical and objective method of ranking the jobs in terms of salaries.

PREREQUISITES OF JOB EVALUATION

In order to establish a job evaluation programme in an organisation, there are some necessary prerequisites which are as follows:

1. Availability of job analysis information, i.e. job description and job specification.
2. Job evaluation system should be simple and easy to understand.
3. The job evaluation should be taken as an adjustment to (but not to prevent) collective bargaining.[3]

4. Active involvement of a trade union and employees is essential.
5. Availability of industry rates (through labour market survey) to know the prevailing salary rates.
6. Selection of groups of employees and jobs to be covered by the evaluation system.
7. Proper communication of objectives and implication of job evaluation to employees and unions to avoid any misunderstanding.
8. Involvement of outsider experts/consultants such as specialists from National Productivity Council, administrative staff college of India, etc. These people have a rich experience in job evaluation.

PRINCIPLES OF JOB EVALUATION

There are certain principles of job evaluation, which are relevant to all jobs and in all organisations. Following principles must be kept in mind before putting the job evaluation programme in actual practice:

1. Execution of job evaluation programme is a mutual co-operation of management and employees, so chosen members of committees must be agreeable to all concerned.
2. Objectives of job evaluation process should be well determined.
3. Objectives should be well communicated to the concerned parties.
4. The system should be transparent. Decision regarding the evaluation system (type of system, why it is chosen, its procedure) should be communicated to concerned parties to avoid misunderstandings.
5. Level of wage rates for the selected jobs must be in conformity with the jobs prevailing in the company and in the industry.
6. It is advisable to see all the concerned parties have an opportunity to fully engage themselves in the job evaluation process.

7. Job evaluation is concerned only with the job, i.e. its contents and not the person or jobholder. This is the iron law of job evaluation.
8. Final appraisal and conclusion should not be formalised until and unless the judgements of different raters agree.
9. There should be the provision of consistency checks in the operating procedure.
10. Special care should be taken in developing a grade structure following a job evaluation exercise to ensure that grade boundaries are placed appropriately and that the allocation of jobs to grades is not in itself discriminatory.[4]

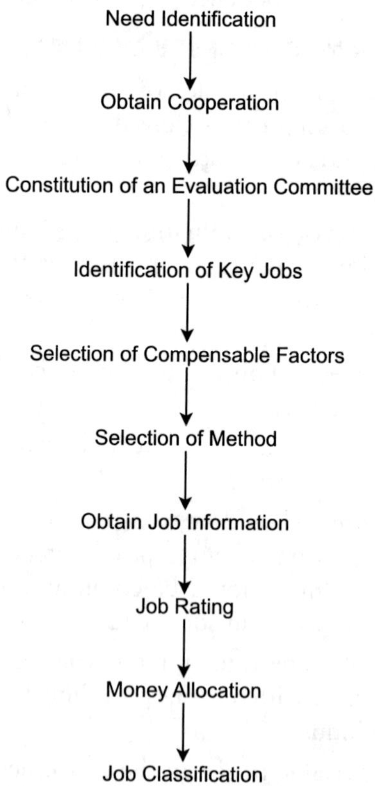

Fig. 13.1: Job Evaluation Process

11. The system should be regularly reviewed in order to ensure that it is being operated properly and it serves its objectives.

PROCESS OF JOB EVALUATION

The main steps in the process of job evaluation are the following:

1. Need identification

First and foremost step is identifying the need for the job evaluation programme in the organisation. For example, dissatisfaction reflected in high turnover, work stoppages or arguments may result from applying employees different rates for similar jobs.[5] This all reflects that there is a need of systematic evaluation of jobs in order to know their worth rather than informally assigning payments to all jobs.

2. Obtain cooperation

Next important step is getting cooperation of employees in the evaluation. For launching job evaluation programme close cooperation among managers, trade unions and employees is essential. Management should ensure the employees that present employees will not be adversely affected due to job evaluation process.

3. Constitution of an evaluation committee

The next step is to constitute a committee comprising about 5 to 8 members. The committee should include several people who are familiar with the jobs in question, each of whom may have a different perspective regarding the nature of the jobs.[6] Generally, committee members include employees, trade union representative, HR specialists and outside specialists. Each committee should be provided with the manuals, which will explain the job evaluation procedure and special instruction for conducting job evaluation.

4. Identification of key jobs

Practically it's not possible to evaluate each and every job. Thus the appointed committee identifies 10 or 15 key benchmark jobs. These jobs will be evaluated and, later on, these will serve as benchmarks or anchors against which the relative value of all other jobs can be obtained.

5. Selection of compensable factors

Now the committee selects the compensable factors. These are the factors that establish how the jobs compare to one another. A compensable factor is a fundamental, compensable element of a job, such as skills, effort, responsibility, and working conditions.[7]

6. Selection of method

This is the most important task of a committee. At this stage committee chooses the most appropriate method of job evaluation. These methods will be discussed next in this chapter.

7. Obtain job information

Next step is to get detailed information about key jobs. This is obtained through job analysis. The products of job analysis, i.e. job description and job specification will provide help to provide job facts. As already discussed in Chapter 3, job description is a statement of duties and responsibilities and job specification is a statement of minimum human qualities needed for the job.

8. Job rating

After the method of job evaluation is selected the next step is the use of that method to study the job description as well as job specification and then assigning a relative score to each key job.

9. Money allocation

It involves assigning a money rate of wages or salary to each key job according to its worth.

10. Job classification

This refers to grading different jobs into certain categories of scales of pay.

JOB EVALUATION SYSTEMS OR METHODS

There are four basic systems or methods of job evaluation. They can be put into two broad categories as shown in Figure 13.2.

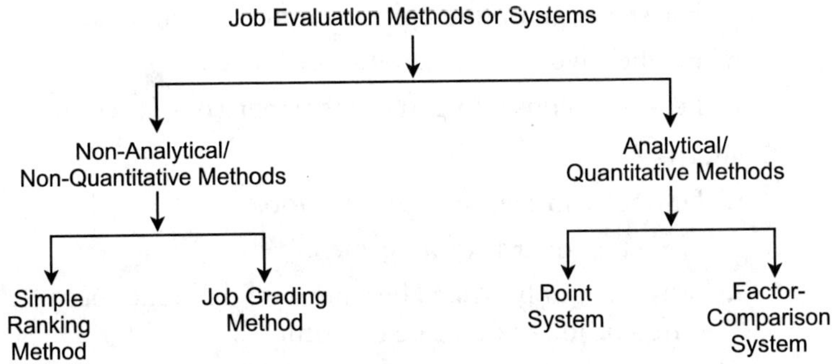

Fig. 13.2: Job Evaluation Methods

I. Non-Quantitative Systems

These include simple methods, which do not use detailed job factors. In these methods, a job is treated as a whole and often job description is used rather than job specification. This category includes the following two methods:

1. Simple ranking system

This is the simplest of the four systems of job evaluation. In this method, the committee evaluates the job description and ranks the jobs in the order of their importance. Here, no specific job factors are selected and worth of each job is assessed on the basis of its contents or title. A simple job-to-job comparison is made and ranks are assigned as shown in the following table:

Table 13.1: Job Ranking

Job	Rank
B	1
D	2
C	3
E	4
A	5

Some merits and demerits of simple ranking system are the following:

Merits

1. Simple and easy to understand.
2. Appropriate for smaller organisations.

3. Easy to explain to employees and trade unions.
4. Inexpensive
5. Less time-consuming and less paperwork is required.

Demerits

1. Difficulty in measuring whole job.
2. No set standards of judgement.
3. Jobs are simply ranked but the exact difference between different jobs cannot be determined.
4. It does not provide a defence in a legal case. Also, employees may resent the arbitrary job ranking.

2. Job grading (or job classification) system

In the simple ranking method there is no predetermined scale of values. But in case of job grading method, there is one such scale consisting of job grades or classes. Jobs are still measured as whole jobs. However, a scale of values is created to which jobs and their descriptions (JD) can be compared. In other words, once a scale of values is established, the process of job evaluation consists of reading the job description, reading the grade descriptions and then allocating the job to a specific grade. Table 13.2 shows the scale consisting of grade and the grade descriptions.

Table 13.2: Job Grading Description

Grade	Description of Job Grading
Unskilled/Manual	No education required, no responsibility, work under supervision, routine work
Semi-skilled	At least 10+2 passed, need some training, work under supervision
Skilled	Graduate, trained and experience holder, need to take initiative and supervise others

Merits

1. Improvement over simple ranking as it has a pre-determined scale of values.
2. Simple and inexpensive to operate.
3. Appropriate for small organisations.

4. Evaluation can be supported by the job description and job grade description.
5. Easy to understand.

Demerits

1. Job grade descriptions are broad and vague and cannot be quantified.
2. Multiple systems are required for different types of jobs. For example, description of production jobs will be entirely different from office jobs.
3. Not appropriate for large organisations.
4. Difficulty in explaining, convincing trade unions and employees regarding the inclusion of a particular job in a broad generality.
5. Human biasness cannot be ruled out, as no set standards are available for preparing.

II. Quantitative/Analytical Methods

This includes a detailed, analytical and quantitative approach to measure job worth.

1. Point system

This method was developed by Meril Latt in 1923. This is most widely used job evaluation system. A series of steps are involved in the procedure of job evaluation under point system. These steps are the following:

(i) *Selection of the job factors*

A job factor is a specific requirement levied upon the job holder, which she or he must contribute, assume or endure.[8] Unlike the simple ranking and grading methods, which measure the whole jobs, the point system deals with job factors or components.

The evaluators first select job factors. Although number of factors selected may vary from organisation to organisation but the most common job factors in use are (i) skill, (ii) responsibility, (iii) effort, and (iv) working conditions. These job factors represent the values for which an organisation provides salary. Then each of these factors is divided into smaller factors as shown in Table 13.3.

Table 13.3: Specific Factors in Job Evaluation System

Skill	Responsibility	Effort	Working Condition
Education Experience Expertise Initiative	Tools, machinery and equipment Material or product Safety of others Accountability	Physical Mental Visual	Risk involved, work surroundings

(ii) *Construction of a scale*

Next step is to construct a scale or yardstick of values for each selected factor so as to measure the factor in each job. First of all, decision is taken regarding the total number of points that will be utilized in the entire system to be followed by the determination of the percentage to be allocated to each factor (as shown in Table 13.4).

Table 13.4: Values of Selected Factors

S.No.	Factor	Number of Points	Percentage
i.	Skill	200	50
ii.	Responsibility	100	25
iii.	Effort	60	15
iv.	Working Conditions	40	10

Once a total value of each factor is determined, now derive a scale or yardstick. The scale or yardstick is composed of points and definitions of degrees of a specific factor. For example, take the experience factor. Let's assume that it has been assigned a total value of 70 points out of 200 allocated to skill factor (as experience is a sub-factor of skill). Figure 13.3 shows the

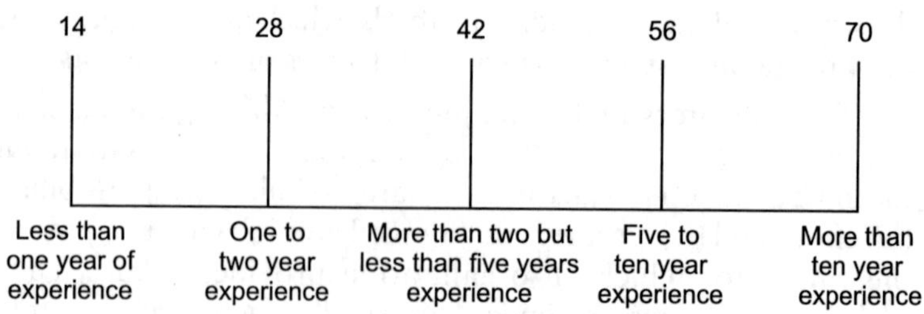

Fig. 13.3: Scale of Values for the Experience Sub-factor

establishment of five degrees of experience with an arithmetic progression of 14 points.

(iii) *Evaluation of the jobs in terms of yardsticks*

After the scales for each factor has been constructed, now the committee members carefully read the job specifications and compare that information with degree of definitions on factor scales and decide at which degree the job falls on each factor. Then a totaling of points for all factors will provide the evaluation of the job in terms of points.

(iv) *Conducting a wage survey*

Once the point values has been arrived, next is to translate these point values into monetary values. This is done by conducting wage surveys. First of all, in a wage survey, key jobs are selected. Key jobs are those jobs whose duties are very clearly defined and these are representative of all levels of job worth. So, a sample of jobs is created. After this, a sample of firms in the labour market area are chosen. Then, next step is to obtain appropriate wage information regarding key jobs from the sampled firm. Next step is to analyse and average the data obtained. Now plot the rupee value of key jobs on a wage chart and draw the wage-trend line that is closed to all the points as shown in Figure 13.4. This line approximates the going rates of all jobs in the structure and wage

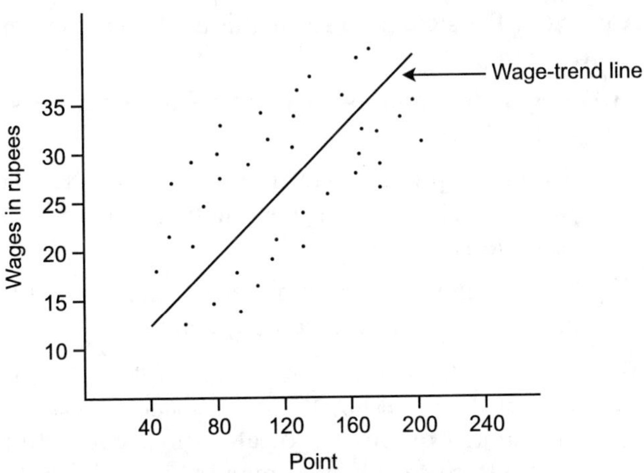

Fig. 13.4: Wage-trend Line

rate for all the other jobs can be interpolated by reading up from the point values to the wage line. The wage line can be drawn by freehand or by using the method of least squares.

Merits

1. Objective and systematic.
2. More accurate as compared to other methods. Each major factor is divided into sub-factor.
3. Easy to understand and operate.
4. Human bias is reduced.
5. Stable method and can be used for a long time.

Demerits

1. Selection of factors and sub-factors is difficult.
2. Employees may resent with the allocation of points and with the factors and degrees identified.
3. Time-consuming method.
4. Expensive and can be used only by big organisations.
5. Allocation of marks to several factors and sub-factors is difficult.

2. Factor-comparison system

This system of job evaluation was developed by Eugene J. Benge in 1962. The steps involved in this method of job evaluation are the following:

(i) First step is same as in case of point system, i.e. selection of job factors.

(ii) Second step is the selection of key jobs. Key jobs are those which are stable, well-defined, fair and relative to other jobs.

(iii) Third step is to determine the correct rates of key jobs as determined in the point system.

(iv) Fourth step is the refinement of the ranking method. Rather than ranking of whole jobs, in this case the jobs are ranked by one factor at a time. For example, the committee of evaluators may rank five key jobs (A, B, C, D, E) as shown in Table 13.5.

Table 13.5: Ranking of Key Jobs

Skill	Responsibility	Effort	Working Conditions
A	C	B	D
B	B	E	E
C	A	C	A
D	E	D	C
E	D	A	B

(v) Fifth step involves the allocation of correct rate of each key job among the job factors. For example, if the pay for job A is Rs. 12, it is divided among skill, responsibility, effort and working conditions as the committee members think that these factors are important in the job. This is shown in Figure 13.5.

(vi) In the next step, jobs are evaluated by comparing them with the yardsticks of key jobs. For example, if a new job F is similar to A in skill (Rs. 6.80), B in responsibility (Rs. 4.00), D in effort(Rs. 1.80) and E in working conditions (Rs. 1.80), then it's correct rate is Rs. 14.40.

(vii) Last step involves adjusting and operating the wage structure.

Merits

1. Most accurate system of job evaluation.
2. More objective and systematic as the weights are not arbitrarily assigned.
3. As limited number of factors is used it avoids overlapping.
4. Difficult nature of jobs can be evaluated with the same set of factors such as supervisory and clerical.

Demerits

1. Expensive and complicated system.
2. Difficult to operate.
3. Cannot be easily understood by non-supervisory staff members.

Skill	Rs. 1.00	2.00	3.00	4.00	5.00	6.00	7.00	8.00
	E	D	CB					
Responsibility	Rs. 1.00	2.00	3.00	4.00	5.00	6.00	7.00	8.00
	ED	C		AB				
Effort	Rs. 1.00	2.00	3.00	4.00	5.00	6.00	7.00	8.00
	A	CBD	E					
Working Conditions	1.00	2.00	3.00	4.00	5.00	6.00	7.00	8.00
	A	BCED						

Correct Job Rate	Skill	Rsponsibility	Effort	Working Conditions
A — Rs. 12.00	A — 6.80	B — 4.00	E — 2.40	D — 2.00
B — Rs. 11.20	A — 4.40	A — 3.60	D — 1.80	E — 1.80
C — Rs. 8.10	C — 3.60	C — 2.40	B — 1.60	C — 1.60
D — Rs. 6.80	D — 2.00	D — 1.00	C — 1.20	B — 1.20
E — Rs. 5.60	E — 3.60	E — 0.60	A — 0.80	A — 0.80
E — Rs. 5.60	E — 3.60	E — 0.60	A — 0.80	A — 0.80

Fig. 13.5: Factor Scales of a Factor Comparison System

Source: Adapted from D.C. Sharma & R.C. Sharma, *Personnel Management & Industrial Relations*, S.J. Publications, Meerut, p. 225.

4. Only big organisations can afford it.
5. Frequent changes in wage level require adjustment in the key job.

LIMITATIONS OF JOB EVALUATION

1. Technology and other changes in the business environment may need to revise the factors selected earlier.
2. It is a time-consuming process and it needs technical personnel.
3. Element of human bias cannot be altogether eliminated.
4. Substantial changes are required in the organisation when job evaluation system is first time introduced.

5. Because of its characteristics such as time-consuming, expensive, experts are required, etc. it is only suitable to large organisations as small firms cannot afford this system.
6. The installation of job evaluation generally results in an immediate increase in number of grievances concerning wages.
7. Usually the trade unions and employees react strongly against the job evaluation system and its results.
8. Often, there is a conflict between management and employees over the selection factors. Management generally considers factors like skill, responsibility, effort and working conditions. On the other hand, workers want inclusion of factors like (i) the type of supervision received, (ii) the congeniality of tightness of incentive standards, (iii) the steadiness of the work, (iv) the amount of overtime, and (v) the tightness of incentive standards.[9] Obviously, no job evaluation system could ever encompass all these factors.
9. In some cases, the selected factors may overlap and this raises questions on their reliability.
10. In case the job evaluation results in substantial changes in the exiting wage structure of the firm then it is difficult to implement these changes in a shorter duration due to financial and other problems.

KEY TERMS

Compensable factors	Job factors
Factor-comparison method	Job grading
Job classification system	Point system
Job evaluation	Ranking system

QUESTIONS

1. Define job evaluation and discuss its importance.
2. Bring out the prerequisites of a job evaluation programme.
3. Describe the principles of job evaluation.

4. Explain the process of job evaluation.
5. Describe the various methods of job evaluation.

ENDNOTES

1. I.L.O., *Job Evaluation—Studies and Reports*, New Series, No. 56, Geneva, 1960, p. 8.
2. Gary Dessler, *Human Resource Management*, Pearson Education, Ninth Edition, Delhi, 2004, p. 310.
3. C.S. Venkataratnam and B.K. Srivastava, *Personnel Management and Human Resources,* Tata McGraw-Hill, 1995, New Delhi, p. 184.
4. Michael Armstrong, *A Handbook of Human Resource Management Practice,* Ninth Edition, Kogan Page, London, 2005, p. 640.
5. Gary Dessler, op. cit., p. 311.
6. *Ibid.*
7. *Ibid.*, p. 310.
8. Edwin B. Flippo, *Personnel Management*, Sixth Edition, McGraw-Hill, New York, 1984, p. 296.
9. *Ibid.*, p. 304.

Employee Compensation 14

LEARNING OBJECTIVES

After studying this chapter, you should be able to:

1. Understand the nature, components and objectives of employee compensation
2. Describe the various wage theories
3. Describe the various factors that influence employee compensation
4. Understand the various concepts of wages
5. Understand the methods of wage payments

Determination of suitable monetary compensation is one of the most difficult and complex duty of human resource manager. This is most important and highly significant to both the organisation and employee. It is significant for the employee as, in most cases, it is the only means of economic survival besides determining their social status. It is important for the organisation as wages and salaries constitute the highest cost of doing business. Also, employee compensation programmes play an important role for organisation in attracting, motivating and retaining the competent employees. There are many options before an organisation from which it has to decide most appropriate pay system. There is no exact and accurate yardstick that can determine the correct pay rate. Although system like job evaluation played a significant role but still lot of decisions has to be taken to arrive at best decision.

MEANING AND DEFINITION

Employee compensation refers to all forms of pay or rewards going to employees and arising from their employment.[1] Employee compensation has three main components and the relative proposition of each component in the total compensation varies by the organisation. Figure 14.1 shows the components of compensation.

Compensation is a comprehensive term which includes everything an employee receives in return for his work such as wages, salaries, allowances, benefits and services. Although there

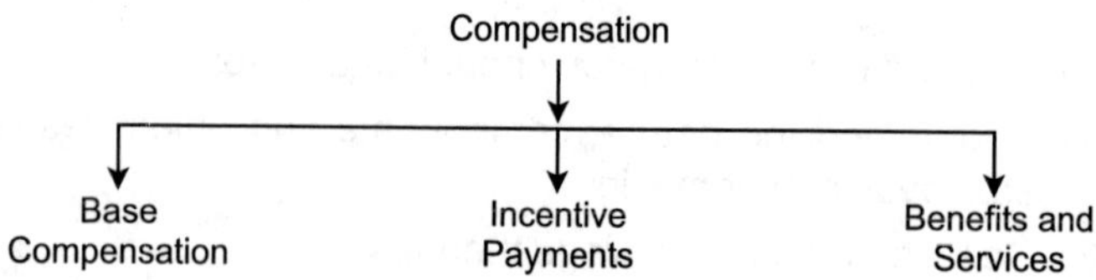

Fig. 14.1: The Components of Compensation

is no basic difference between the term 'wages' and 'salaries', but generally 'salary' is used for compensation to white-collar employees while 'wages' is used to denote the payment made to blue-collar workers. Another difference is salaries are paid on monthly basis whereas wages may be paid on hourly or daily basis.

OBJECTIVES OF EMPLOYEE COMPENSATION

The main objectives of employee compensation are the following:

1. To attract well-qualified and competent personnel.
2. To motivate them for higher levels of performance by making arrangement of incentive payments.
3. To retain the present workforce by keeping their pay levels at the competitive levels.
4. To raise the morale of workforce.
5. To establish internal as well as external equity. Internal equity refers to payment of similar wages for similar work. External equity means payment of similar wages to similar jobs in comparable firms.
6. To maintain the labour and administrative costs in line with the ability of the organisation to pay.

7. To comply with wage legislation.
8. To project a good image of company.
9. To satisfy employees and to reduce the incidents of grievances, absenteeism and quitting.
10. To reward the desired behaviour such as good performance, loyalty, dedication, etc.

FACTORS INFLUENCING EMPLOYEE COMPENSATION

The significant factors affecting the employee compensation can be grouped together into two broad categories: (I) external and (II) internal factors (Figure 14.2).

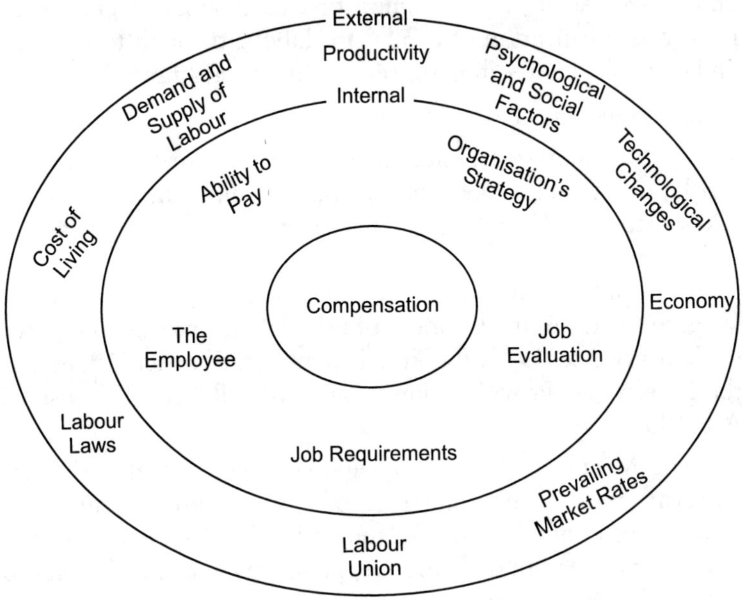

Fig. 14.2: Factors Influencing Compensation

I. External Factors

External factors include demand and supply of labour, cost of living, labour laws, bargaining power of trade unions, prevailing market rates, economy, psychological and social factors and technological developments.

1. Demand and supply of labour

The conditions of labour market, i.e. demand for and supply of labour influence the fixation of compensation. In case the supply exceeds the demand then wages may be fixed at lower levels. On the other hand, if there is great demand for a particular skill but supply is less, in that case, higher wages will be fixed in order to attract and retain skilled personnel.

2. Labour unions

Labour unions influence wages by controlling the supply of labour. Often there are strikes by labour unions for higher wages. Further, to strengthen their control over the supply of labour, unions seek such goals as union or closed shops, regulated or restricted substitution of capital for labour through technology and controlled entry into apprenticeship programmes.[2]

3. Government

Government influence compensation through various legislations, policies regarding wages, wage differentials, dearness allowance, etc. Government has enacted a number of labour legislations, which have a bearing on employee compensation. These include the Minimum Wages Act, 1948, the Payment of Wages Act, 1936, the Payment of Bonus Act, 1965, the Payment of Gratuity Act, 1972, the Equal Remuneration Act, 1976, and the Employees' Provident Funds and Miscellaneous Provisions Act, 1952.

The Minimum Wages Act enables the Central and State Government to fix minimum rates of wages payable to employees in a selected number of sweated industries. The Payment of Wages Act was passed with the aim to regulate the payment of wages to certain classes of persons employed in industry. Also, it protects workers against irregularities in payment of wages and unauthorised deductions by the employer. The Payment of Bonus Act ensures the payment of bonus to persons employed in certain establishments. The Payment of Gratuity Act provides for the payment to an employee after his or her retirement whether the retirement is the result of the rules of superannuation or of some physical disability. The Equal Remuneration Act provide for the payment of equal remuneration to men and women workers for same or similar work and prevents the discrimination on the ground of sex, against women workers. The Employees' Provident Funds and Miscellaneous Provisions Act provides for the institution of provident funds, family pension and deposit-linked insurance schemes for employees.

Apart from these legislations, government also influences wage fixation through wage boards, pay commission, wage committees and adjudication (see Exhibit 14.1). Recently Sixth Pay Commission has been set up.

Exhibit 14.1: Sixth Pay Commission Set Up

In October, 2006 the government announced the constitution of a four-member sixth Central Pay Commission thus paving the way for the revision of salaries of over 33 lakh Central Government employees and raising hope among public sector and State Government employees for revision of salaries at a later stage. In addition to Central Government employees, the Commission would also recommend new pay structure of officers and employees of the regulatory bodies and personnel of armed forces among others.

The Commission, headed by Justice B.N. Sri Krishna, has been set up following Prime Minister Manmohan Singh's announcement to set up the commission to review the salary structure of the public sector, which is facing poaching of professional by the private sector through higher pay packets. The terms of reference of the Commission also include making recommendations for pension, gratuity for those employees appointed before Jan 1, 2004, as after this date new recruits are under the defined contributory pension scheme instead of defined benefit. The pay panel will also make recommendations on bonus payment and feasibility of introducing productivity-linked incentive scheme. The revision of the salaries is expected to put an additional burden of at least Rs. 20,000 crore on the central exchequer annually.

Source: *The Tribune*, October 6, 2006.

4. Prevailing market rates

Going rate of pay or comparable wage rates also influence the employee compensation. Prevailing market rates are those, which are paid by different organisations in an industry. Every organisation tries to conform to the wage rates being paid by the industry, community and the adjoining organisations. Oftenly this is the only way of fixing wages during the initial stages of any organisation. Also, it helps in attracting and retaining the competent personnel and helps in the prevention and settlement of industrial disputes related with wages.

5. Cost of living

The present cost of living also influences the wage rates considerably. This matters a lot during the periods of rising prices. This criterion immediately calls for wage adjustments based on increase in the cost of living index. And the justification for this criterion is that the real wages of employees should not go down by the increase in price levels. Adjustment in the wages is made in such a way that basic pay remains undisturbed and the rise in cost of living is compensated by the payment of dearness allowancc. In some organisations there is a provision for automatic adjustment of dearness allowance with the cost of living index (see Exhibit 14.2).

Exhibit 14.2: 5pc hike in DA for Punjab Staff

As a Diwali bonanza to its employees, the Punjab Government has hiked dearness allowance (DA) for them by 5 per cent from July 1, 06 on the Union Government pattern. DA has now been enhanced from 24 per cent to 29 per cent. The enhanced DA would be added to the salaries of the employees. However, with the enhancement of DA, the annual liability on the state exchequer would be Rs. 168.88 crore.

Source: *The Tribune*, October 11, 2006.

6. Economy

The state of economy also influences the wage and salary fixation. Wage rates will be different in a stable economy than in a depressed economy. In case of depressed economy there may be increase in supply of labour and this results in the fixation of lower wage rates.

7. Technological changes

Technological changes also influence the fixation of wage levels. Due to the advancements in the technology there may be shortage of skilled manpower in that area. So, the organisation will provide high wages for skilled personnel. For example, information technology (IT) industry in India and abroad is suffering from the shortage of IT experts.

8. Psychological and social factors

Both the psychological and social factors have a great influence on employees' perception regarding their job and success in life. An organisation cannot ignore these factors. Psychological needs of employees should be taken into consideration before fixing wages such as security. The employees should feel succeeding in life and they can take pride from their work. Sociologically and ethically, people feel that "equal work should carry equal wages", that, "wages should commensurate with their efforts", that "they are not exploited" and that "no distinction is made on the basis of caste, colour, sex or religion."[3] So, the management should take these factors into consideration.

9. Productivity

Productivity refers to output per man-hour. Increase in productivity depends upon the contribution of all the resources, i.e. men, machines, materials, methods and management. Improvement in technology, better management, latest machines and equipment, efficient methods of production, etc. can raise the productivity. However, there is no productivity index that can be devised which can measure only the productivity of a specific factor of production. So, productivity due to individual effort cannot form a criterion of wage fixation.

II. Internal Factors

These factors include the following:

1. Ability to pay

This is one of the most significant factor influencing employee compensation. Generally, a firm, which is prosperous and successful, has the ability to pay more than the competitive rate. This way it can attract a superior caliber of personnel. Oftenly the labour unions also demand an increase in compensation on the grounds that the organisation is prosperous and is able to pay more.

2. Employee

Numerous employees related factors also influence his or her compensation. These include the following:

(a) **Performance**—It is always rewarded with pay increase and as a result it motivates the workers to do better in future.

(b) **Experience**—This makes a person perfect by providing valuable insights and thus rewarded also.

(c) **Seniority**—Trade unions always prefer this objective criterion for pay rises.

(d) **Potential**—Firms also pay their employees, especially young ones on the basis of their potential.

3. Job requirements

Wages are also influenced by the requirements of a job such as physical and mental requirement. Jobs, which demand more skill, responsibility, efforts and are of hazardous in nature, will carry high wage tag with them.

4. Job evaluation

Job evaluation establishes a consistent and systematic relationship among base compensation rates for all jobs. In other words, it establishes the satisfactory wage differentials.

5. Organisation's strategy

The organisation's strategy regarding wages also influences employee compensation. For example, an organisation, which wants rapid growth, will set higher wages than competitors. On the other hand, organisations that want smooth going and just maintain the current earning will pay average or below average.

PRINCIPLES OF COMPENSATION ADMINISTRATION

Compensation administration refers to process of determining a cost-effective pay structure that will attract and retain competent employees, provide an incentive for them to work hard and ensure that pay levels will be perceived as fair.[4] Some basic principles of compensation administration are the following:

1. Different jobs require different kinds and levels of skills, knowledge and abilities and these vary in their value to the organisation.[5] So, efforts should be made to ensure that differences in pay are according to these variations.

2. Compensation administration should always be consistent with the overall organisational plans.
3. Wage structure should be flexible enough to accommodate the changes in internal and external environment.
4. Compensation administration plans should be carefully designed and developed by considering the best interests of all the concerned parties such as management, trade unions, employees, society and government.
5. There should be equal pay for equal work.
6. Wage plans should be clearly defined and written to ensure stability and uniformity.
7. The level of wages should be in line with the prevailing rates in labour market.
8. The employees should receive a guaranteed minimum wages in order to maintain a reasonable standard of living.
9. There should not be any secrecy in the establishment of wage rates. Employees and trade unions should be well-informed regarding the procedure of setting wage rates.
10. There should be a provision of hearing and adjusting grievances related with wages.
11. Wages should be received and revised periodically and for this a wage committee should be appointed.
12. Finally, wages should be such that it attracts and motivates and retains competent personnel.

CONCEPT OF WAGES

There are different concepts of wages that are considered while evolving wage policies and plans. Their brief description is as follows:

1. Money wages and real wages

The monetary form of wage payment refers to money wages. On the other hand, real wages means the purchasing power of money wages. Money wages only express the amount in terms of currency but the real wages gives the actual worth of that amount.

2. Minimum wage

Minimum wage refers to that amount which not only provides for the bare sustenance of life but also for the preservation of the efficiency of the worker. The International Labour Organisation (ILO) lists three criteria for fixing the minimum wage. These are: (i) the needs of workers, (ii) the capacity to pay, and (iii) wages paid for comparable work elsewhere in the economy or more generally the standard of living of other social groups.[6] The Committee on Fair Wages (1948) emphasized that minimum wages must also provide for some measure of education, medical requirements and amenities.[7]

3. Fair wage

A wage rate is fair in the narrower sense when it is equal to the current rate for similar workmen in the same trade and neighbourhood and fair in the wider sense when it is equal to the predominant rate for similar work throughout the country and in the generality of trades.[8] According to Fair Wage Committee the fair wage is something between a minimum wage and a living wage. The lower limit of the fair wage must obviously be the minimum wage; the upper limit is equally set by what may broadly be called the capacity of the industry to pay. Between these two limits the actual wage will depend on: (i) the productivity of labour, (ii) the prevailing rates of wages in the same or similar occupations in the same or neighbouring localities, and (iv) the place of the industry in the economy of the country.[9]

4. Living wage

This is the highest level of wages and obviously it would include all amenities, which a person living in a modern civilised society is entitled and expects when the economy of the country is sufficiently advanced and the employer is able to meet the expanding aspirations of his workers. After considering various views expressed by Indian and foreign authorities, the Committee on Fair Wages observed that "the living wage should enable the male earner to provide for himself and his family not merely the bare essentials of food, clothing, and shelter but a measure of frugal comfort including education for the children, protection against ill-health, requirement of essential social needs and a measure of insurance against the more important misfortunes including old age.[10] However, living wage must be fixed only after taking into consideration the national income and capacity to pay of the industry concerned.

THEORIES OF WAGES

For better understanding of various components of employee compensation it is essential to understand the theories of wages. The main theories of wages are the following:

1. Subsistence theory

This theory is also known as 'Iron Law of Wages'. This theory was propounded by David Ricardo (1772–1823). This theory states that in the long run, wages would tend toward that sum which is necessary to maintain a worker and his family. If the wages rise above the subsistence level, then it would result in increase in population, which will bring down wages to the subsistence level. On the other hand, if the workers are paid below the subsistence level then their number will decrease as many of them would die due to hunger, malnutrition, etc. and many of them will not marry and as a result the wage rate would go up to the subsistence level.

2. Wage fund theory

This theory was propounded by Adam Smith (1723–1790). According to this theory, there is a fixed amount of wage fund available for distribution at any one time and the level of wages depends on the number of workers seeking employment. If the wage fund is large, wages will be high and if the fund is small then the wages will be low, just enough for the subsistence. Thus, this theory provides a rigid demand and supply explanation of wages.

3. Surplus value theory

This theory was propounded by Karl Marx (1818–1883). According to this theory, labour was to be considered as an article of commerce, which could be purchased on the payment of subsistence price. The price of any product was determined by the labour time needed for producing it. The labour was not paid in proportion to the time spent on work but subsistence wages which is much less. The surplus went to the capitalist.

4. Residual claimant theory

This theory was propounded by Francis A. Walker (1840–1897). He was known as one of the chief opponents of the wage fund doctrine. According to this theory, after the payments has been made to all other factors of production, i.e. land, capital and entrepreneur/organisation whatever the surplus remains, represents the wages. So, the workers get the residual. According to Walker, rent, interest and profits are determined by the definite laws but there is no specific law, which determine wages. Thus, workers get the residual.

5. Marginal productivity theory

Alfred Marshall and J.R. Hicks are the main exponents of this theory. This theory takes into account demand, supply and competition as the main regulators of wages. The theory postulates a relationship between wages, productivity and employment. In other words, this theory postulates that any industry would go on employing additional labour so long as it pays to employ them, i.e. addition of labour must result in increase of production. After a certain point additional employment will become counter productive. And the workers are paid only what they are economically worth and the employer will stop hiring when it becomes uneconomical for him.

6. Bargaining theory

According to this theory, wages are determined by the relative bargaining power of the employees or trade unions and employers. Collective bargaining is a system in which the union and the management participate together to regulate the terms and conditions of employment.

7. Equity theory

This theory was developed by J. Stacy Adams. According to this theory, employees perceive what they get from a job in relation to what they put into it and then compare their input-output ratio with the input-output ratios of relevant others. When the workers perceive their ratios to be equal to those of relevant others with whom they compare themselves then a state of equity exits. Then they perceive fair situation. A 'fair day work for fair day pay' situation prevails. But when employees perceive inequity then they view themselves either under-rewarded or over-rewarded. They will attempt to correct inequities through increase absenteeism, turnover, lower or higher productivity, improved or reduced quality of output, voluntary resignation, etc.

8. Expectancy theory

This theory was developed by Victor Vroom. According to this theory an individual tends to act in a certain way on the basis of the expectation that this act will be followed by a given outcome and the attractiveness of that outcome to the individual. Vroom suggested the following formula:[11]

Motivational force = Valence × Expectancy

If money or any other reward has to motivate the behaviour of an employee then the employee must desire it and also believe that it will be forthcoming if they act or behave in the prescribed manner. Thus, the actual effect of its influence comes from employee assessment of (i) valence or value of money in meeting personal needs and (ii) the strength of expectancy that the prescribed behaviour will actually result in the obtainment of the preferred reward.

9. Agency theory

According to this theory, the employers and the employees both are the stakeholders of a business unit. The employers acquire the role of principals and the employees assume the role of agents. Compensation payable to employees is the agency cost. Obviously, employers will try to keep this as low as possible whereas employees expect high agency costs. According to this theory the principal must choose a contracting scheme that aligns the interests of the agents with the principal's own interests.

10. Reinforcement theory

This theory states that behaviour is a function of its consequences. According to this theory individuals can be motivated by proper design of their work environment and praise for their performance and that punishment for poor performance produces negative results. High employee performance followed by monetary reward will make employee performance likely high in future also. Similarly, high performance not followed by monetary reward will make its recurrence in future very unlikely.

THE COMPENSATION DETERMINATION PROCESS

An employee's pay determines his or her purchasing power. Paychecks are very important for every employee. Compensation affects a person economically and psychologically.[12] Thus, compensation should be determined very systematically by following the steps mentioned below:

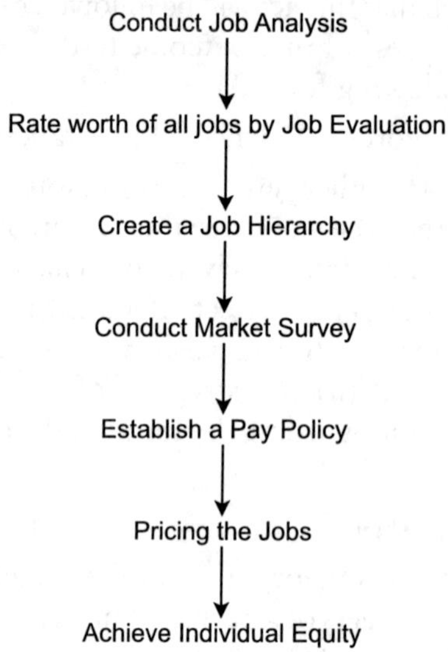

Fig. 14.3: The Compensation Determination Process

1. Conduct job analysis

It provides crucial information in designing pay systems. It describes the duties, responsibilities and other important job characteristics. Thus it helps to determine and weigh the compensable factors (experience, skill, responsibility, effort etc.).

2. Rate worth of all jobs by job evaluation

Next step is to determine the worth of jobs with the help of job evaluation. This is to achieve internal equity. This is already explained in detail in Chapter 13. For each degree of a compensable factor, some points are assigned.

3. Create a job hierarchy

In this stage, all the points assigned to all compensable factors are aggregated. The listing of jobs is done in terms of their importance to the organisation (starting from highest point to lowest point).

4. Conduct market survey

After job hierarchy is created, the next step is determining the prevailing wage rates. This is done to achieve external equity. Usually, a survey is conducted on a sample of selected key jobs and selected companies in the industry. Thus, the rates of key jobs in the labour market are determined.

5. Establish a pay policy

The market survey may provide wide wage and salary rates thus an organisation has to decide its pay policy. Whether the organisation wants to pay above, below or at the market rate for its jobs.

6. Pricing the jobs

In this step, the job evaluation worth is matched with labour market worth. First, appropriate pay levels for each job are established and then different pay levels are grouped into pay grades.

7. Achieve individual equity

Individual equity refers to fairness in pay decisions for employees holding the same job.[13] At this stage, each employee is assigned a pay rate within the range established for his or her job. Generally firms use previous experience, seniority and performance appraisal ratings to determine how much an employee should be paid within that job's pay range.

CRITERIA FOR DEVELOPING COMPENSATION PLAN

In order to develop a suitable compensation plan certain criteria are to be taken into consideration. These are the following:

1. Fixed versus variable pay

Organisations can choose the compensation to be paid monthly on a fixed basis (through base salaries) or it will fluctuate according to some predetermined criterion.

2. Below-market versus above-market compensation

Organisation can decide to pay the employees at below-market rate, at market level, or at above-market level. This is very important decision due to two reasons. First, it directly impacts the organisation's ability to attract and retain workers from others. Secondly, this choice has an important cost component. To pay above-market rate definitely enables an organisation to hire the cream layer of candidates, minimise labour turnover and create a good environment but only large companies can afford this. Also, the companies that want to grow rapidly in a competitive labour market requires to pay above-market rate.

3. Monetary versus non-monetary rewards

An organisation can decide to motivate its workforce through monetary rewards such as pay and stock options or through non-monetary rewards such as interesting work, public recognition, challenging assignments and medical benefits.

4. Elitism versus egalitarianism

Firms must decide whether to place most of their employees under the same compensation plan (an egalitarian pay system) or to establish different compensation plans by organisational level and or employee group (an elitist pay system).[14] For example, in some organisations only the managing director or CEO is eligible for stock options whereas in other companies even the lowest-paid employees are also offered stock option. The trend in recent years has been toward more egalitarian compensation systems.[15] These systems give organisations more flexibility to deploy employees in different areas without having to change their pay levels. Also, it reduces barriers between people who need to work together. These systems are common in highly competitive business environment, where organisations frequently take business risks and try to expand their market share by investing in new products, ventures and technologies. The advantage with the elitist system is that they tend to result in a more money only by moving up through the organisation. These systems are common among older, well-established organisations with mature products, a relatively stable market share and limited competition.

5. Open versus secret pay

An organisation can decide whether the employees can have assess to information about all other workers' compensation levels or not. It means whether employees can get information how compensation decisions and plans are made (open pay) or this knowledge cannot be open to employees (secret pay).

Open pay has some distinct advantages. It results in fair and effective administration. Hidden data about pays always create an environment of conflicts and misunderstanding and results in greater pay dissatisfaction among employees.

6. Centralisation versus decentralisation

An organisation may choose to make compensation decisions in a controlled central location (headquarter) or they will be delegated to managers of the organisation's units. Centralised pay is more appropriate when it is cost-effective and efficient to hire compensation specialists who can be located in a single place and made responsible for salary surveys, benefits administration and record keeping.[16] However, large and diverse organisations are better served by decentralised pay system.

7. Performance versus membership

An organisation should decide that whether compensation emphasize performance and tie pay to individual or group contributions, or it will emphasize membership in the organisation, i.e. logging in a prescribed number of hours each week and progressing up to the organisational ladder.[17] The main forms of performance based compensation are piece-rate plans, sales commissions and award for cost-saving suggestions.

8. Job-based versus skill-based pay

An organisation may establish compensation system on the basis of either contribution of each job or how well the employee performs it. Under job-based pay policy the job becomes the unit of analysis for determining base compensation. This means that the minimum and maximum values of each job are set independently of individual workers, who must be paid somewhere in the range established for that job.[18]

On the other hand, in knowledge-based pay or skill-based pay system, employees are paid on the basis of the jobs they can do or the talents they can be successfully applied to a variety of tasks and situations.[19]

METHODS OF WAGE PAYMENTS

The important wage systems are as follows:

1. Time Wage System

This is the oldest and popular method of wage payment. Under this system, the wages are paid on the basis of time the employee puts on the work without considering the output of the employee. The wage rates are fixed for an hour, a day, a week, a month, etc. So, the wages are calculated on the basis of attendance. Wages are calculated as follows:

Wages = Number of days/hours worked × Rate per day/hour

Illustration

In a factory, a wage rate of Rs. 100 per day is fixed. A worker 'A' attends work for 30 days and another worker 'B' work for 20 days, respectively.

Wages of worker 'A' = 30 × 100 = Rs. 3000

Wages of worker 'B' = 20 × 100 = Rs. 2000

Advantages

1. Simplicity

This is the simplest method. This is very easy for the workers to understand.

2. Security

This provides a sense of security to workers as wages are paid irrespective of output.

3. Better quality of work

As there is no hurry to complete the work, the worker will handle the work with care and maintain quality.

4. Trade union support

This system has full support of trade unions, as this system does not distinguish between employees on their performance.

5. Economy in costs

As the workers are not in a hurry to finish the task, so the materials, machinery and equipment are handled with care. This results in less wastage.

6. No need of standardisation

This system does not create the necessity for standardisation.

7. Good for the beginner

This system is beneficial for the beginners as they may not be able to reach a specific level of production in the early years of their careers.

Disadvantages

The demerits of time wage system are the following:

1. No incentive for efficiency

Under this system, efforts and rewards are not correlated. Thus, this system works as a disincentive to efficient workers.

2. More supervision is required

The workers do not care for time and they consume time uselessly. Thus to make them work, there is a need for more supervision and control.

3. Low production

As wages are not related to output, employees may be producing at slower rate.

4. Dissatisfaction among workers

As efficient and inefficient employees get equal wages, thus efficient workers lose their enthusiasm for more efforts.

5. Difficulty in measuring labour cost

As wages are not related to output, labour cost is uncertain, thus it creates difficulty in determining labour cost per unit.

2. Piece Wage System

Under this system, the wages are paid on the basis of output without considering the time taken by the workers in performing the work. Workers are paid on the basis of quantity of work produced. Wages can be calculated as follows:

Wages = Number of units produced × Rate per unit

Illustration

If the rate per unit is Rs. 10/- and if a worker produces 10 units, then the worker will get 10 × 10 = Rs. 100 as wages.

Advantages

1. Increased production

As wages are paid according to number of units produced, workers are encouraged to produce more.

2. Differentiate between efficient and inefficient employees

Under this system, the efficient worker will work more as wages are linked to the efforts.

3. Less supervision is required

As workers are paid on the basis of performance so less control and supervision is required.

4. Optimum utilisation of machinery

Under this system, workers may not like to keep their machines idle, this results in the optimum utilisation of machines and equipment.

5. Effective cost control

Increase in output will result in the reduction of overhead costs per unit. This alternatively results in the form of lower price of goods, which is beneficial for customers.

6. Act as an incentive

This system works as an incentive to employees to produce more. So, it maximises the output.

7. Breakage is minimised

Under this system, the worker handles the machines and equipment with great care thus loss of breakage is minimised. Workers know that breakage will reduce their output, which means reduced wages.

Disadvantages

1. No guaranteed wage

Under this system, workers are not guaranteed minimum wages as wages are directly linked to their efforts not to the time spent.

2. Poor quality

Workers are encouraged to have quantity at the cost of quality. Workers are always in a hurry to produce more and this results in sub-standard products.

3. Deterioration of health of workers

This system motivates workers to produce more and more, this affects health of workers adversely.

4. Opposition of trade unions

This system creates unhealthy competition among workers and also it does not provide any sense of security thus trade unions opposes this method of wage payment.

5. Determination of piece rate is difficult

Difficulty arises in determining the piece rate and generally disputes arise between labour and management in this regard.

6. Not suitable for beginners

Due to lack of experience, the newcomers may not be able to produce more goods.

7. Discontentment

This system frustrates the inefficient workers. People who get fewer wages may feel jealous of the others. This all results in discontent among workers.

KEY TERMS

- Ability to pay
- Compensation
- Cost of living
- Egalitarian compensation
- Elitism compensation
- Job-based pay
- Living wage
- Money wage
- Piece rate system
- Productivity
- Real wage
- Skill-based pay
- Time wage system

QUESTIONS

1. Define employee compensation. What are its components?
2. Bring out the main objectives of employee compensation.
3. What are the factors influencing employee compensation?
4. Describe the principles of compensation administration.
5. Bring out the various concepts of wages.
6. Discuss various theories of wages.
7. What are the various steps involved in determining compensation?
8. What are the different criteria need to be considered while developing compensation plans?

ENDNOTES

1. Thomas Patten Jr., *Pay: Employee Compensation and Incentive Plans*, 1977, Free Press, New York, p. 1.
2. Edwin B. Flippo, *Personnel Management*, Sixth Edition, McGraw-Hill, New York, 1984, p. 283.
3. C.B. Mamoria and S.V. Gankar, *Personnel Management*, Himalaya Publishing House, Mumbai, Twenty-fifth Edition, 2005, p. 443.
4. Stephen P. Robbins and David A. Decenzo, *Fundamentals of Management*, Third Edition, Pearson Education, Delhi, 2002, p. 202.
5. J. Alley, "Where the Jobs Are", *Fortune*, September 18, 1995, pp. 53-55.
6. International Labour Organisation, "Minimum Wage Fixing and Economic Development", Geneva, 1968, p. 59.

7. Report of the Committee on Fair Wages, 1948, p. 9.
8. Pigou quoted in Express Newspaper V. Union of India, 1961–ILLJ 363.
9. Report of the Committee on Fair Wages, 1948, p. 11.
10. *Ibid.*, p. 5-7.
11. V.H. Vroom, *Work and Motivation*, John Wiley and Sons, New York, 1964, p. 183.
12. C. Duff, "Wage—Benefit Increase Sets 14-Year Low", *The Wall Street Journal*, 1996, A2.
13. Luis R. Gomez-Mejia, David B. Balkin and Robert L. Cardy, *Managing Human Resources,* Third Edition, Pearson Education, Delhi, 2003, p. 345.
14. *Ibid.*, p. 331.
15. S. Branch, "The 100 Best Companies to Work for in America", *Fortune*, 1999, January 11, p. 118.
16. David. B. Balkin and Luis R. Gomez-Mejia, "Matching Compensation and Organisational Strategies", *Strategic Management Journal*, 1990, Vol. 11, pp. 153-169.
17. Luis R. Gomez-Mejia, David B. Balkin and Robert L. Cardy, op. cit., p. 326.
18. *Ibid.*, p. 330.
19. H. Tosi and L. Tosi., "What Managers Need to Know About Knowledge Based Pay", *Organisational Dynamics*, 1986, Vol. 14, No. 3, pp. 52-64.

Incentive Systems

15

LEARNING OBJECTIVES

After studying this chapter, you should be able to:

1. Understand the nature and importance of incentive payments
2. Describe the prerequisites of an effective incentive system
3. Describe the various types of incentive systems

The preceding chapter highlights the significance of equitable and competitive base pay in attracting competent personnel to an organisation. But in order to motivate the personnel an organisation needs to establish incentive schemes under which the payments are made on the basis of employee performance.

MEANING AND DEFINITION

Incentive system is related with wage payment plans which tie wages directly or indirectly to standards of productivity or to the profitability of the organisation or to both criteria.[1] So, the incentive plan refers to all the plans that provide extra pay for extra performance in addition to regular wages for a job. Such payments are also called as payment by results.

IMPORTANCE OF INCENTIVE PAYMENTS

The incentives schemes are beneficial for both the employer and the employees in the following stages:

I. Benefits to Employees

1. Due to incentives the earnings of the employees increase, as they will get besides the prescribed wages the premium also.

2. As a result of additional money, workers standard of living goes up.
3. It results in the improvement of the work capacity of employees. To get the incentives employees work hard to finish the job in the prescribed time or before time.
4. Employees are encouraged to become innovative in the ways of doing work. For example, they can inform management regarding wasteful practices.
5. A spirit of mutual cooperation and teamwork is created among the employees.
6. The morale of the employees goes up when rewards are tied with the performance.

II. Benefits to Employers

1. It motivates the workers for higher efficiency and hence production increases rapidly.
2. There is reduction in production cost per unit and also the overall cost.
3. Minimum supervision is required.
4. All incentive schemes are based upon the scientific work-study. Thus, it brings improvement in workflow, work methods, man-machine relationship, etc.
5. It brings improvement in the overall climate of the organisation. Workers become more responsible and disciplined and discourage misuse of time.
6. It results in the adoption of good practices by the employees. For example, reduced wastage, better utilisation of wastage, reduced absenteeism and turnover and increased output.

LIMITATIONS OF INCENTIVE PAYMENTS

The disadvantages of the incentive payments are the following:

1. In order to maximise the output, quality of products may deteriorate until and unless a strict checking and inspection is maintained.

2. Incentive systems may provoke jealousy, conflict and competition while discouraging cooperation. When employees believe they have important information and it can help them go ahead they withhold that information from their colleagues.
3. Workers cannot control all of the factors affecting their performance. For example, factors beyond an employee's control are the supervisor, performance of other work group members, the quality of material's the employee is working with, working conditions, the amount of support from management and environmental factors.[2]
4. In some cases, employees tend to overwork and this affects their health.
5. Employees may disregard the safety regulations in order to produce more output thus increasing risk of accidents.
6. In group-incentive systems, hard working and active employees may be dissatisfied from slow and old workers.
7. Difficulties arise for appraisers in measuring the performance whether at individual employee level or at group or team level. Accurate measures of performance are not easy to achieve and pay to inaccurate measures is likely to create problem.[3]
8. Once the incentive scheme is implemented it becomes difficult to change the scheme even when the conditions call for a change due to workers' opposition.
9. Pay-for-performance systems may lead to greater productivity but lower job satisfaction.[4]
10. Establishment and administration of incentive plans requires additional time and cost.

PREREQUISITES OF AN EFFECTIVE INCENTIVE SYSTEM

In order to be a successful incentive system, the system should possess some essential characteristics. These are the following:

1. The incentive system should be simple enough to operate and easy to understand.

2. The incentive system should be installed with the cooperation of workers and trade unions.
3. There should be climate of mutual trust and faith between employer and employee for the successful implementation of the incentive system.
4. The incentive system should be based on scientific work measurement.
5. Top management support is essential for meeting cost and time requirement.
6. There is a need for careful and detailed planning for the installation of an incentive scheme.
7. The scheme should have constant attention of competent supervisors.
8. The scheme should be economical.
9. The standards once fixed should not be frequently changed except where there are changes in methods, materials or equipment used in the production process.
10. The scheme should be comprehensive in nature. It means the scheme should cover all the employees.
11. There should be the provision of prompt payment of incentives when they are due.
12. A minimum wage rate should be guaranteed to every employee irrespective of security to employees.
13. Provision should be made for quick and fair redressal of grievances arising from the implementation of the scheme.

TYPES OF INCENTIVE SCHEMES

An organisation may use a variety of incentive schemes. It can be designed to reward the performance of the individual, group, business plant, entire organisation or any combination of these. The main incentive schemes are the following:

A. Individual Incentive Systems

These are the most widely used incentive systems in industry. Here, an organisation attempts to identify and reward the contribution of individual employees.

Incentive Systems

Individual Incentive Systems

I. Straight Piece Work System
II. Standard Hour System
III. Time-based Systems
  (i) Halsey Plan
  (ii) Halsey-Weir Plan
  (iii) Rowan Plan
  (iv) Beadeaux Plan
  (v) Barth Variable Sharing System
IV. Differential Piece Rate Plans
  (i) Taylor's Differential Piece Rate System
  (ii) Merrick's Differential Piece Rate System
  (iii) Gantt's Task and Bonus Plan
  (iv) Emerson's Efficiency Plan
  (v) Accelerated Premium System

Group Incentive Systems

I. Priestman's Production Bonus Plan
II. Profit Sharing Plan
III. Scanlon Plan
IV. Rucker Plan
V. ESOPs
VI. Improshare Plan
VII. Waste Reduction Plan

Fig. 15.1: Types of Incentive Systems

I. Straight Piece Work System

This is the oldest and simplest method. It is also most commonly used method. In this, the rate per unit of output is fixed and the total wages of a worker are arrived at by multiplying the total output by the rate per unit. The total output is measured in terms of unit. For example, if the rate per unit is Re. 1 and the total output of an employee is 50 units, then his or her wages will be 50 × 1 = Rs. 50.00. However, employee's time-rate is guaranteed here.

II. Standard Hour System

In this system, standard time in terms of hours is fixed for the job completion. Rate per hour is determined. An employee is paid according to standard time wages. If the employee takes more than the standard time then he or she will be paid the same wages unless it is guaranteed time wages. If time wages are guaranteed, the employee is paid on the basis of time taken multiplied by the time-rate.

For example:

Standard time = 8 hours

Rate per hour = Re. 1

Ist Case

Time Taken = 6 hours

Wages = 8 × 1 = Rs. 8.00

IInd Case

Time taken = 10 hour

(a) Wages if time wages are not guaranteed = 8 × 1 = Rs. 8.00

(b) Wages if time wages are guaranteed = 10 × 1 = Rs. 10

III. Time-based systems

(i) Halsey Plan

This plan was developed by F.A. Halsey. Under Halsey plan, a standard time is fixed in advance for completing the job. An employee taking standard or more time is paid for the time taken by him. An employee completing his or her job in less than the standard time is paid for some of the time saved. In other words, if the worker completes the job in less than the standard time, he or she will receive a bonus payment at his or her time rate for a specific percentage of the time saved. This percentage may vary anywhere from 30 per cent to 70 per cent, but usually it is fixed at 50 per cent (the rest 50 per cent goes to the employer).

$$\text{Wages} = T \times R + \left(\frac{S-T}{2}\right) \times R$$

Where

S = Standard time

T = Time taken

R = Hourly rate

For example:

Standard time = 12 hours

Rate per hour = Re. 1

Ist Case

Time taken = 12 hours

Wages = 12 × 1 = Rs. 12.00

IInd Case

Time taken = 13 hours

Wages = 13 × 1 = Rs. 13.00

IIIrd Case

Time taken = 10 hours

$$\text{Wages} = 10 \times 1 + \left(\frac{12-10}{2}\right) \times 1$$

= Rs. 11.00

Merits

1. Halsey plan guarantees minimum wage to all workers, this creates a sense of security.
2. The wages of time saved are divided between the employer and employee. Thus, this plan benefits the employer also.
3. This plan is simple to introduce and easily understood by the workers. They can easily make their calculations.
4. Workers can utilise their saved time in doing other jobs and earn more.

Demerits

1. Difficulty arises in fixing standard time for completing a job.
2. Quality of goods may suffer as workers may try to finish the work in the shortest possible time.
3. More supervision is required to ensure that workers in their eagerness to complete the work fast do not waste materials unduly or damage the machines and tools.
4. Workers do not receive full benefits for their efforts as usually they are paid for half of the time saved, the other half goes to employer.

(ii) Halsey-Weir Plan

This plan was developed by Messers G & J Weir Ltd of Glasgow in 1900. This plan is just another form of Halsey plan. Under this plan, a worker receives 30 per cent of the time saved (i.e. standard time–actual time taken). Similar to Halsey plan, a minimum wage is guaranteed here also.

(iii) Rowan Plan

This plan was developed by Mr. James Rowan in 1898. In this plan also a standard time and rate per hour are fixed. This plan differs from Halsey plan only in respect of the determination of the bonus. The bonus is calculated on the basis of the proportion which the time saved bears to the standard time.

$$\text{Bonus} = \frac{\text{Time saved}}{\text{Standard time}} \times \text{Time taken} \times \text{Hourly rate}$$

For example:

Standard time = 12 hours

Rate per hour = Re. 1

Ist Case

Time taken = 12 hours

Wages = 12 × 1 = Rs. 12.00

IInd Case

Time taken = 13 hours

Wages = 13 × 1 = Rs. 13.00

IIIrd Case

Time taken = 10 hours

Wages = 10 × 1 = Rs. 10.00

$$\text{Bonus} = \frac{2}{12} \times 10 \times 1 = 1.66$$

Total wages = 11.66

Merits

1. It guarantees minimum wages to workers.
2. Increase in production reduces overhead cost per unit.
3. It enables the employer of the share in the benefits of increased output.

Demerits

1. This plan is more complex and expensive than the Halsey plan.
2. This plan's incentive value is low at high production levels, thus this is unjust to efficient workers.

(iv) Bedeaux Plan

This plan was developed by Mr. Charles E. Bedeaux in 1911. In this plan, each minute of the allowed time is called a Bedeaux point or 'B' in short. There are 60 B's in one hour. Each job has a standard number of B's and the hourly rate is also determined. In addition to hourly rate, a worker receives a bonus calculated at 75 per cent of the points earned in excess of 60 per hour, multiplied by one-sixtieth of the worker's hourly rate.

For example:

Standard time = 12 hours

Rate per hour = Re. 1

Time taken = 10 hours

Standard B's = 60 × 12 = 720 B's

Actual B's = 60 × 10 = 600 B's

Saving in terms of B's = 120 B's

Wages = 10 × 1 = Rs. 10.00

$$\text{Bonus} = \frac{75}{100} \times \frac{120 \times 1}{60}$$

= Rs. 1.50

Total wages = 10 + 1.50 = Rs. 11.50.

(v) Barth Variable Sharing System

Unlike other plans, this plan does not guarantee a time rate. The worker's earning are computed by multiplying the standard hour by the number of hours actually taken to do the job, taking square root of the product and multiplying it by the worker's hourly rate.

$$\text{Earning} = \text{Rate per hour} \times \sqrt{\text{Standard hours} \times \text{Actual hours taken}}$$

Difficulty arises in explaining the plan to the workers. It just provides incentives only to beginners and not to efficient workers. Thus, it is not a popular plan.

For example:

Standard time = 12 hours

Rate per hour = Re. 1

Time taken = 10 hours

$$\text{Earning} = 1 \times \sqrt{12 \times 10} = 1 \times 10.95$$

$$= \text{Rs. } 10.95$$

IV. Differential Piece Rate Plans

Under these plans different piece rates are set for different amounts of outputs which may be recognised either by actual numbers or pieces or as percentage of tasks. The important ones are the following:

(i) Taylor's Differential Piece-Rate System

This system was developed by F.W. Taylor in 1880. Under this plan, there are two piece rates namely, high rate and a low rate for each job or task. For each job standard output and task time are established. If the output of workers is equal to or exceeds the standard, he or she receives wages at the higher rate to enable them to get the bonus. On the other hand, if the output of the worker is less than the standard, then he or she receives wages at the lower rate. Then standard is determined on the basis of time and motion studies. This plan is basically designed to encourage the especially efficient worker with a higher rate of payment and to penalise the inefficient by a lower rate of payment. However, this plan is rarely used now.

Illustration:

Standard output = 10 units

Rate (i) High rate = Rs. 5 per unit

(ii) Low rate = Rs. 2 per unit

Case (i) actual output = 10 units

In case actual output equal or exceeds standard output

Wages = 10 × 5 = Rs. 50.00

Case (ii) in case actual output is below the standard output (actual output = 8 units)

Wages = 8 × 2 = Rs. 16.00

(ii) Merrick Differential Piece-Rate system

This system was developed by Mr. D.V. Merrick. This system is the modification of Taylor's system. Merrick realised that it was unreasonable and unrealistic to classify all the employees into two broad categories only, i.e. workers of high efficiency and workers of lower efficiency because there are various degrees of efficiency and there are many workers who actually put their efforts to produce more. These kind of persons need to be encouraged. This system introduces three piece rates and made the lowest piece rate equal to the ordinary rate which becomes the base piece rates. The rates introduced by Merrick are the following:

S.No.	Output (percentage of task)	Piece Rate Wage
1.	Less than 83%	Basic piece rate
2.	From 83 % to 100%	110% of basic piece rate
3.	Over 100%	120% of basic piece rate

For the potentially high producer, this plan is a good incentive system. This plan pays a production bonus at 10 per cent of the basic rate to the workers when they reach 83 per cent task and further 10 per cent bonus on reaching over 100 per cent.

(iii) Gantt's Task and Bonus Plan

This system was developed by H.L. Gantt, a close associate of F.W. Taylor, in 1901. Gantt is considered as one of the pioneers of scientific management. Gantt modified Taylor's plan considerably. The significant modification is the substitution of Taylor's punitive wage rate by a guaranteed basic wage. Under this plan, a worker's wage consists of two parts, these are the following:

(a) A guaranteed minimum wage on time rate, which is usually an hourly rate.

(b) A bonus, which is paid to the worker when output is equal to or more than the task. The bonus is a percentage of the guaranteed wage. Bonus varies from 20 per cent to 50 per cent of the guaranteed wage.

(iv) Emerson Efficiency Plan

This plan was developed by Mr. Harrington Emerson in 1919. Under this plan, whenever the efficiency of a worker reaches 67 per cent, he or she will get a bonus. Then as the efficiency increases the bonus also increases. When a worker's efficiency varies from 67 per cent to 99 per cent, he or she receives a bonus at different percentages of their basic wages. And when the efficiency is 100 per cent, the worker's bonus is 20 per cent of the basic wage. Further, when the efficiency is more than 100 per cent for every 1 per cent increase in efficiency there is a 1 per cent increase in bonus. Just like other incentive plans, a minimum wage is guaranteed also in this plan. The efficiency of a worker should be determined on the basis of the monthly or at least worker's weekly output.

Merit

1. This plan is simple and easily understood by workers.
2. Minimum wages are guaranteed.
3. In this plan, whenever the efficiency of a worker reaches 67 per cent he or she will get bonus. In addition, the rate of bonus increases progressively. Thus it provides a stimulus to employees for increasing their efficiency.

Demerits

1. Wage calculations require careful attention.
2. Employees may not be encouraged to increase their output beyond the standard level, as rewards may be nominal.

(v) Accelerated Premium Plans

Under this system, the earnings of the employees increase with output, the rate of increase itself rising progressively with the output. The employees receive a strong reward or incentive to increase their output in order to obtain increased earnings. However, this is a complicated system and not easy to understand and administer.

B. Group Incentive Systems

Earlier discussion has covered incentive plans for individual workers. However, in many cases the output of individual workers cannot be measured although output as a group of workers can be conveniently measured. In such situations group incentive systems are very useful. Under situations where workers are engaged in the assembly work, for example automobiles, textiles, etc. in the grinding and welding, etc. group incentive schemes are followed.

Advantages of group incentive plans:

1. It creates cooperation and a team spirit among workers.
2. There is less need of inspection and supervision.
3. The calculation of wages requires less clerical work.
4. It raises production and reduces wastage.
5. It reduces absenteeism.
6. It guarantees time wages and thus it creates a sense of security in the workers' mind.

Disadvantages of group incentive plans:

1. It does not distinguish between efficient and inefficient workers in a group for the purpose of proper distribution of bonus.
2. The incentive may be insignificant to motivate the workers.
3. Difficulty arises in the determination of the basis of distribution of bonus.
4. Jealousy and rivalry among workers defeats the very purpose of teamwork and cooperation.

Types of Group Incentive System

There are a number of different group incentive systems, some of these are the following:

1. Priestman's Production Bonus Plan

This plan was adopted by Messers Priestman Bros., Ltd., in 1917. Under this plan, a committee representing the management and the workers' union sets in advance the standard production (or performance) for the whole factory. Bonus becomes payable to a department which gives results higher than the standard output. It is calculated on the basis of the ratio of excess production to standard one. This is calculated as follows:

$$\text{Percentage of bonus} = \frac{\text{Increased production}}{\text{Standard production}} \times 100$$

For example, if the standard production in a year is 2000 units and the actual output come to 3000 units, the workers will be given a bonus equivalent to 50 per cent for their wages

2. Profit-sharing plan

Employee profit sharing plans constitute one of the more glamorous forms of monetary compensation used in business.[5] The International Cooperative Congress in 1897 defines employee profit sharing as an agreement freely entered into, by which the employees receive a share, fixed in advance of the profits. The employee profit sharing plans are mainly of two types. These are (i) cash or current distribution and (ii) trust or deferred distribution. In the cash or current arrangement, the benefits are distributed among participants in cash at least once each year. The deferred type involves a trust fund, the benefits from which are distributed in the event of death, retirement or disability. Some managements prefer to place a part the profit share in trust and distribute the remaining part in the form of cash each year.[6]

Features of profit-sharing

The main features of profit-sharing are the following:[7]

1. The profit-sharing arrangement is voluntary but based on an agreement between employer and employee.
2. The amount to be distributed amongst the participants depend upon the profits earned by the enterprise, and
3. The proportion of the profits to be distributed is determined well in advance.

Objectives of profit-sharing

The major objectives of profit-sharing plan are the following:

1. To secure employee cooperation and to maintain industrial harmony.
2. To promote employee loyalty towards organisation by supplementing his or her earning.
3. To promote increased employee effort.
4. To strengthen unity of interest between the employer and employees.

Advantages of profit-sharing

Some of the merits of profit-sharing scheme are the following:

1. It effects an increase in productive efficiency through reducing costs and increasing output.[8]
2. This scheme is relatively easy and less expensive to adopt.
3. It improves employee morale.
4. It results in cordial relations between employees and employer.
5. It reduces labour turnover.
6. It provides security for the employee in the event of disability, death and retirement.
7. It provides additional earning to employees.
8. It constitutes a mechanism for employee economic educaton.[9]
9. It enhances team spirit among employees.

Disadvantages of profit-sharing

Some of the disadvantages of profit-sharing scheme are the following:

1. This scheme does not distinguish among individuals on the basis of effort and contribution. In other words, it does not differentiate between efficient and inefficient workers.
2. Besides labour there are many other factors that affects profits. For example, economic and social factors, government policies, demand of the product, etc.

3. The employer may indulge in the manipulation of accounts.
4. Under this scheme, the extra compensation is not paid immediately after the employee effort is made.
5. The main disadvantage against this scheme is its high discontinuance rate. These discontinuances are caused by such factors as employee apathy to profit-sharing appraisal, lack of profits, insufficient share, union opposition and unintelligent plan administration.[10]

3. Scanlon Plan

This plan was developed by Joseph Scanlon of the United Steel Workers of America in 1927. It is a plant-wide incentive scheme. The underlying concept of this plan is that efficiency depends upon plant wide cooperation. The main aim of this plan is to devise a formula, which will most adequately reflect the prospective efforts of workers and employers as a whole. This plan has two major aspects, namely (i) adopting a measure for increasing the productivity and (ii) sharing the gains accrued from that productivity.

This plan invites suggestions from the workers. Suggestions regarding cost reduction, improvement in working methods and sharing in the gains of increased productivity. Thus this plan is essentially a suggestion system. Usually, a committee of employees, trade unions and top management is appointed to evaluate the suggestions (e.g. cost cutting) offered by workers, supervisors and management. When the actual labour costs are lower than the expected/standard labour costs over an agreed upon period (generally one year), then the difference is shared between the employees (who, as a group, usually receive 75 per cent of the savings) and the organisation (which usually receives the remaining 25 per cent of the savings). Some of the prerequisites for the success of the plan are the following:

(i) Relatively small numbers of participants are required for the success of this plan. For example, this plan is successful in small plants.

(ii) Stable product lines and costs are required.

(iii) Cordial labour-management relations are required.

(iv) Good supervision is required.

(v) Top management's support and commitment is required.

4. Rucker Plan

This plan is based on the same philosophy as that of the Scanlon plan, however, the bonus computed is based on a more sophisticated basis. There are two main differences between the Rucker plan and Scanlon plan, these are the following:

(i) Under the Rucker plan, the standard is based upon a careful study of the accounting records and is not considered bargainable; and

(ii) The Rucker plan offers incentives/rewards for saving in wide areas (e.g. in production process) rather than only savings in labour costs under Scanlon plan.

5. Employee Stock Ownership Plans (ESOPs)

ESOPs reward employees with company stock, either as an outright grant or at a favourable price that may be below market value.[11] These plans are more common among major insurance companies, commercial banks, gas and electric companies and those with over one-half billion dollars in sales.[12] The main objective of ESOPs is to promote a mutuality of interests. Other possible values are the promotion of thrift and security, the creation of an added incentive to work productively and cooperatively and the creation of an additional source of investment capital.[13]

Features of ESOPs

Some salient features of ESOPs are the following:

1. Generally, a mechanism is adopted through which certain eligible employees may purchase the stock of the company at a reduced rate.
2. Usually, the eligibility is determined by the salary level or years of continuous service or both.
3. There is a provision for installment buying. The employee authorizes a payroll deduction and stock is periodically purchased for her or him in the market by the company.[14]

4. Sometimes, there is also a provision of a right to purchase a certain amount of stock in the future at a stated price.
5. ESOPs are most widely used in executive compensation plans rather than with the rank and file workers.

6. Improshare Plan

This is relatively a new plan. This means improved productivity through sharing. It has proved easy to administer and communicate. Under this plan, first of all, a standard is developed. This standard is based on either studies by an industrial engineering group or some set of base period experience data—that identifies the expected number of hours required to produce an acceptable level of output.[15] Any saving arising from production of this agreed on output in fewer than the expected hours are shared between the firm and the workers.[16]

7. Waste Reduction Plan

The aim of this plan is to provide incentives to employees with a view to reduce material waste to a minimum. Generally, this plan is used in the industries where cost of materials is very high.

KEY TERMS

Accelerated premium system
Barth variable sharing plan
Bedeaux plan
Emerson's plan
ESOPs
Gantt's plan
Halsey plan
Halsey-Weir plan
Improshare plan
Incentive systems
Merrick plan
Priestman's plan
Profit-sharing plan
Rowan plan
Scanlon plan
Taylor plan

QUESTIONS

1. Define incentives. Discuss the importance of incentive payments.
2. Bring out the limitations of incentive payments.

3. Bring out the prerequisites of an effective incentive system.
4. Describe the various types of incentive systems.

ENDNOTES

1. Wendell French, *The Personnel Management Process: Human Resources Administration*, 1974, p. 521.
2. P.R. Scholtes, *An Elaboration on Deming's Teachings on Performance Appraisal*, 1987, Madison, WI: Joiner Associates.
3. Luis R. Gomez-Mejia, David B. Balkin and Robert L. Cardy, *Managing Human Resources,* Third Edition, Pearson Education, Delhi, 2003, p. 361.
4. D.P. Schwab, "Conflicts Impacts of Pay on Employee Motivation and Satisfaction", *Personnel Journal*, 1974, Vol. 53, No. 3, pp. 190-206.
5. Edwin B. Flippo, *Personnel Management*, Sixth Edition, McGraw-Hill, New York, 1984, p. 320.
6. *Ibid.*
7. A.M. Sarma, *Understanding Wage System,* Himalaya Publishing House, Bombay, Third Edition, 1992, p. 60.
8. Edwin B. Flippo, op. cit., p. 321.
9. *Ibid.*
10. *Ibid.*, p. 322.
11. R. Edelman, "Record Amount of Stock Awards Allocated for Compensation Plans", 1996, ACA News, 5.
12. S.S. Singhvi, "Motivation through Employee Stock Option Plans", *Personnel Administration/Public Personnel Review*, 1973, Vol. 1, No. 3, p. 61.
13. Edwin B. Flippo, op. cit., p. 326.
14. *Ibid.*
15. Luis R. Gomez-Mejia, David B. Balkin and Robert L. Cardy, op. cit., p. 374.
16. *Ibid.*

Benefits and Services

16

LEARNING OBJECTIVES

After studying this chapter, you should be able to:

1. Understand the nature and importance of employee benefits and services programmes
2. Describe the principles of employee benefits and services programmes
3. Identify the types of fringe benefits
4. Describe the various steps in administration of benefits and services

As discussed in the beginning of Chapter 14, employee compensation consists of direct as well as indirect components. Chapter 14 and 15 dealt with direct compensation. This chapter is devoted to a discussion of indirect compensation, i.e. benefits and services. Today, benefits and services have become crucial in attracting, retaining and motivating employees.

MEANING AND DEFINITION

Employee benefits or indirect compensation are group membership rewards that provide security for employees and their family members.[1] Benefits-indirect financial and non-financial payment employees receive for continuing their employment with the company—are very important part of just about every employee's compensation.[2]

Benefits and services are alternatively known as supplementary compensation, service programmes, non-wage payments, employee benefits and hidden payroll. Generally, they are known as fringe benefits. In the broadest sense, such "fringes" can be constructed to include all expenditures designed to benefit employees over and above regular base pay and direct variable compensation related to output.[3]

For the success of employee benefits and services programmes, the management should ensure the following:

1. To provide employees meaningful choices of benefits that exactly match their needs;
2. To keep the costs of these programmes under control; and
3. To ensure that employees are fully informed regarding the various options of these benefits and services.

SOME BASIC TERMS

There are some basic terms used in employee benefits and services programme. These are the following:

1. Cafeteria programme/system

This is also known as flexible benefit programme. This programme is based upon the principle of individual differences. This system allows employees to choose from a variety of benefits that are most valuable to him or her. This is a flexible programme, which offers a menu, or a package of different benefits and allows the employees to select from them.

2. Coinsurance

These are the payments made to cover health-care expenses. Usually these are spilt between the employer's insurance company and the insured employee. For example, the company will pay 70 per cent of employee's health care costs and the employee will pay the remaining 30 per cent.

3. Contributions

This refers to the payment made for the benefits coverage. Depending on the type of benefits, contributions are made from employer, employee or both. For example, premiums for health-care insurance are usually paid from both the parties. Whereas vacations are an employer-provided benefit.

IMPORTANCE OF BENEFITS AND SERVICES

Employee benefits and services programmes are valuable because of the following reasons:

1. Benefits are helpful in most effective recruitment.
2. Benefits are helpful in retaining the talented and skilled employees.
3. They improve the morale and loyalty.
4. They reduce absenteeism and labour turnover.
5. They reduce the influence of trade unions.
6. They reduce the threat of government intervention.
7. They are helpful in maintaining harmony in the industry.
8. They are helpful in maintaining good public relations.
9. They protect employees against certain hazards, e.g. life insurance, pension, etc.

FEATURES OF BENEFITS AND SERVICES

The main features of fringe benefits are the following:

1. These are supplementary to regular wages. These are extra payment other than wages.
2. These are regularly payable, not in piece-meal.
3. These benefits are indirect compensation. These are not directly related to employee performance.
4. These benefits have a direct relation to the real wages of the workers during a given period of time.
5. These benefits constitute a labour cost for the employer and are not meant directly to improve efficiency.
6. These benefits provide help in raising the standard of living of employees.
7. These benefits may be statutory or voluntary. For example, housing and educational facilities are a voluntary benefit whereas gratuity and provident fund is a statutory benefit.

PRINCIPLES OF EMPLOYEE BENEFITS AND SERVICES PROGRAMMES

The main principles of employee benefit programme are the following:[4]

1. The employee benefit should satisfy a real need.
2. Benefits should be confined to activities in which the group is more efficient than the individual.
3. The benefit programme should be characterised by sufficient flexibility to enable adaptation to varying employee needs.
4. If the firm is to receive values from providing employee services, it must undertake an extensive and well-planned communication programme.
5. The cost of the benefit should be calculable and provision should be made for sound financing.

TYPES OF EMPLOYEE BENEFITS AND SERVICES (FRINGE BENEFITS)

Various kinds of employee benefits and services offered by the organisations are the following:

1. Legally required benefits

This includes the following:

(a) Social security benefits such as benefits during sickness, accident compensation, maternity benefit, old-age pension, provident fund and gratuity.

(b) Workers' compensation.

(c) Unemployment insurance or compensation.

(d) Severance pay (this refers to one time payment which an employer provides when terminating the services of an employee).

These benefits are compulsory to be provided under legislation.

2. Labour welfare benefits

These includes (i) canteens, (ii) subsidized food and other supplies, (iii) subsidies to co-operative stores and fair price shops,

(iv) housing facilities, (v) creches, (vi) schools, (vii) holiday homes, (viii) recreation (parties & picinics), (ix) birth, marriage and death grants, (x) aid towards buying or constructing homes, (xi) transportation facilities, etc.

3. Payments for time not worked

These include: (i) vacations, (ii) leave with pay, (iii) holidays, (iv) voting time, (v) paid rest periods, (vi) clothes change time, (vii) get ready time, (viii) sick leave, (ix) jury duty, etc. These types of benefits are the most expensive benefits for an employer.

4. Employee services

These are tax-free or tax-preferred services that enhance the quality of employees' work or personal life.[5] These include (i) education subsidies, (ii) travel expenses (car reimbursement, food and entertainment reimbursement), (iii) parking privileges, (iv) discounts on company products, (v) physical awareness and fitness programmes, (vi) clothing allowance, (vii) tool allowance/reimbursement, (viii) relocation expenses, (ix) emergency loans, (x) on-site health services, (xi) credit union (it is an organised group of people who pool their money and agree to make loans to one another), and (xii) counselling services.

5. Hazard protection

These include payment made to maintain income of the employees during the periods of hazards such as injury, illness, disability, unemployment, etc.

ADMINISTRATION OF BENEFITS AND SERVICES

Usually the HR department takes the lead in designing and administering benefit and service programmes, however, the managers provide help in communicating the various options to employees and in keeping records (e.g. sick days, vacation timings, etc.) of employees. The main steps involved in the administration process are as follows:

1. Establishment of objectives

First of all, the management should establish the clear-cut objectives of benefits and services programmes. Generally the main objectives are:

(a) To meet the real needs of employees
(b) To meet the legal requirements
(c) To show organisation's social responsibility
(d) To increase cost effectiveness
(e) To foster external competitiveness
(f) To attract and retain competent employees.

2. Assessment of environment

Both the external as well as internal environment factors influence the benefit and service programs. External factors include economic factors, government policies and regulations and labour unions. Internal factors include employee preference and demographics, organisational objectives and strategies and organisation's ability to pay. Employees have different benefits and services needs depending on a number of factors such as age, marital status, whether spouse works or not, presence of kids, etc.

3. Assessment of competitiveness

This is very essential to assess the benefits and services offered by the competitors in order to match or outplay them. Usually, this is assessed by the market survey conducted by the professional associations.

4. Communication

The benefit and service programmes should be communicated properly to all employees with the help of brochures, calendars, slide presentations, booklets and meetings.

5. Evaluate and control

The last step involves the assessment of fringe benefits. It is checked whether organisation has been able to attract and retain the competent employees or not, whether employees earnings have been improved or not, whether labour-management relations are better or not, whether morale of employees is raised or not, whether the programmes were cost effective or not, etc.

KEY TERMS

Cafeteria system	Credit union
Coinsurance	Fringe benefits
Contribution	Severance pay

QUESTIONS

1. Describe employee benefits and service programmes.
2. Bring out the importance of fringe benefits.
3. Outline the key features of employee benefits and service programmes.
4. Describe the various types of employee benefits and service programmes.
5. What are the steps involved in the proper administration of benefits and service programmes?

ENDNOTES

1. Luis R. Gomez-Mejia, David B. Balkin and Robert L. Cardy, *Managing Human Resources,* Third Edition, Pearson Education, Delhi, 2003, p. 395.
2. L.K. Beatty, "Pay and Benefits Break Away from Tradition", *HR Magazine*, 1994, Vol. 39, No. 11, pp. 63-68.
3. Edwin B. Flippo, *Personnel Management*, Sixth Edition, McGraw-Hill, New York, 1984, p. 331.
4. *Ibid*., p. 334.
5. Luis R. Gomez-Mejia, David B. Balkin and Robert L. Cardy, op. cit., p. 399.

Motivation

17

LEARNING OBJECTIVES

After studying this chapter, you should be able to:

1. Understand the nature and importance of motivation
2. Describe the various types of motivation
3. Describe the various theories of motivation

Once the employees are hired, trained, developed and compensated, the next task is to motivate them for better performance. All organisations', whether small or large, are concerned with what should be done to attain sustained high levels of performance through its employees. Every organisation desires its employees to go to work willingly and enthusiastically.

MEANING AND DEFINITION

The term motivation is derived from the word 'motive'. Motive can be defined as that which makes a person active in a particular way. Some of the main definitions of motivation are as follows:

1. Motivation is the act of stimulating someone to get a desired course of action, or push the right button to get desired results.[1]
2. Motivation can be defined as the willingness to exert high levels of effort to reach organisational goals, conditioned by the effort's ability to satisfy some individual need.[2]
3. Motivation can be defined as willingness to expand energy to achieve a goal or reward.[3]

There is a well-accepted truism that performance is a function of motivation × ability.[4] This can be expressed algebraically as follows:

$$\text{Performance} = f\,(\text{Motivation} \times \text{Ability})$$

The above said truism simply captures the logic that ability in the absence of motivation or motivation in the absence of ability is insufficient to yield performance. Ability involves knowledge and skill. Whereas motivation is influenced by individual's needs, physical and social conditions. Knowledge involves education, experience, training and interest, while skills relate to aptitude and personality. Individual needs include psychological, social and egoistic needs, which embrace general variables. Physical conditions include light, temperature, safety, whereas social conditions include leaders, informal groups and formal organisations.[5]

THE MOTIVATION PROCESS

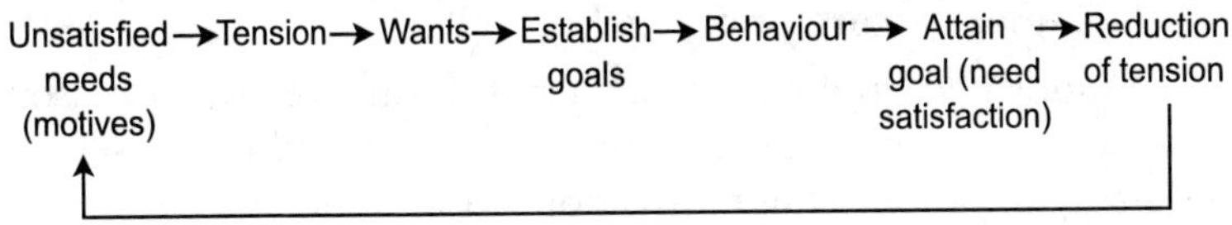

Fig. 17.1: The Process of Motivation

As Figure 17.1 suggests, the motivation is initiated by the recognition of the unsatisfied needs. Need is the feeling that something is required. This creates tension in the mind and transforms itself into want. It can be said that motivated employees are in a state of tension. Wants are the desires to attain something. Then goals are established which it is believed will satisfy these needs and wants. A behaviour pathway is selected which is expected to achieve the goal. When the goal is achieved, the need will be satisfied and tension is reduced. The behaviour ends the moment the tension is released. However, the satisfaction of one need leads to a feeling of another need and this way the process keeps on going.

CHARACTERISTICS OF MOTIVATION

The main features of motivation are as follows:

1. Motivation is an internal feeling. It is a psychological phenomenon, which generates within an individual.
2. An individual in totality, not in part, is motivated.
3. It produces goals-directed behaviour.
4. It is a continuous process as human needs are unlimited.
5. It can be either positive or negative. Positive motivation refers to pay, rewards, bonus, etc. while negative motivation emphasises penalties, for example, disciplinary action, threat of demotion, fear of loss of job, etc.
6. It sustains the behaviour in progress. It persists until and unless the satisfaction of the need occurs.

IMPORTANCE OF MOTIVATION

The importance of motivation can be judged from the following:

1. Higher performance level

A motivated employee put higher performance in comparison to other employees. High performance from individual is essential for an organisation. Thus motivation is a vital tool for the success of an organisation.

2. Optimum utilisation of resources

A motivated employee will make best possible use of different factors of production. By this wastage is minimised and cost is reduced thus benefits the organisation.

3. Low absenteeism and employee turnover

A motivated employee remains on the job for longer duration and his or her rate of absenteeism is also very low.

4. Facilitates change

In order to survive and thrive, an organisation has to cope up with various changes. Changes may be technological, social, etc. Motivation helps to reduce resistance to change. Highly motivated employees accept these changes with zeal and enthusiasm. They provide support in the proper introduction and implementation of the changes in the organisation.

5. Better industrial relations

Motivation creates optimum integration of individual interests with organisational objectives. Motivation results in increased labour productivity, which in turn results in higher wages and rewards for employees. This reduces labour unrest and raises a sense of belongingness and loyalty. This results in healthy labour-management relations.

TYPES OF MOTIVATION

Basically there are two types of motivation which are as follows:

1. Intrinsic motivation

It is concerned with self-generation factors that influence individuals to behave in a particular way. These factors include recognition, appreciation, responsibility, autonomy, status, respect, etc.

2. Extrinsic motivation

It is concerned with what is to be done for the employees in order to motivate them. It has an immediate effect but it may not necessarily last long. A manager can motivate his or her employees by the following ways:

(i) **Positive Motivation**—this includes offering rewards, promotion, praise, increased pay etc.

(ii) **Negative Motivation**—this includes punishments, reprimands, disciplinary action, criticism, loss of job etc.

Apart from the above types, the motivation can classified as follows:

(a) *Financial motivation*

This is concerned with money. Money is assumed to be a very potential motivator. This includes production bonus, profit-sharing scheme, higher salary, etc.

(b) *Non-financial motivation*

This provides psychological and emotional satisfaction. It is concerned with psychic rewards, i.e. the inner felt satisfaction. This includes status, job security, team spirit, participation, recognition, etc.

THEORIES OF MOTIVATION

There are numerous approaches to the study of motivation. All approaches to motivation are underpinned by the motivation theory. All the theories can be classified into three broad categories as follows:

I. Instrumentality Theory

This states that rewards or punishments serve as the means of ensuring that employees behave in the desired ways.

II. McGregor's Theory X and Theory Y

III. Contemporary Theories

These can be further classified into two categories.

A. *Content (needs) theory*

This focuses attention on the identification of the main needs of individuals that influence their behaviour or act and take action to satisfy these needs.

B. *Process theory*

This focuses attention on psychological processes that affect motivation. Figure 17.2 provides a list of various theories of motivation.

I. Instrumentality Theory

Instrumentality refers to the belief that if we do one thing it will lead to another. This focuses on the use of rewards and penalties in order to induce the desired behaviour. This is known as carrot and the stick approach of motivation. This is based upon an old story that to make a donkey move, one must put a carrot in front of him or jab him with a stick from behind. Despite all the research on the theories of motivation that have come to the fore in recent years, reward and punishment are still considered strong motivators.[6] Reward prefers to salary rise, promotion, bonus, etc. Punishment refers to fear of loss of job, loss of income, reduction of bonus, demotion, disciplinary action, etc.

II. McGregor's Theory X and Theory Y

Douglas M. McGregor identified two opposing sets of assumptions about the nature of human beings. One is basically

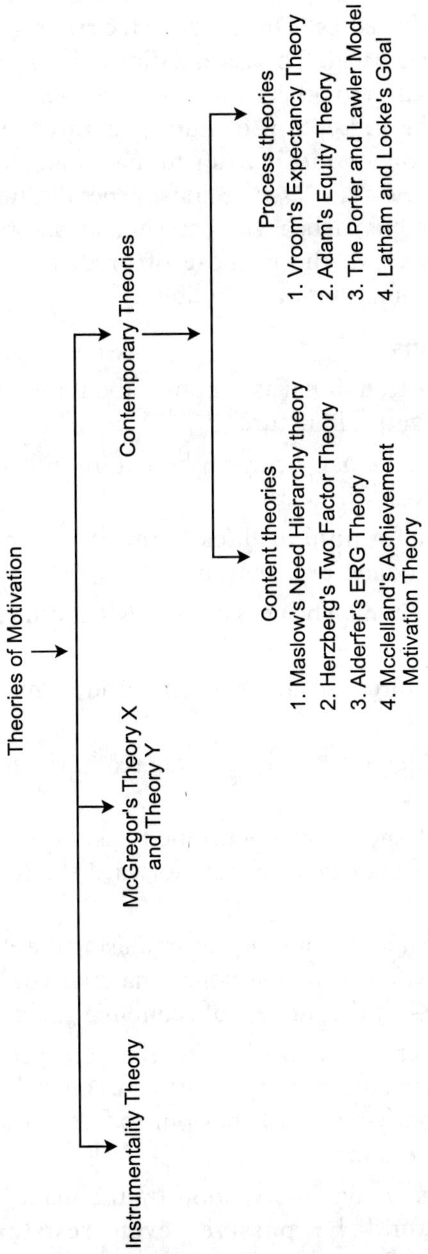

Fig. 17.2: Various Theories of Motivation

the negative view, labelled as 'Theory X' and another is basically the positive view, labelled as 'Theory Y'.[7] McGregor suggested that managing must start with the basic question of how managers see themselves in relation to others. Now this viewpoint requires some thought on the perception of human nature. In detail, management's action of motivating human beings in the organisation involves certain assumptions, generalisations and hypotheses relating to human behaviour and human nature. These assumptions simply serve the purpose of predicting human behaviour. These assumptions are as follows:

Theory X assumptions

These include the traditional assumption about the nature of people. These are negative in nature.

1. The average human being is, by nature indolent and will avoid work if he can.
2. The average human lacks ambition, dislikes responsibility and prefers to be led.
3. The average human being is inherently self-centered and indifferent to organisational goals.
4. He is by nature resistant to change and want security above all.
5. He is gullible, not very bright, the ready victim of the schemer.

On the basis of the above-mentioned assumptions, the conventional view of management puts forward the following propositions:

1. Management is responsible for organising the elements of productive enterprises—money, material, equipment, and people—in the interest of economic gains.
2. With respect to human beings, this is a process of directing their efforts, motivating them, controlling their actions, modifying their behaviour to fit/suit the needs of the organisation.
3. Without the active intervention by the management, people would be passive, even resistant, to organisational needs. They must be persuaded,

rewarded, punished, coerced, controlled and their activities must be directed.

According to McGregor, an organisation which is built upon Theory X assumptions will be the one in which the managers attempt to structure, control and closely supervise their employees. There will be high centralisation of authority and leadership will tend to be autocratic. Control is considered to be more appropriate in dealing with the irresponsible and immature employees.

Theory Y assumptions

The assumptions under Theory Y are as follows:

1. The expenditure of physical and mental effort in work is as natural as play or rest. Average human being does not inherently dislike work. Depending upon the controllable conditions, work may be a source of satisfaction or a source of punishment.
2. External control and the threat of punishment are not the only means of bringing about efforts toward organisational objectives. People will exercise self-direction and self-control in the sense of objectives to which they are committed.
3. The degree of commitment to objectives is a function of the rewards associated with their achievement.
4. The average human being learns under proper conditions not only to accept but also to seek responsibility.
5. The capacity to exercise of relatively high degree of imagination, ingenuity and creativity in the solution of organisational problems is widely, not narrowly distributed in the population.
6. Under the conditions of modern industrial life, the intellectual potentialities of the average human beings are only partially utilised.

Theory Y presents an optimistic, dynamic, modern and flexible nature of human beings. In this theory, there is an emphasis on self-direction and the integration of individual needs with organisational demands. It emphasises on the mutual cooperation between management and employees. The aim is to get maximum output with minimum amount of control and direction. From the motivation point of view and in relation to Maslow's need hierarchy (to be discussed next in this chapter), theory X assumes that physiological and safety needs dominate the individual whereas Theory Y assumes that social and esteem needs are dominant.[8]

COMPARISON BETWEEN THEORY X AND THEORY Y

These theories are based on certain assumptions about the nature of human beings. The key differences between the two sets of assumptions are given in Table 17.1.

THEORY Z

This theory was developed by William Ouchi after making a comparative study of the Japanese and American management practices (see Table 17.2). According to this theory large complex organisations are human systems and their effectiveness depends on the quality of humanism used. Theory Z represents an integrated model of motivation. Theory Z takes into account the strengths of both Japanese management as well as American management. The letter 'Z' does not stand for anything, it just

Table 17.1: Comparison between Theory X and Theory Y

Theory X	Theory Y
1. Inherent dislike for work	1. Work is as natural as play
2. No ambitions and prefers to be directed by others	2. Ambitious and prefer self-direction
3. Little capacity for creativity	3. Creativity is widely distributed
4. Focus on lower level needs (physiological and safety) to motivate people	4. Focus on both the lower and higher level needs (social and esteem needs) for motivation
5. Avoid responsibility	5. Accept and seek responsibility under proper conditions
6. Lack self-motivation	6. People are self-motivated
7. Emphasis scalar system and centralisation of authority	7. Emphasis decentralisation and greater participation in the decision-making
8. External control and close supervision is required to get maximum output from people	8. Self-direction and self-control
9. Autocratic leadership	9. Democratic and supportive leadership

Table 17.2: The Japanese and US Management Approaches

Japanese Management	U.S. Management
	Planning
1. Long-term orientation	1. Primarily short-term orientation
2. Collective decision making (*ringi*) with consensus	2. Individual decision making
3. Involvement of many people in preparing and making the decision	3. Involvement of a few people in making and "selling" the decision to persons with divergent values
4. Decision flow from bottom to top and back	4. Decisions initiated at the top, flowing down
5. Slow decision making; fast implementation of the decision	5. Fast decision making; show implementation requiring compromise, often resulting in suboptimal decisions
	Organising
1. Collective responsibility and accountability	1. Individual responsibility and accountability
2. Ambiguity of decision responsibility	2. Clear and specific decision responsibility
3. Informal organisation structure	3. Formal, bureaucratic organization structure
4. Well-know common organization culture and philosophy; competitive spirit toward other enterprises	4. Lack of common organization culture; identification with profession rather than with company
	Staffing
1. Young people hired out of school; hardly any mobility of people among companies	1. People hired out of schools and from other companies; frequent company changes
2. Slow promotion through the ranks	2. Rapid advancement desired and demanded
3. Loyalty to the company	3. Loyalty to the profession
4. Very infrequent performance evaluation for new (young) employees	4. Frequent performance evaluation for new employees
5. Appraisal of long-term performance	5. Appraisal of short-term results
6. Promotions based on multiple criteria	6. Promotions based primarily on individual performance
7. Training and development considered a long-term investment	7. Training and development undertaken with hesitation (for fear of turnover)
8. Lifetime employment common in large companies	8. Job insecurity prevailing

Leading	
1. Leader acting as a social facilitator and group member	1. Leader acting as decision maker and head of the group
2. Paternalistic style	2. Directive style (strong, firm, determined)
3. Common values facilitating cooperation	3. Often divergent values; individualism sometimes hindering cooperation
4. Avoidance of confrontation, sometimes leading to ambiguities; emphasis on harmony	4. Face-to-face confrontation common; emphasis on clarity
5. Bottom-up communication	5. Communication primarily top-down
Controlling	
1. Control by peers	1. Control by superior
2. Control focus on group performance	2. Control focus on individual performance
3. Saving face	3. Fixing blame
4. Extensive use of quality control circles	4. Limited use of quality control circles

Source: H. Koontz and H. Weihrich, *Essentials of Management,* Tata McGraw-Hill, New Delhi, 2002, p. 495.

denotes the state of affairs in an organisation and human behaviour. The main features of Theory Z are as follows:

1. Trust

According to Theory Z, trust, integrity and openness are essential ingredients of an effective organisation. In the environment of trust and openness between employees, work group, union and management, conflicts are reduced to the minimum and employees fully cooperate to attain organisational goals.

2. Strong relationship between employees and organisation

For establishing strong bonds between employees and organisation, several techniques may be adopted such as lifetime employment, great concern for the individual employee and emphasis on seniority. In situations of adverse business environment, the shareholders may forgo dividends to prevent the lay-offs and retrenchment of workers. In such situations, promotions may be delayed. Rather than vertical movement of employees more emphasis should be given to the horizontal movement that reduces stagnation.

3. Employee involvement

Employee involvement refers to the meaningful participation of employees in the decision-making process of the organisation. This is built on the concept that change and new ideas should come primarily from below. This also generates a sense of responsibility and enthusiasm among employees. Although the decision-making process is time-consuming, the implementation of the decision—because of the general consensus at various levels of management—is swift and does not require additional selling.[9]

4. Integrated organisation

Theory Z focuses on structureless organisation. It puts greater emphasis on sharing of information and resources, team work and understanding. This concept of integrated organisation focuses on job rotation, which will improve understanding about independence of tasks.

5. Coordination

Proper coordination of human effort is essential to develop a common culture. In order to coordinate the subordinate efforts, the leader must be ready to give his time and energy in sharing their ideas openly in breaking class barriers and in creating opportunities for employees to realise their potential.

6. Informal control system

Theory Z puts emphasis on informal organisational control system. It suggests that the focus should be on mutual trust and cooperation rather than on superior-subordinate relationships.

III. Contemporary theories

A. *Content theories*

Content theories are concerned with what factors within individuals cause them to behave in a certain way. These theories emphasize that if you want to understand what motivates employees you must identify their needs. In other words, the content theories of motivation are concerned with identifying the

Table 17.3: Contemporary Theories to Motivation

Theory	Characteristics	Theories	Managerial Examples
A. Content	Concerned with what factors within individuals cause them to behave in a certain way	1. Need Hierarchy theory	Motivation by satisfying
		2. Two-factor theory	individual needs for money,
		3. ERG theory	status and achievement
		4. Achievement motivation theory	
B. Process	Concerned not only with what factors within individuals cause them to behave in a certain way, but also how individuals are motivated	1. Expectancy theory	Motivation through clarifying
		2. Equity theory	an individuals perception
		3. Porter and Lawler model	of work inputs, performance
		4. Goal theory	requirements and rewards

Source: Adapted from Andre D. Sizilagyi, Jr. and Marc J. Wallace, Jr., *Organizational Behaviour and Performance*, Santa Monica; Cal.; Good year Publishing, 1980, p. 114.

needs/drives that people have and how these needs/drives are prioritized. The four content theories which have generated strongest interest are Maslow's need hierarchy theory, Herzberg's two-factor theory, Alderfer's ERG theory and McClelland's achievement theory.

1. Maslow's Need Hierarchy Theory

The need hierarchy theory was propounded by Abraham Harold Maslow. This is one of the most simple, popular and widely known theories of motivation. Figure 17.3 shows the basic human needs placed by Maslow in an ascending order of importance.

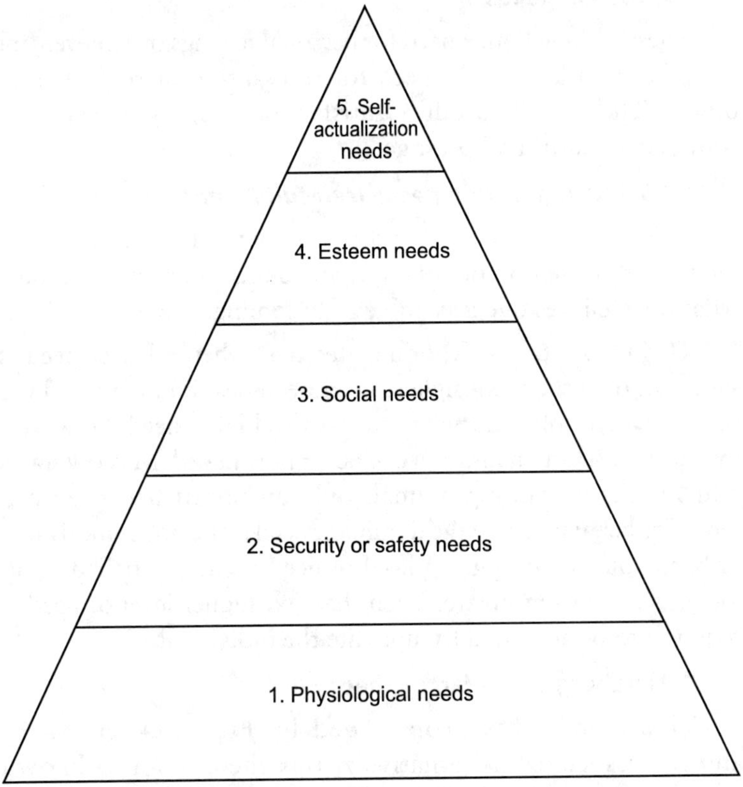

Fig. 17.3: Maslow's Hierarchy of Needs

(i) *Physiological needs*

These are the basic needs for sustaining human life itself. These include the needs for food, water, air and sex.

(ii) *Security or safety needs*

These are the needs for protection against danger. These are the needs for safety, stability and protection from the fear of losing a job, property, food and shelter.

(iii) *Social needs*

These include need for love, affection, friendship, interaction and acceptance by others.

(iv) *Esteem needs*

These include both a need for personal feelings of achievement or self-esteem and also a need for recognition or respect from others. These needs produce satisfaction such as power, self-confidence, status and prestige.

(v) *Self-actualization needs (self-fulfillment)*

This is the highest need in the need hierarchy. These include the need to develop potentialities and skills in order to become what one believes one is capable of becoming.

This theory of motivation states that when a lower need is satisfied, then the next highest need becomes dominant and the person's attention is turned to satisfy this higher need. However, the need for self-actualisation can never be satisfied. Maslow states that man is a wanting animal, only an unsatisfied need can motivate behaviour and the dominant need is the prime motivator of behaviour. Once a given level of need became satisfied, it no longer served to motivate. Then the next higher level of need is required to be activated to motivate the individual.

2. Herzberg's two-factor theory

This theory was propounded by Frederick Herzberg and his associates. Alternatively, this theory is also known as motivation- hygiene theory and dual-factor theory (Table 17.4).

Table 17.4 shows that one group of needs includes company policy and administration, supervision, quality of supervision, interpersonal relations, working conditions, salary, status and job security. Herzberg and his associates found these as only

Table 17.4: Herzberg's Two-factor Theory

Hygiene Factors	Motivators
1. Company policy and administration	1. Challenging work
2. Supervision	2. Achievement
3. Quality of supervision	3. Advancement
4. Interpersonal relations	4. Responsibility
5. Working conditions	5. Growth in the job
6. Salary	6. Work itself
7. Status	7. Recognition
8. Job security	

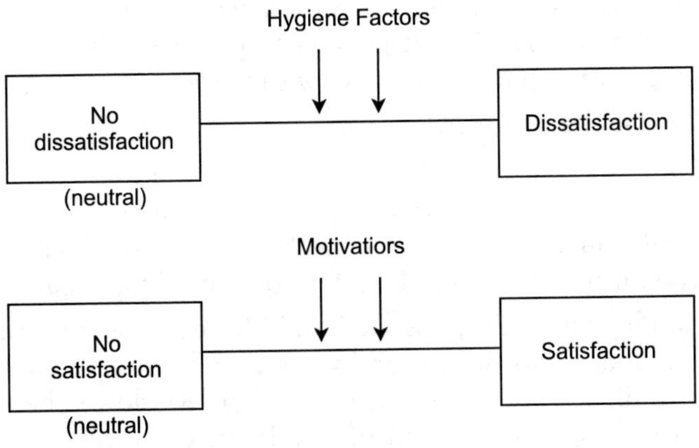

Fig. 17.4: Herzberg's Views of Job Satisfaction and Dissatisfacton

dissatisfiers and not motivators. Their existence does not motivate in the sense of yielding satisfaction, but their lack of existence causes dissatisfaction. These are known as hygiene, maintenance or job content factors.

On the other side is the list of motivators (or satisfiers). These are related with job content. They include challenging work, achievement, advancement, responsibility, growth in the job, work itself and recognition. Their existence motivates human beings on the job. According to this theory, it is only the presence of these motivators which produces employee satisfaction and performance. Whereas the presence of hygiene factors merely prevents employee dissatisfaction (Fig. 17.4).

3. Alderfer's ERG theory

This theory of motivation was developed by Clayton P. Alderfer. He has formulated Maslow's five need level into three more general need levels.[10] E stands for existence, R for relatedness and G for growth.

(i) *Existence needs (E)*

These includes both physiological and safety needs. This category is similar to the lowest two needs of Maslow's need hierarchy.

(ii) *Relatedness needs (R)*

These needs emphasise the importance of interpersonal and social relationships. This category is comparable to the social and certain ego-esteem needs of Maslow's theory.

(iii) *Growth needs (G)*

These are concerned with the individual's intrinsic desire for personal development. These relate to the development of human potential. This category is comparable to the self-actualization and certain ego-esteem needs of Maslow's need hierarchy.

Although ERG theory is similar to Maslow's theory in that it posits that needs form a hierarchy based on an abstraction from lower to higher. However, this differs from Maslow's theory in three respects. First, instead of five levels of needs, the ERG considered only three. Second, the ERG theory does not place much emphasis on the successive prepotency of needs. It hypothesises that all needs may be active at the same time. Third, it has incorporated a need frustration regression process. It means that when a person is repeatedly frustrated in his or her efforts to satisfy a higher-order need then greater importance is placed on the preceding lower level.

4. McClelland's achievement motivation theory

This theory was developed by David C. McClelland and his associates. He has contributed to the understanding of motivation by identifying three types of basic motivating needs. These are the need for power (n/PWR), need for affiliation (n/AFF) and the need for achievement (n/ACH).

(i) *Need for power*

People with a high need for power have a great concern for exercising influence and control.[11] The satisfaction is derived from being in a position of influence and control. Individuals with a high power derive often seek position of leadership, they are forceful, good conversationalists, good public speaker and they enjoy teaching.

(ii) *Need for affiliation*

Individuals with a high need for affiliation oftenly derive pleasure from being loved and tend to avoid the pain of being rejected by a social group. Usually, they need to form strong interpersonal ties and to get close to others psychologically. They enjoy a sense of intimacy and understanding with others.

(iii) *Need for achievement*

Individuals with a high need for achievement have an intense desire for success and an equally intense fear of failure. They set moderately difficult goals (but achievable) for themselves and they want to be challenged. They adopt a realistic approach to risk. They are not gamblers, they dislike succeeding by chance. In other words, they prefer the challenge of working at a problem rather than leaving the outcome to chance. High achievers are tend to be restless, they like to work for long hours and have strong desire to do things better.

McClelland and his associates found, in their research studies, that entrepreneurs showed a very high need for achievement and fairly high need for power drives but were quite low in their need for affiliation. Managers generally showed high achievement and power need but low affiliation need but not as high or low as was of entrepreneurs. The research work of McClelland and his associates has a number of practical applications. Upto some extent the managers can increase the achievement need level of their subordinates by creating a proper work environment. This includes increasing responsibility, autonomy and by offering challenging work.

The relationship among the four content theories is shown in Figure 17.5. Maslow's and Alderfer's theories of motivation are based upon levels of need hierarchy. Whereas Herzberg developed two discrete continua for two need categories. The hygiene factors,

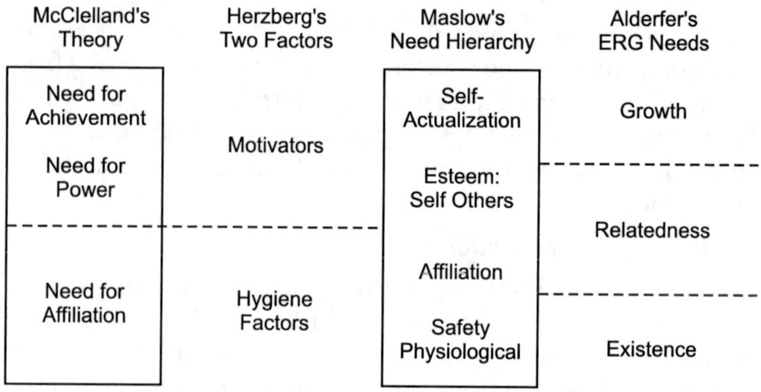

Fig. 17.5: Relationship among the Content Theories

of Herzberg's two-factor theory, correspond to the three lower need levels of Maslow's hierarchy. The motivators correspond to upper two levels of the need levels.

As far as Maslow's need hierarchy and ERG theories are concerned, the existence needs of ERG theory correspond to the two lower need levels of Maslow's theory. The relatedness needs overlap with the interpersonal needs and the need for respect from others in the Maslow's need hierarchy. Lastly, the growth needs correspond to the self-actualization and self-esteem needs.

In case of McClelland's theory the need for affiliation correspond with the relatedness needs of ERG theory, affiliation in Maslow's theory and interpersonal relations in Herzberg's theory. The need for power overlaps with Alderfer's relatedness and growth needs. Whereas the need for achievement correspond with growth needs of ERG theory and self-actualisation needs of Maslow's theory.

All these content theories highlight a variety of individual's needs. These theories suggest how to make a job design. For example, with the help of techniques such as job enlargement, enrichment, autonomous work teams, etc. These all serve various needs of people. In addition, the manager should identify the best compensation package to satisfy different individual needs.

B. *Process Theories*

The content theories of motivation attempted to identify what motivated individuals at work (e.g. power, achievement, esteem, etc.). In other words, content theories were mainly concerned with what factors within individuals cause them to behave in a certain way. In contrast, the process theories are more concerned with identifying the variables that go into motivation. In addition, these variables are related with one another. In process theories, the emphasis is on the psychological processes or forces that affect motivation as well as on basic needs.[12] There are four process theories, these are, namely, Vroom's expectancy theory, Adam's equity theory, the Porter and Lawler model, and Latham and Locke's goal theory.

1. Vroom's expectancy theory

This theory of motivation was advanced by the psychologist Victor H. Vroom. According to him people will be motivated to do things to reach a goal if they believe in the worth of that goal and if they can see that what they do will help them in achieving it.[13] This theory states that individual's motivation toward doing anything will be determined by the value they place on the outcome of their effort (whether positive or negative), multiplied by the confidence they have that their efforts will help in achieving a goal. Algebraically, Vroom's theory may be stated as:

$$\text{Force} = \text{Valence} \times \text{Expectancy}$$

Where

Force is the strength of a person's motivation,

Valence is the strength of an individual's preference for a particular outcome

Expectancy is the probability that a particular action will lead to a desired outcome.

Working of the expectancy theory

Figure 17.6 presents a very simplified version of the expectancy theory.

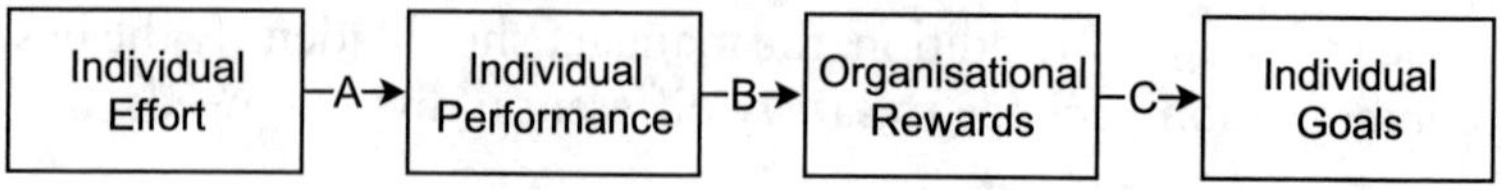

A = Effort-performance linkage
B = Performance-reward linkage
C = Attractiveness

Fig. 17.6: Simplified Version of ExpectancyTheory

Source: Stephen P. Robbins and David A. Decenzo, *Fundamentals of Management,* 3rd Edition, Pearson Education, Delhi, 2001, p. 324.

As the Figure 17.6 shows there are three variables or relationships:[14]

(i) *Effort-performance linkage*

This relates to the probability perceived by an individual that exerting a given amount of effort will lead to performance.

(ii) *Performance-reward linkage*

This refers to the degree to which an individual believe that after performing at a particular level will lead to the achievement of a desired outcome.

(iii) *Attractiveness*

This refers to the importance that an individual places on the potential reward that can be achieved on the job.

In totality, the strength of an individual to perform depends on how intensely that individual believes that he or she can attain what is being attempted. Once this goal is attained the individual will be adequately compensated by the organisation, this will satisfy his or her individual goals.

2. Adam's equity theory

This theory was developed by J. Stacey Adams. This theory states that employees perceive what they get from a job situation (outcome) in relation to what they put into it (inputs) and then compare their input-outcome ratio with the input-outcome ratios of relevant others. The relevant others may be one person (e.g. a colleague), a group (e.g. workers on other shift) or someone from a previous or even hypothetical, work situation. There is one important point in this theory of motivation, i.e. here the emphasis is on 'perceived' as compared to 'actual' equity. It hardly matters that whether an individual's evaluations are based on subjective perception or objective reality.

Figure 17.7 shows the various relationships in equity theory. When the employees perceive their ratio to be equal to those of

Perceived Ratio Comparison	Individual's Assessment
1. $\frac{O_A}{I_A} < \frac{O_B}{I_B}$	Inequity exists (under rewarded)
2. $\frac{O_A}{I_A} = \frac{O_B}{I_B}$	Equity exists
3. $\frac{O_A}{I_A} > \frac{O_B}{I_B}$	Inequity exists (over rewarded)

Individual A is the employee and Individual B is a relevant other.
O and I stands for outcome and input.

Fig. 17.7: The Equity Theory Relationships

the relevant others (with whom they are comparing themselves) then a state of equity exists. Then they perceive that the situation is fair and justice prevails. However, when the ratios are unequal, then inequity exists. In this case the employees consider themselves either under-rewarded or over-rewarded. In these cases, employees tried to correct the situation. There is considerable evidence that employees make comparisons of their job inputs and outcomes relative to others and that inequities influence the degree of effort that employees exert.[15]

In greater detail, an employee, on the basis of his or her inputs like education, experience, effort and competence compares outcomes like raise in pay, salary grade, recognition, status, etc. When the employees perceive imbalance in their input-outcome ratio relative with the others, then they experience tension. Now this tension provides the basis for motivation. Employees will work for what they perceive to be equity and justice. The result might lower or higher productivity, improved or reduced quality of output, increased absenteeism or voluntary resignation.[16]

3. The Porter and Lawler model

This is a very comprehensive model of motivation. This model was developed by Lyman W. Porter and Edward E. Lawler III. They have applied this model primarily to managers in their study.[17]

Figure 17.8 depicts the multivariate model of Porter and Lawler. As the figure shows the amount of effort depends on the value of a reward and the probability of receiving the reward. Also, this perceived effort and probability of getting a reward in reality are in turn, also influenced by the record of actual performance. As the figure shows that though the actual performance on a job is determined by the amount of effort but it is also influenced by the ability of an individual to do the job and by the person's perception of what the required task is. Then the performance leads towards the intrinsic rewards (like sense of accomplishment) and extrinsic rewards (like status, working conditions). These rewards lead to satisfaction. Also, the actual value of reward will be influenced by satisfaction.

This comprehensive model of motivation has practical implications for a practising manager. This model clearly shows that motivation is not a simple cause and effect matter. It means, too, that managers should carefully assess their reward structures and that through careful planning, managing by objectives and clearly defining duties and responsibilities through a good organisation structure, the effort-performance-reward-satisfaction system can be integrated into an entire system of managing.[18]

4. Latham and Locke's goal theory

This theory was developed by G. Latham and R. Locke. This theory states that motivation and performance are higher when individuals are set for specific goals, when goals are difficult but accepted and when there is a feedback on performance.[19] This theory suggests that the process of goal setting in itself is motivating provided the goal is perceived as realistic, just as a challenging task, provided it is achievable, is more motivating than an easy task.[20] Two important things to mention here are, first, it is important to set demanding goals as they will lead to better performance. Second, it is equally important to get feedback.

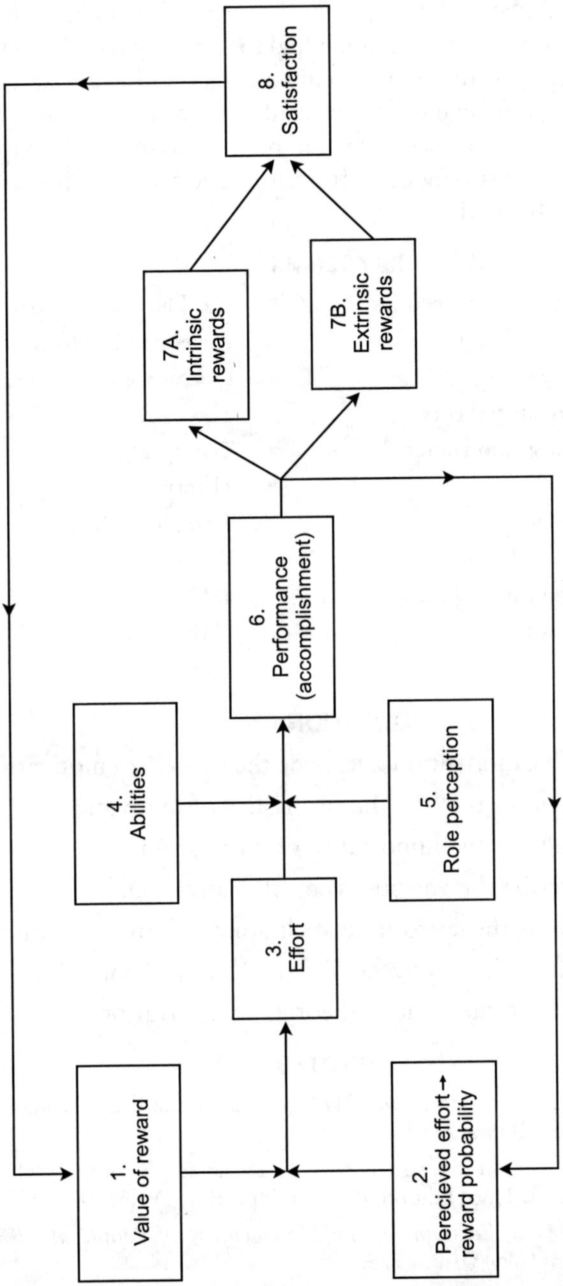

Fig. 17.8: The Porter and Lawler Model of Motivation

This theory is just in line with the concept of management by objectives. The goals inform individual to achieve particular levels of performance, in order for them to direct and evaluate their actions, while performance feedback allows the individual to track how well he or she has been doing in relation to the goal, so that, if necessary, adjustments in effort, direction or possibly task strategies can be made.[21]

KEY TERMS

Contemporary theories	Need hierarchy theory
Content theories	Porter and Lawler model
Equity theory	Process theories
Expectancy theory	Theory X
Extrinsic motivation	Theory Y
Force	Theory Z
Goal theory	Two-factor theory
Hygiene factors	Valence
Instrumentality theory	n/PWR
Intrinsic motivation	n/AFF
Motivators	n/ACH

QUESTIONS

1. Define motivation. Describe the process of motivation.
2. Bring out the key characteristics of motivation.
3. Bring out the importance of motivation.
4. Describe the various types of motivation.
5. Discuss the carrot and stick approach of motivation.
6. Differentiate between Theory X and Theory Y.
7. Describe the various theories of motivation.

ENDNOTES

1. Michael J. Jucius, *Personnel Management,* Richard D. Irwin, Inc., Homewood, Illinois, 1975.
2. Stephen P. Robbins and David A. Decenzo, *Fundamentals of Management*, Third Edition, Pearson Education, Delhi, 2002, p. 313.
3. Dale S. Beach, *Personnel—The Management of People at Work*, Macmillan, New York, 1975.

4. J.P. Campbell, R.A. Cloy, S.H. Oppler and C.E. Sager, "A Theory of Performance", N. Schmitt and W.C. Borman (Eds.), *Personnel Selection in Organisations*, 1993, pp. 35-70, Jossey-Bass, San Francisco.
5. Gurpreet Randhawa, *Education and Human Resource Management*, APH Publishing Corporation, New Delhi, 2007, p. 3.
6. Harold Koontz and Heinz Weihrich, *Essentials of Management*, Fifth Edition, Tata McGraw-Hill, New Delhi, p. 321.
7. Douglas McGregor, *The Human Side of Enterprise*, 1960, McGraw-Hill, New York.
8. "The Way We Were", *Management Today*, June 1998, pp. 111-12.
9. Harold Koontz and Heinz Weihrich, *Essentials of Management*, Fifth Edition, Tata McGraw-Hill, New Delhi, p. 493.
10. C.P. Alderfer, "An Empirical Test of a New Theory of Human Needs", *Organisational Behaviour and Human Performance*, 1969, Free Press, New York. pp. 142-175.
11. D.C. McClelland and D.H. Burnham, "Power in the Great Motivator", *Harvard Business Review*, 1976, pp. 100- 110.
12. Michael Armstrong, *A Handbook of Human Resource Management Practice,* Ninth Edition, Kogan Page, London, 2005, p. 220.
13. V.H. Vroom, *Work and Motivation*, John Wiley and Sons, New York, 1964.
14. Stephen P. Robbins and David A. Decenzo, op. cit., p. 324.
15. J.S. Adams, "Inequity in Social Exchanges," in L. Berkowitz, Ed., *Advances in Experimental Social Psychology*, Vol. 2, Academic Press, New York, 1965, pp. 267-300.
16. Stephen P. Robbins and David A. Decenzo, op. cit., p. 320.
17. L.W. Porter and E.E. Lawler III, *Managerial Attitudes and Performance*, Irwin, Homewood, 1968, p. 165.
18. Stephen P. Robbins and David A. Decenzo, op. cit., p. 326.
19. G. Latham and R. Locke, "Goal Setting—A Motivational Technique That Works", *Organisational Dynamics*, 1979, Autumn, pp. 68-80.
20. D. Guest, "Motivation After Maslow", *Personnel Management*, March 1976, pp. 29-32.
21. I.T. Robertson, M. Smith and D. Cooper, *Motivation,* IPM, 1992, London.

Industrial Relations

18

LEARNING OBJECTIVES

After studying this chapter, you should be able to:

1. Understand the nature and features of industrial relations
2. Describe the various approaches to industrial relations
3. Identify the factors influencing industrial relations

Industrial relations refer to the collective relationship between management, employees and government in any organisation. It deals with the people at work. Industrial relations in reality is a more comprehensive field of study, subtle as well as gross, a vast area of interactions, actions and reactions which affect not just a company or an industry, but also the economy. In turn, it is also affected by economic, social and historical factors making it a dynamic subject.[1]

MEANING AND DEFINITION

1. According to the *Encyclopaedia Britannica*, "The concept of industrial relations has been extended to denote the relations of the state with employers, workers and their organisations. The subject, therefore, includes individual relations and joint consultations between employers and work people at their work place, collective relations between employers and their organisations and trade unions and the part played by the state in regulating these relations."[2]
2. The ILO has used the term industrial relations in a wide sense to denote such matters as freedom of association and the right to organise, the application of the principle

of the right to organise, right of collective bargaining, of conciliation and arbitration proceedings and the machinery for co-operation between the authorities and the occupational organisations at various levels of the economy.

3. The term 'industrial relations' has been described as relationship between management and employees or among employees and their organisations that characterize or grow out of employment.[3]
4. Industrial relations is the study of all aspects of job regulation—the making and administering of the rules which regulate employment relationships—regardless of whether these are seen as being formal or informal, structured or unstructured.[4]

The above definition highlight that the term industrial relations means a set of relations arising out of the employer-employee relationship in the modern industrial society. The concept of industrial relations is a dynamic concept, which keeps on changing according to the development of new situations.

FEATURES OF INDUSTRIAL RELATIONS

The main features of industrial relations are as follows:

1. Industrial relations has two faces, just like a coin, conflict and cooperation. The relationship starting with cooperation soon changes into conflict and after its resolution again changes into cooperation.[5]
2. Industrial relations do not emerge in vacuum. They are born out of employment relationship in an industry. They involve two parties, i.e. management and labour.
3. Industrial relations is dynamic in nature. It does not operate in isolation. It is a part of large system. It considers the nation's socio-economic and political environment, technology, attitudes of trade unions, demand and supply, etc.

4. Industrial relations focuses on the study of conditions conducive for the cooperation between labour and management.
5. Industrial relations also include the study of rules, regulations, laws, awards and settlements, customs and traditions for maintaining harmonious relationship between labour and management.

OBJECTIVES OF INDUSTRIAL RELATIONS

The main objectives of industrial relations are as follows:

1. To promote mutual understanding and goodwill among employees and management.
2. To raise the productivity of labour and organisation as a whole.
3. To establish and maintain industrial democracy through workers' participation in management, labour copartnership, collective bargaining, etc.
4. To minimise all forms of industrial conflict for example, strikes, lockouts, gheraos, etc.
5. To promote smooth and healthy labour-management relations.
6. To promote mutual cooperation between employers and employees.
7. To integrate the interests of labour and management.
8. To minimise absenteeism and labour turnover.
9. To promote the welfare of the workers.
10. To encourage and develop strong trade unions.
11. To bring about government control over plants and units running into losses.
12. To ensure that the government endeavour to bridge the gap between the unbalanced, disordered and maladjusted social order.

SCOPE OF INDUSTRIAL RELATIONS

The scope of industrial relations can be classified under the following categories:

I. Relations within the Industry

This includes:

1. Individual relations

These are concerned with:

(a) Management of grievances of individuals' or group

(b) Matters pertaining to discipline.

2. Collective relations

These include:

(a) Negotiation

(b) Collective bargaining

(c) Working of joint committees

(d) Prevention and settlement of industrial disputes.

II. Role of State

This refers to the labour legislations and other rules and regulations, framed by both state as well as Central Governments.

III. International Aspects

This refers to international organisations' of workers and employers such as ILO. These organisations represent interests of various member countries.

COMPONENTS/MAIN ACTORS IN INDUSTRIAL RELATIONS

There are three actors in an industrial relations system, these are as follows:

1. Workers and their organisations

One actor in the industrial relations is workers and their organisations, i.e. unions. Basically, worker's organisations are political institutions. They safeguard workers interests, both within and outside the plant.

2. Management

Another actor in industrial relations is management/employer. They provide employment, lay down terms and conditions of employment and administer labour welfare and social security programme. For managing its workforce, a manager may adopt various leadership styles such as autocratic, exploitative, consultative and participative.

3. Government

In industrial relations, the government acts as a regulator. Both the State and Central Government affect industrial relations through labour legislations, rules, policies, regulations, etc.

FACTORS INFLUENCING INDUSTRIAL RELATIONS

The main factors affecting industrial relations are the following:

1. Institutional factors

These institutional factors include factors such as labour policy of the government, labour legislation, employers' and employees' organisations and their policies, collective bargaining agreements, voluntary codes, implementation machinery, etc.

2. Social factors

These include factors like norms, customs, beliefs, traditions, values, social status, level of education, level of awakening, etc.

3. Economic factors

These include factors such as system (capitalist, socialist, communist, mixed economy), economic conditions and policies, source of labour supply, nature and composition of workforce, labour market relative status, level and structure of wages, dearness allowance, incentives, price level, nationalisation of industries, rationalisation, level of unemployment, etc.

4. Psychological factors

These factors are like perception of workers, attitude and behaviour towards management, unions, fellow workers, living and working conditions respectively, workers interest, morale, motivation, boredom, dissatisfaction, etc.

5. Technological factors

These factors include type of technology used, work methods, technology development, etc. The technological factors influence directly the wage levels and employment status.

6. Political factors

These factors include the ideology and philosophy of the ruling party, political institutions, attitude of oppositions, etc.

7. Organisation-related factors

These are also known as internal factors. These include industrial relations policy of the organisation, working environment, prevailing management style, living conditions, organisational culture, climate and health, trade unions (their attitude, political affiliation, policies, leadership, etc.), wage and salary administration, various human resource management policies (e.g. recruitment and selection methods, training and development techniques, promotion policies, incentive schemes, grievance redressal procedures, composition of workforce, etc.).

8. Global factors

These include international relations, international trade agreements, role of ILO, economic and trading policies of power blocks, etc.

APPROACHES TO INDUSTRIAL RELATIONS

The main approaches to industrial relations are as follows:

1. Psychological approach

This approach suggests that the conflicts between labour and management are deeply rooted in the perception and attitudes of all the participants. Differences in the perception of the parties are due to their individual perception. Conflicts between them arise, as they negatively perceive each other's behaviour. They view and interpret the situations differently and these differences create problems of industrial relations.

2. Sociological approach

Industry is a part of society. So, various sociological factors such as value system, norms, customs, traditions and status symbols affect relations among the parties. The social consequences of industrialisation like organisation, social mobility, migration generate many social evils like family disintegration, stress and strain, delinquency, personal and social disorganisation (leading to growing incidence of gambling, drinking, prostitution, drug abuse, etc.) do influence workers' efficiency and productivity that in turn influence industrial relations of an industry.[6]

3. Human relations approach

This approach focuses on human beings as a key factor of production in industry. Unlike other resources such as finance and material, human beings have emotions, sentiments, desires, perceptions, attitudes, personality, etc. For harmonious industrial relations there is a need for the proper integration of individuals' need with the organisation's requirements. Management should motivate the employees in order to raise productivity.

4. Socio-ethical approach

This approach to industrial relations emphasises that besides having a sociological base it does have some ethical ramification. As good industrial relations can be only maintained when both the labour and management realise, their moral responsibility in contributing to the said task through mutual cooperation and greatest understanding of each other's problems.[7]

5. V.V. Giri approach

This approach to industrial relations was given by Sh. V.V. Giri, the late President of India. V.V. Giri emphasises collective bargaining, voluntary arbitration and mutual negotiations between employers and employees for the settlement of industrial disputes. This approach stresses on the internal settlement in comparison to compulsion from outside. Voluntary arbitration should be preferred to compulsory arbitration and compulsory adjudication.

6. Gandhian approach

This approach to industrial relations is based upon fundamental principles of truth, non-violence and non-possession. This approach presumes the peaceful co-existence of capital and labour. Gandhiji emphasised that if the employers follow the principle of trusteeship then there is no scope for conflict of interest between labour and management. Gandhiji accepted the workers' right to strike, but cautioned that they should exercise this right for a just cause and in a peaceful and non-violent manner and this method should only be resorted to when all other methods failed in getting employer's response.

7. Systems approach

A system is an organised or complex whole, an assemblage or combination of things or parts forming a complex unitary whole.[8] The systems approach tells us that no one single element or phenomenon should be dealt with without regard for its interacting consequence with other elements.[9] This suggests that there is always an interaction between the four basic elements, i.e. input, transformation, output and feedback.

In the field of industrial relations, the systems approach to industrial relations was developed by John T. Dunlop. Dunlop described an industrial relations system (IRS) consisting of three actors: unions, employers and the state. According to him, an IRS at any one point in its development is regarded as compressed of certain actors, certain contexts, ideology that binds the IRS together, and body of rules created to govern the actors at the work place and community.[10] The equation of the systems model is as follows:

$$r = f(a, t, e, s, i)$$

where

r = the rules of the industrial relations system

a = the actors

t = the technical context of the work place

e = the economic context of budgetary constraints

s = the power context and the status of the parties

i = the ideology of the system.

According to Dunlop, an IRS is dynamic in nature. An IRS would be in a state of equilibrium in a given environment where there are shared views of the parties but any change in one element would result in a transmission chain. The changes would work through the system as a whole, including all forms of interaction and the rules that are generated. Dunlop's model of IRS is shown in Figure 18.1.

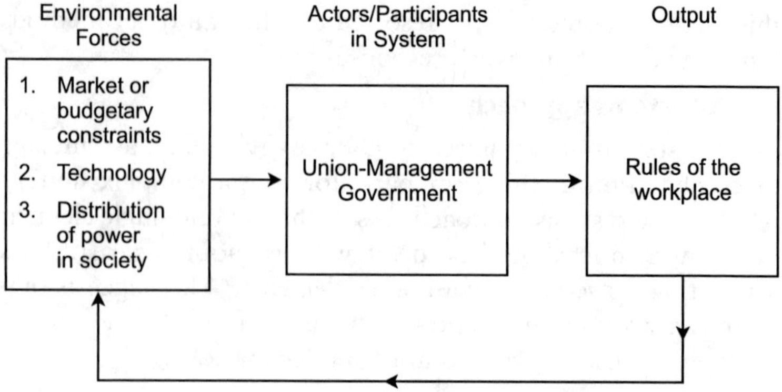

Fig. 18.1: Dunlop's Model of Industrial Relations System

The main elements in IRS are as follows:

1. Actors/Participants in the system

These are:

(a) Workers and their organisations

(b) Management and their representatives

(c) Government agencies (such as labour courts, tribunals)

2. Ideology of the system

Ideology regulates the relations among the participants. An ideology is a set of ideas and beliefs commonly held by the actors that helps to build or integrate the system tighter as an entity.[11]

3. The context or environment

As shown in the Figure 18.1, the actors do not operate in isolation. Their interaction takes place under the influence of, and in the context of, various types of factors and within certain environments.[12] Three types of environment relevant to industrial relations are as follows:

(i) *Technological environment*

Industrial relations would be different in a labour-intensive industry as compared to a capital-intensive industry. Changes in technology bring changes in work methods, new techniques are adopted that result in higher productivity.

(ii) *Market or economic constraints*

Economic factors such as inflation have a great impact on industrial relations. Every inflationary situation generally leads to higher incidences of industrial unrest and every recessionary situation usually leads to a decline of industrial action. This potentially disruptive issue is dealt with by devising rules for its automatic adjustment.[13] Other economic and market factors also influence industrial relations, for example, demand of product is considered important for deciding the need for labour.

(iii) *The locus and balance of power in society*

In an IRS, the power centers lies in workers and their organisation and the employers and the government. Usually, workers and employers demonstrate their strength to further their interests and the regulatory role of the government becomes important in shaping the patterns of industrial relations.

PRE-REQUISITES FOR A SUCCESSFUL INDUSTRIAL RELATIONS PROGRAMME

The necessary prerequisites for establishing good industrial relations are as follows:

1. Top management support

The industrial relations is basically a staff function, thus the officers or managers in charge of industrial relations work should derive authority from the line executive, i.e. President or Vice President as the case may be. For the success of industrial relations programme, support of top management is essential.

2. Constructive attitude

Both management and trade unions should develop constructive attitude towards each other. Mutual understanding and cooperation is necessary for the smooth conduct of industrial relations programme. On the one hand, the management must recognise their union as the spokesman of the workers' grievances and as custodian of their interests. It should accept workers as equal partners in the industry. On the other hand, the workers and their trade unions must also consider and appreciate the rights, authority and responsibility of the management.

3. Developing sound policies and procedures

The policies and procedures relating to industrial relations should be well-designed and revised timely for maintaining good industrial relations in an organisation. All the policies and procedures should be clear to everybody in the organisation including union leaders. The HR or industrial relations managers must make certain that the line people well-understand and agree with these policies.

4. Development of effective practices

The implementation of various policies pertaining to man-management selection calls for developing effective practices so that various policies could be translated into action.[14]

5. Good communication system

There must be a good and prompt communication system in an organisation in order to avoid any suspicion, rumour, doubt and misunderstanding between both the parties. Efficient communication system removes distrust between management and union leaders. HR or IR managers should play a key role in bringing both the parties together.

6. Adequate supervisory training

To a large extent the problem of industrial relations is a human problem. So, in order to deal with the human beings in the organisation and also, to ensure that organisational policies and procedures are properly implemented by the industrial relations staffs, it is necessary that all the supervisors and foreman should be provided with sufficient training. These are the people who come in direct contact with the employees so these people should be well trained in the tools and techniques of human relations. Success of industrial relations programme is largely determined by the attitude and dealing of supervisors. Thus they should be trained in motivation, communication and leadership.

7. Development of right kind of union leadership

On the pattern of developing good supervisors, management should also encourage the development of right type of union leadership. Although the management should not interfere with the union activities but it can create conditions, which would stimulate the growth of constructive and competent union leadership.

8. Follow-up of results

This refers to the constant review of industrial relations so that existing practices may be evaluated and also the problems and undesirable tendencies can be identified. Along with the regular follow up of various industrial relations policies and procedure, special emphasis should be placed upon gathering relevant information related with absenteeism, employee turnover, morale, job satisfaction, grievances, disputes, accident rate, wage and salary administration, etc. If the turnover rate is high then exit interviews should be conducted to identify the reasons.

KEY TERMS

Gandhian approach
Giri approach
Human relations
Ideology
Industrial relations
Systems approach

QUESTIONS

1. Define the term industrial relations and discuss its importance.
2. Bring out the objectives of industrial relations.
3. Bring out the factors influencing industrial relations.
4. Describe the various approaches to industrial relations.
5. What are the pre-requisites for a successful industrial relations programme?

ENDNOTES

1. Ratna Sen, *Industrial Relations in India: Shifting Paradigms*, Macmillan, 2003, p. 1.
2. *Encyclopedia Britannica*, Vol. 12, London, 1961, p. 297.
3. Dale Yoder, *Personnel Management &Industrial Relations*, Prentice-Hall of India, New Delhi, 1967.
4. H.A. Clegg et al., "A Strategy for Industrial Relations Research in Great Britain", *British Journal of Industrial Relations*, Vol. XII, No. 1, 1974, p. 85.
5. R.C. Singh, "Determinants of Industrial Relations", *Indian Journal of Labour Economics*, Vol. XII, p. 91.

6. C.B. Mamoria, Satish Mamoria and S.V. Gankar, *Dynamics of Industrial Relations,* Fifteenth Edition, Himalaya Publishing House, 2005, p. 194.

7. *Ibid.*, p. 196.

8. R.A. Johnson, F.E. Kast and J.E. Roserwig, *The Theory and Management of Systems*, McGraw-Hill, New York, 1973, p. 4.

9. H. Koontz and C. O'Donnell, *Management*, McGraw-Hill, Tokyo, 1976, pp. 14-19.

10. John T. Dunlop, *Industrial Relations System*, Henry Holt and Company, 1958, New York.

11. *Ibid.*

12. Ratna Sen, op. cit., p. 11.

13. C.B. Mamoria, Satish Mamoria and S. V. Gankar, op. cit., p. 204.

Industrial Disputes

19

LEARNING OBJECTIVES

After studying this chapter, you should be able to:

1. Understand the nature, types and causes of industrial disputes
2. Identify the various forms of industrial disputes
3. Describe the methods of settling the industrial disputes

Disputes have become a common feature of industrial life. They may take the form of strikes, lockouts, bandhs and gheraos. The result of industrial disputes are loss/delay of production, loss of man-hours, loss of profits, loss of market and shut down or closure of working place. The economic growth of a nation is vitally bound with industrial peace. Thus for the progress of industry and overall economy of a nation, the causes of industrial disputes should be identified and preventive measures should be taken in order to maintain industrial peace.

NATURE AND MEANING OF INDUSTRIAL DISPUTES

Industrial disputes refer to any conflict and unrest between employees and management on any ground. According to Industrial Disputes Act, 1947, Section 2 (k) industrial disputes means any dispute or difference between

(i) Employers and employers, or

(ii) Employers and workmen, or

(iii) Workmen and workmen, which is connected with

(a) The employment or non-employment, or

(b) The terms of employment, or

(c) The conditions of labour of any person.

According to the above said definition, following are the main elements of an industrial dispute:

1. Dispute must be related to workers and employers, or among workers and employers themselves.
2. The parties to the dispute must have direct and substantial interest in the dispute.
3. The causes of the dispute must be related with the work or terms of employment, etc.
4. Dispute can also be among the employers.

CLASSIFICATION/TYPES OF INDUSTRIAL DISPUTES

Industrial disputes may be classified as follows:

1. Individual disputes

The disputes about the compensation for wrongful dismissal, reinstatement, etc. are individual disputes. Section 2-A of Industrial Disputes Act, 1947 provides that where any employer discharges, dismisses, retrenches or otherwise terminates the services of an individual workman, any dispute or difference between the workman and his employer connected with or arising out of, such discharge, dismissal, retrenchment or termination shall be deemed to be an industrial dispute even if no other workman nor any union of workmen is the party to the dispute.

2. Interest disputes or economic disputes

These disputes usually come up when trade unions demand improvement in their wages, dearness and other allowances, fringe benefits and other terms of employment. As these demands are generally made on the behalf of the body of workers so these are also known as collective disputes.

3. Grievance disputes or legal disputes

These disputes arise when the workers feel that their rights have been violated or an act of injustice has been done to them. For these reasons, these are also called disputes of rights. Usually, these disputes are related with day-to-day workers' grievances or complaints, for example, working and employment conditions, promotion, etc.

4. Disputes pertaining to unfair labour practices

These disputes arise due to the unfair practices adopted by the employers against trade unions such as discrimination against office-bearers, victimisation of union leaders, restraining the workers from organising, etc.

5. Recognition disputes

These disputes arise due to reluctance or refusal shown by the employers in recognising the worker's union.

FORMS OF INDUSTRIAL DISPUTES

The major forms of an industrial dispute are the following (Fig. 19.1):

I. Strike

According to Section 2(q) of Industrial Disputes Act, 1947, strike means:

(i) a cessation of work by a body of persons employed in any industry acting in combination, or

(ii) a concerted refusal of any number of persons who are or have been so employed to continue to work or to accept employment, or

(iii) refusal under a common understanding of any number of such persons to continue to work or to accept employment.

A strike is a weapon in the hands of employees. Strikes can be classified as following:

A. Primary Strikes

The strikes generally aimed against the employer with whom the dispute exists are known as primary strikes.

B. Secondary Strikes

These are the strikes in which the pressure is applied not against the primary employer with whom the primary workers have a dispute but against some third person who has good trade relations with him which are severed and the primary employer incurs a loss.[1]

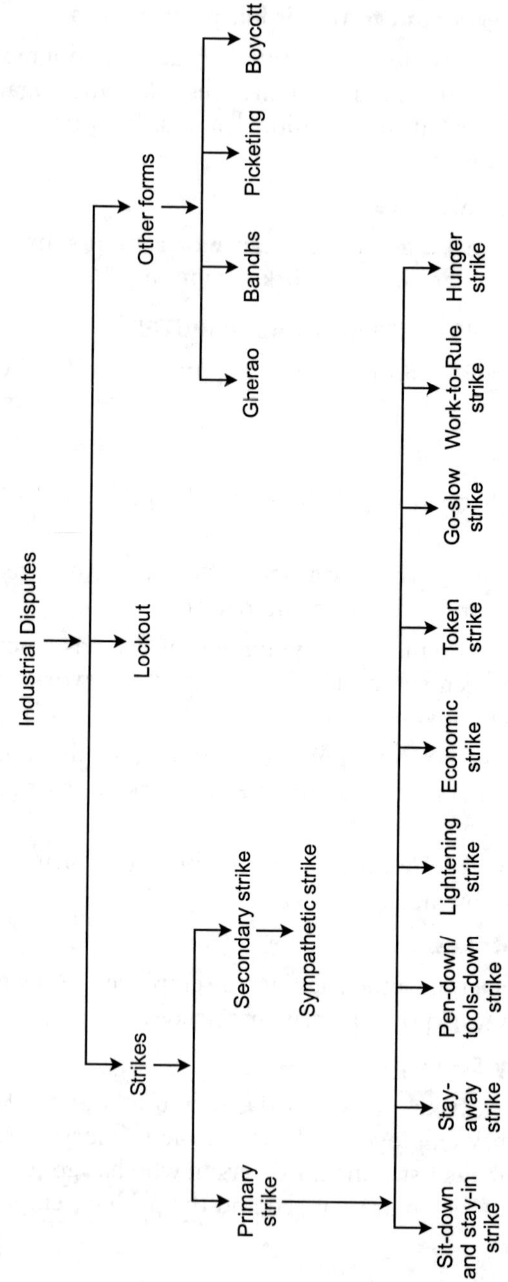

Fig. 19.1: Various Forms of Industrial Disputes

A. Primary Strikes

Following are the common forms of primary strikes:

1. Sit-down and stay-in strike

These strikes amount to trespass upon the property of the employer. A sit-down strike is said to have occurred whenever a group of employees or other interested in attaining certain objectives in a particular business take possession of property of that business, establish themselves in the plant, stop its production and refuse access to the owners or to others desiring to work.[2] Whereas, a stay-in strike is one which develops when the demands of the workers are not met on the strike day and the workers remain determined on the sit-down-strike and do not leave the plant.[3]

2. Stay-away strike

In this strike, workers organise rallies and hold demonstrations outside to draw attention of employers as well as general public towards their grievances. They do not come to their place of work during the working hours.

3. Pen-down or tools-down strike

In these types of strikes, workers report for duty but they lay down their tools or pen and do not work thereby preventing the employer from engaging other workers to carry on his business. In a stay-in, sit-down, tools-down or pen-down strike workmen report for duty but do not work thereby preventing the employer from engaging other workers to carry on his business.

4. Lightening or wildcat or catcall strike

This strike is announced suddenly. Workers may go on a strike without any notice or at a very short notice. Generally, there is an element of surprise in such strikes. Usually, this type of strike takes place because of some provocation and the real cause may be some other fundamental issue between employees and employer.

5. Token or protest strike

This is a short duration strike with the clear intention of not disrupting the business of the employer but to provide a signal for the danger ahead. This is taken up to communicate the emotions and sentiments of the workers on some matters. Such a strike is readily accompanied by threats of a strong dose of direct action on the part of workmen and their purpose is simply to inform the employer about the feelings of the employees against any decision taken by him.[4]

6. Go-slow strike

In this type of strike, the workers intentionally reduce their speed of work but pretend to be engaged in the factory. This strike is usually adopted by the workers when the union does not want to resort to a full-fledged strike but still wants to take some alternative action which may be less risky but equally effective.[5]

7. Work-to-rule strike

In this type of strike, the workers perform the work literally in accordance with the rules or procedures laid down for the purpose. Workers follow the rules of work in such a manner that they result in dislocation of work.

8. Hunger strike

In this type of strike, the workers may decide to forgo food for a specific period. In this the leaders of the union or some workers all at a time or in small batches go on a hunger strike. The main aim of this type of strike is to create sympathy of the employer and to attract public attention.

9. Economic strike

In this type of strike, the workers and union stop work to enforce their economic demands like wages, bonus, incentives, share in profits, etc.

B. Secondary Strikes

One form of secondary strike:

1. Sympathetic strike

In this type of strike, the workers collectively stop work in order to express their sympathy with other members/workers of who are on strike in other undertakings. In such strikes, the workers have no grievances against their employer but they may go on strike for the purpose of supporting others in their cause.

II. Lockout

According to Section 2(l) of Industrial Disputes Act, 1947, lockout means the temporary closing of a place of employment or the suspension of work, or the refusal by an employer to continue to employ any number of persons employed by him. Lockout is the counterpart of strike, i.e. the corresponding weapon in the hands of the employer to enforce his terms or show resistance towards the collective demands of workmen. The essentials of lockout are as follows:[6]

(a) There is a temporary closing of the place of employment, or suspension or withholding of the work by the employer in some form;

(b) There is an element of demands for which the place of employment is locked-out or closed; and

(c) There is an intention to reemploy the workers if they accept the demands.

III. Other Forms

The other forms of industrial disputes are the following:

1. Gherao

This refers to the encirclement of the employers or managers or supervisory staff with intention to criminally intimidate them to accept the demands of workers. The main aim of gherao is to compel the persons to submit to workers demand without any recourse to the machinery provided by the law. This is resorted to achieve their objectives by violence. This involves criminal conspiracy; commission of offences thus has been considered unconstitutional and illegal.

2. Bandhs

This means closed or locked. This conveys the idea that everything is to be closed or blocked. Call for and holding of bandh is unconstitutional as this violates the fundamental rights guaranteed to workers. Under bandhs, a worker is coerced not to attend his or her work, which is a violation of his or her fundamental right at the instance of others. Generally, when certain workers do not report for work then the employer follows the principle of no work, no wages.

3. Picketing

This means watching and dissuading those who go to work during a strike.[7] Under picketing, some of the union workers are posted at the factory gate for the purpose of persuading visitors and others not to enter premises but when the persuasion is done by physical force or obstruction, threat, or violence, picketing can no longer be peaceful.[8] However, peaceful picketing is not lawful.

4. Boycott

The aim of boycott is to disrupt the normal functioning of the organisation. It is an appeal for the workers to voluntary withdraw the cooperation. This is persuasive in nature but negative in approach.

CAUSES OF INDUSTRIAL DISPUTES

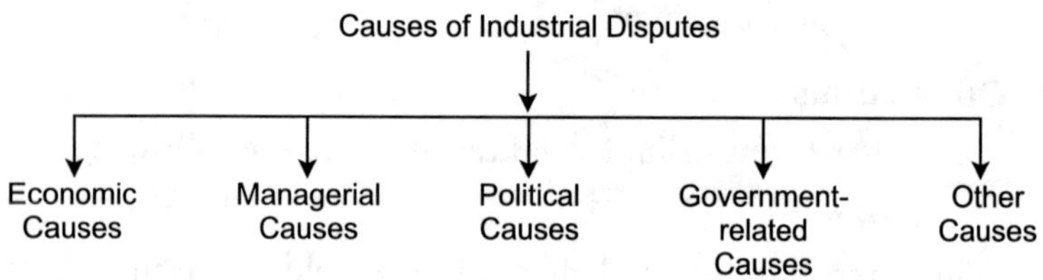

Fig. 19.2: Various Courses of Industrial Disputes

The main causes of industrial disputes can be divided into the following categories:

I. Economic Causes

Generally, most of the reasons for industrial disputes are the economic reasons such as demand for high wages, bonus, etc. The main economic causes are as follows:

1. Low wages

This is the main reason for industrial disputes. There is demand for rise in wages. Due to high cost of living and inflation unions periodically put up the demand for increase in their compensation in order to maintain their real income.

2. Dearness allowance (DA)

The price rise always leads to demand for wage rise, as these are co-related. Whenever prices are increased then demand for DA always come. Also, the workers want a proportionate share in the profits of the industry in the form of bonus. If these demands are not met then these may lead to labour unrest.

3. Working conditions

Working conditions in Indian industries are not proper. Usually adequate arrangements of light, water, safety are not made, so, these are also responsible for industrial disputes.

4. Working hours

Working hours are longer in India so the workers have to work more but the wages are not accordingly paid. So, they demand for less working hours and rest breaks/intervals.

5. Modernization

As a result of modernization, automation, reengineering and restructuring sophisticated machines are replacing workers. Hence, this has become another reason for industrial disputes.

6. Demand for other benefits

Besides wages, dearness allowance and bonus, workers also demand other facilities such as medical, housing, educational, etc.

II. Managerial Causes

These causes include wrongful managerial decisions, treatment and wrong labour polices and procedures. These are the following:

1. Non-recognition of trade unions

When management does not want to recognise a particular trade union or its rival trade union, this leads to labour unrest. Employers attitude towards trade unions has never been sympathetic this leads to conflicts between them.

2. Defective recruitment policies

Defective recruitment policies such as recruitment through contractors who exploit workers, etc. creates many problems in industry.

3. Violation of agreements

Workers oppose the violation of agreements reached through collective bargaining or terms of settlement arrive through conciliation proceedings.

4. Disobedience of codes

When the management does not abide code of discipline and code of conduct this leads to industrial disputes.

5. Defective HR policies

Defective promotion, transfer, demotion, placement, separation policies and authoritarian administration cause dissatisfaction of the workers.

6. Forced leave

During depression, the employers in the hope of economic loss try to force workers to go on leave. This causes resentment among workers towards management.

7. Defective leadership

Defective leadership and ineffective managerial leadership is one of the main causes of industrial disputes. Defective leaders do not attempt to improve and maintain good human relations, they do not care about the problems faced by workers at workplace this leads to industrial disputes.

8. Misbehaviour by supervisors

Supervisors are the persons with whom workers come in direct contact in day-to-day working. So, misbehaviour by supervisors at the workplace has been a source of conflict.

III. Political Causes

Almost all the trade unions in India are affiliated with the political parties. The political parties use trade unions as weapons in order to satisfy their own selfish interests or motives. They usually initiate strikes, gheraos, bandhs, etc.

IV. Government-Related Causes

These include changes in economic policies, improper and inadequate implementation of labour laws, growing irrelevance of government's conciliation machinery, etc.

V. Other Causes

Other causes include strike call given by opposition parties, sympathetic strikes, inter-union rivalry, legal complexities, lack of proper communication, rampant corruption in industry, etc.

EFFECTS OF INDUSTRIAL DISPUTES

Industrial disputes in the form of strikes, lockout, gherao, bandhs, etc. disturb the normal and routine life of the industry in particular and also economic, social and political life of the country in general. They effect all the participants of an industrial relation system in the following way[9]:

1. Effect on workers

Due to industrial disputes, workers suffer as follows:

(i) Direct loss of wages
(ii) Victimisation by the management once the strike is over
(iii) Personal injuries due to lathi-charge, firing, etc. by the police
(iv) Set-back in their own careers
(v) Get indebted to meet their current requirements
(vi) Also, suffer from health point of view.

2. Effect on employers

They suffer in the following way:

(i) Loss of production and output
(ii) Loss of profits
(iii) Damage to the property of the company
(iv) Damage to good human relations
(v) Damage to organisational climate
(vi) Feelings of suspicion and mutual distrust
(vii) Loss of good image of the company
(viii) Promote a negative attitude towards the company in general public.

3. Effect on society

The impact of industrial disputes on the overall society is as follows:

(i) Loss of economic development
(ii) Loss of national property because of violence by the workers
(iii) Fall in per capita income
(iv) Scarcity of essential commodities
(v) Rise in price of commodities
(vi) Unemployment
(vii) Inconvenience in public utility services, etc.

4. Effect on government

The impact of industrial disputes on the state is as follows:

(i) Loss of revenue (low recovery of excise duty, sales tax, income tax, etc. due to low output)
(ii) Total wastage of time and efforts in settling the industrial disputes
(iii) Earn less respect and displeasure from the both the parties, i.e. workers and employers.

In spite of all the above said bad effects of industrial disputes, certainly there are a few good effects also, these are the following:

(i) Industrial disputes bring a sense of cooperation among workers; this results in growth of workers' unity.
(ii) They bring improvements in working conditions and other facilities.
(iii) They bring more membership to trade unions with the hope of gains in the end.
(iv) They pressurise government to enact more labour laws and properly implement them.
(v) They bring a change in the behaviour of the industrialists' towards workforce.

SETTLEMENT OF INDUSTRIAL DISPUTES

The Industrial Disputes Act, 1947 provides elaborate and effective machinery for bringing about industrial peace by setting up various authorities for the investigation and settlement of industrial disputes. The act provides the following modes of settlement of disputes:

I. Conciliation Machinery

Under the Act, the authorities that make use of conciliation as a method of settlement of industrial disputes are works committees, conciliation officer, boards of conciliation and courts of inquiry. These authorities can only promote the settlement of industrial disputes or inquire into them but cannot make any awards, which are binding on the parties.

1. Works committees

In any industrial establishment in which 100 or more workmen are employed or have been employed on any day in the preceding 12 months, then the appropriate government may require the employer to constitute a works committee. The works committee will consists of representatives of employers and workmen equal in number. Works committee encourages voluntary settlement of industrial disputes. The main objectives of works committee is to secure industrial harmony and to promote amity and good relations between an employer and the workmen by removing the causes of friction between them in the day-to-day working of establishment. The main function of the works committee is to ascertain the grievances of the workers and to arrive at some agreement when the occasion so arises.

2. Conciliation officers

The State and the Central Government may appoint conciliation officers to mediate in and promote the settlement of industrial disputes. He may be appointed either permanently or for a limited period. The conciliation officer shall be deemed to be a public servant within the meaning of Section 21 of the Indian Penal Code, 1860. He enjoys all the powers of a civil court. The main duty of a conciliation officer is to hold conciliation proceedings where any industrial dispute exists or is apprehended. In order to bring about a settlement of the dispute, the conciliation officer will investigate the dispute and all maters affecting the merits and the right settlement thereof. When the settlement of the dispute is arrived then the conciliation officer shall send a report to the appropriate government. He shall also send a memorandum of the settlement signed by the parties to the dispute to the appropriate government. In case no settlement is arrived

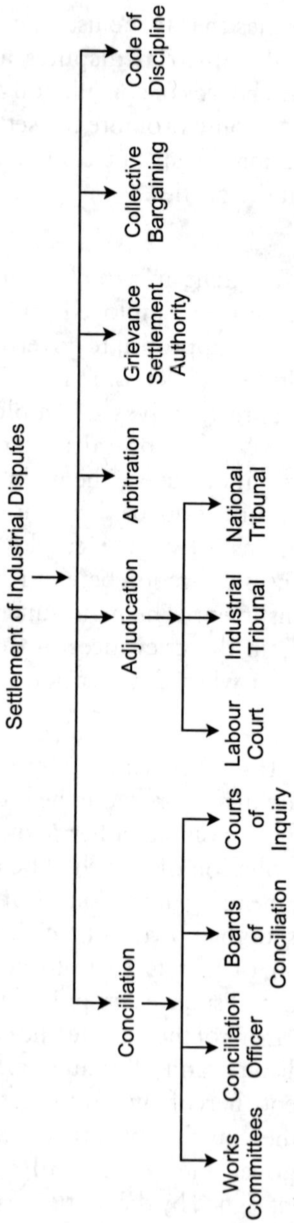

Fig. 19.3: Various Models of Dispute Settlement

then also the conciliation officer shall send a full report to the appropriate government showing the steps taken by him for ascertaining the facts and circumstances relating to the dispute and for bringing about a settlement thereof. The conciliation officer shall submit the report within 14 days of the commencement of the conciliation proceedings.

3. Boards of conciliation

The Central and the State Government may constitute a board of conciliation for promoting the settlement of an industrial dispute. This board shall consist of a chairman and 2 or 4 other members as the appropriate government thinks fit. The chairman shall be an independent person, whereas the other members shall be persons in equal numbers to represent the parties to that industrial dispute. Once an industrial dispute has been referred to the board, then the appropriate government may prohibit the continuance of any strike or lockout connected with such dispute, which may be in existence on the date of reference. The board enjoys the powers of a civil court.

The main duty of the board is to bring about a settlement of the dispute. Once a settlement is arrived then the board shall send a report to the appropriate government along with a memorandum of the settlement, signed by the parties to the dispute. In case no settlement is arrived then the board shall send a full report to appropriate government regarding the details of conciliation proceedings and steps taken by the board. The board shall submit the report within 2 months of the date on which the dispute was referred to it.

4. Courts of inquiry

The Central and the State Government may constitute courts of inquiry for inquiring into any matter appearing to be connected with or relevant to an industrial dispute. The court may consist of one independent person or such number of independent persons as the government may think fit. In case the court consists of 2 or more members, then one of them shall be appointed as the chairman of the court. All the members of the court shall be deemed to be public servants within the meaning of Section 21 of the Indian Penal Code, 1860. They enjoy the powers of a civil court. The main duty of the court is to inquire into the matters referred to it. It should submit its report within a period of 6 months from the commencement of its inquiry. The report shall be signed by all the members of the court and also, any member may record any minute of dissent. This report shall be published within a period of 30 days of its receipt by the appropriate government.

II. Adjudication Machinery

The various adjudication authorities are as follows:

1. Labour courts

The Central and the State Government may constitute one or more labour courts for the adjudication of industrial disputes relating to any matter specified in the second schedule under the Industrial Disputes Act, 1947. These matters include the following:

(i) The legality of any order passed by an employer under standing orders.

(ii) The application and interpretation of standing orders.

(iii) Discharge or dismissal of workmen.

(iv) Withdrawal of any customary concession or privilege.

(v) Illegality of a strike or lockout.

A labour court shall consist of only one person to be appointed by the appropriate government. The person to be appointed as the presiding officer of a labour court should be either a judge of a high court or he has for a period of not less than 3 years, been a district or additional district judge or he has held any judicial office in India for not less than 7 years or he has been the presiding officer of a labour court constituted under any provisional or state act for not less than 5 years. The presiding officer of a labour court shall be deemed to be a public servant. He or she enjoys all the powers of a civil court. The appropriate government refers the industrial dispute to labour court for adjudication when the dispute is related with the matters given in the second schedule. But where the dispute relates to any matter specified in third schedule and is not likely to affect more than 100 workmen then the appropriate government may make the reference to the labour court itself.

The main duty of a labour court is to adjudicate upon industrial disputes relating to any matters specified in the second schedule and to give award within the specified period. The award shall be signed by its presiding officer and within the period of 30 days from the date of its receipt by the appropriate government it shall be published. Once a dispute has been referred to a labour court then the appropriate government may prohibit the continuance of any strike or lockout in connection with such dispute, which may be in existence on the date of reference.

2. Industrial tribunals

The Central and the State Government may constitute one or more industrial tribunals for the adjudication of industrial disputes relating to any matter whether specified in the second schedule or the third schedule and for performing any other function as may be assigned to it. The matters mentioned in the third schedule of the Industrial Disputes Act, 1947 are the following:

(i) Wages (including the period and mode of payment)
(ii) Compensatory and other allowances
(iii) Hours of work and rest intervals
(iv) Leave with wages and holidays
(v) Bonus, profit-sharing, provident fund and gratuity
(vi) Shift working
(vii) Classification by grades
(viii) Rules of discipline
(ix) Rationalisation
(x) Retrenchment of workers
(xi) Closure of establishment.

The industrial tribunal shall consist of only one person appointed by the appropriate government. The person to be appointed as the presiding officer of an industrial tribunal should be either a judge of a high court or he has, for a period of not less than 3 years been a district judge or additional district judge.

The presiding officer shall be deemed to be a public servant. The main duty of the presiding officer is to adjudicate upon the dispute referred to it and submits its award to the appropriate government. Further, it is the duty of a tribunal to decide the matter before it on the merits after taking into consideration all the material facts and circumstances brought on the record. This award shall be signed by its presiding officer and it shall be published within a period of 30 days from the date of its receipt by the appropriate government.

3. National tribunal

The Central Government may constitute one or more national tribunals for the adjudication of industrial disputes, which involve the questions of national importance or are of such a nature that industrial establishments situated in more than one state are likely to be interested in or affected by such industrial disputes.

The national tribunal shall consist of only one person to be appointed by the Central Government. The person to be appointed as the presiding officer of a national tribunal should be a judge of high court. Further, if the Central Government thinks fit then it may also appoint 2 persons as assessors to advise the national tribunal in its proceedings. The presiding officer shall be deemed to be public servant and enjoys all the powers of a civil court.

Once an industrial dispute has been referred to a national tribunal then no labour court or industrial tribunal shall have jurisdiction to adjudicate upon any matter which is under adjudication before the national tribunal. Also, the appropriate government may prohibit the continuance of any strike or lockout in connection with such industrial disputes, which may be in existence on the date of reference to national tribunal.

The main duty of a national tribunal is to adjudicate upon the industrial disputes referred to it and submit its report to appropriate government within specified period. It shall be signed by the presiding officer and shall be published within a period of 30 days from the date of its receipt by the appropriate government.

III. Arbitration

It refers to a process in which a dispute is submitted to an impartial outsider known as arbitrator who makes a decision which is binding on both the parties. Arbitrator means any person who is appointed to determine differences and disputes between two parties. The arbitrator, while giving his decision, takes into consideration the fact that the decision must be based upon some sound principle of natural justice, it must be workable and it must be based upon a "spilt the difference" approach.[10]

Advantages

The main advantages of arbitration are the following:

1. Both labour and management tend to have great faith and confidence in this settlement machinery as they establish it.
2. This procedure is relatively expeditious as compared to labour court and tribunals. Delays are cut down and results are prompt.
3. It is flexible in its approach. It can be adjusted to the views and desires of the parties.
4. It is informal in nature due to absence of lawyers, etc.
5. It is less expensive than other procedures.
6. Awards are capable of implementation.
7. As it is based upon the mutual consent of both the parties so it helps to build up harmonious industrial relations.

Disadvantages

Inspite of the above said advantages, there are few weaknesses also associated with arbitration. These are as follows:

1. The judgement is often arbitrary and ill advised.
2. Usually the chosen arbitrators are not well versed in the technical and economic aspects of the industry.
3. Too much arbitration is also not a good sign of smooth industrial relations. This just means that both the parties have still not learnt how to solve their problems mutually.
4. Usually the arbitrators are biased against the labour class.

TYPES OF ARBITRATION

Arbitration is basically of two types:

(i) Voluntary arbitration

Voluntary arbitration implies when the parties are unable to solve their dispute by themselves or through conciliation decided to submit the dispute to an impartial authority whose decision they are ready to accept.

(ii) Compulsory arbitration

Compulsory arbitration implies when the parties are required to accept arbitration without any willingness on their part.

Voluntary reference of disputes to arbitration under Industrial Disputes Act, 1947

Under Section 10-A of Industrial Disputes Act, 1947 where any industrial dispute exists or is apprehended and the employer and the workmen agree to refer the dispute to arbitration, they may by giving a written agreement refer the dispute to arbitration. In case an arbitration agreement provides for a reference of the dispute to an even number of arbitrators then the agreement shall provide for the appointment of another person as umpire. Further, if the arbitrators are equally divided in their opinion then the award of the umpire shall prevail and shall be deemed to the arbitration award.

Proceedings

When an industrial dispute has been referred to arbitration and the appropriate government is satisfied that the persons making the reference represent the majority of each party then the appropriate government may within one month from the date of the receipt of a copy of agreement issue a notification. When the notification is issued then the employers and workmen who are not parties to the arbitration agreement but are concerned in the dispute, shall be given opportunity of presenting their case before the arbitrators. The arbitration award shall be signed by the parties and the arbitration agreement shall be forwarded to the appropriate government and the conciliation officer. Then the appropriate government shall within one month from the date of receipt of such copy publish it. Further, where an industrial dispute has been referred to arbitration then the appropriate government may prohibit the continuance of any strike or lockout in connection with such dispute, which may be in existence on the date of such reference.

IV. Grievance Settlement Authority

Under Industrial Disputes Act, 1947, Section 9C provides that employer in relation to every establishment, which employs 50 or more workmen or have been employed on any day in the preceding 12 months, shall provide a grievance settlement authority for the settlement of industrial disputes connected with an individual workman. When an industrial dispute connected with an individual workman arises then the workman or any trade union of workmen of which that workman is a member may refer that dispute to the grievance settlement authority for settlement. No reference of disputes shall be made to the boards of conciliation, courts of inquiry and tribunals unless:

(i) Such dispute has been referred to the grievance settlement authority and

(ii) The decision of the grievance settlement authority is not acceptable to any of the parties to the dispute.

V. Collective Bargaining

The phrase collective bargaining is a combination of two words—collective, which means group action through its representatives and bargaining which means negotiating. The term collective bargaining refers to a contract between employees' representatives on one-side and employer's representatives on the other side. The main objective of collective bargaining is rule-making, i.e. reaching on agreement by specifying the rules related with employment relationship. These rules basically emphasise on the terms and conditions of employment. The essence of collective bargaining lies in the readiness of the two parties to a dispute to reach an agreement or mutually satisfying settlement.[11] It is device for discussion and negotiation between labour and management. Collective bargaining helps both the parties to secure a prompt and fair redressal of grievances. Collective bargaining creates new and varied procedures for solving the problems when they arise. It helps to maintain industrial peace. It is a peace treaty between two parties in continual conflict.

VI. Code of Discipline

Although there are a number of labour laws but due to complex judicial formalities and legalities, the Indian industrial relations has not been harmonious. There was need felt by both labour and management for some other alternative way to maintain industrial peace. Hence, Code of Discipline came into force from June 1, 1958. The main features of Code of Discipline are as follows:[12]

(i) It is government induced self-imposed and mutually agreed voluntary principle of discipline and relations between management and workers.

(ii) It aims at preventing disputes by providing for voluntary and mutual settlement of disputes through negotiation, conciliation, and voluntary arbitration without the interference of adjudication machinery.

(iii) It compels the parties not to indulge in strikes and lockouts without notice.

(iv) It requires constructive cooperation between workers and management at all levels.

(v) It enjoys upon the management to take prompt action for the settlement of grievances and implementation of awards and agreements.

(vi) It induces both the parties to make the best use of the existing machinery for the settlement of disputes.

Objectives of Code of Discipline

The objectives of the Code of Discipline are as follows:

(i) To ensure that employers and employees recognise each other's rights and obligations;

(ii) To promote constructive cooperation between the parties concerned at all levels;

(iii) To secure settlement of disputes and grievances by negotiation, conciliation and voluntary arbitration;

(iv) To eliminate all forms of coercion, intimidation and violence in industrial relations;

(v) To avoid work stoppages;

(vi) To facilitate the free growth of trade unions; and

(vii) To maintain discipline in industry.

KEY TERMS

Adjudication	Gherao
Arbitration	Grievance settlement authority
Bandhs	Industrial disputes
Boycott	Lockout
Code of Discipline	Picketing
Collective bargaining	Strike
Conciliation	Unfair labour practices

QUESTIONS

1. Define industrial disputes. Bring out the various types of industrial disputes.
2. Explain the various forms of industrial disputes.
3. Describe the various causes of industrial disputes.
4. Bring out the effects of industrial disputes.
5. Describe the following:
   (i) Conciliation
   (ii) Adjudication
   (iii) Arbitration

ENDNOTES

1. C.B. Mamoria, Satish Mamoria and S.V. Gankar, *Dynamics of Industrial Relations,* Fifteenth Edition, Himalaya Publishing House, 2005, p. 229.
2. *Ibid.*
3. Teller, *Labour Disputes and Collective Bargaining*, Vol. I, p. 311.
4. C.B. Mamoria, Satish Mamoria and S.V. Gankar, op. cit., p. 231.
5. Susa Misa Sugar Workers Pvt. Ltd. vs. Shobrati Khan, 1959, II LLJ at 393 (SC).

6. N.D. Kapoor, *Handbook of Industrial Law,* Twelfth Edition, Sultan Chand & Sons, 2006, New Delhi, p. 385.
7. B.E.S.T. Undertaking, Bombay vs. Mushaffe Ahmed Khalil, 1961, ICR 845 (IC Maharashtra).
8. C.B. Mamoria, Satish Mamoria and S.V. Gankar, op. cit., p. 231.
9. D.C. Sharma and R.C. Sharma, *Personnel Management &Industrial Relations*, First Edition, S.J. Publications, Meerut, p. 464.
10. C.B. Mamoria, Satish Mamoria and S.V. Gankar, op. cit., p. 404.
11. *Ibid.*, p. 349.
12. *Ibid.*, p. 334.

Employee Grievances

20

LEARNING OBJECTIVES

After studying this chapter, you should be able to:

1. Understand the nature and causes of grievances
2. Understand the importance of grievance handling procedure
3. Describe the principles of handling grievances
4. Describe the grievance handling procedure

In an organisation employees have complaints against their employers such as dissatisfaction from the quantum of wages, mode of payment for overtime work, working conditions, promotion, transfer, dismissal or discharge, poor quality of food in canteen, etc. These types of complaints should not be allowed to aggravate. A HR manager should try to identify and resolve them as they come to his knowledge. Identification of grievances and their proper handling is necessary for maintaining harmonious industrial relations.

MEANING AND NATURE OF GRIEVANCES

A grievance can be any discontent or dissatisfaction, whether expressed or not, whether valid or not, arising out of anything connected with the company that an employee thinks, believes or even feels is unfair, unjust or inequitable.[1] This dissatisfaction may be either stated or unvoiced, written or oral, legitimate or ridiculous but the only thing is that the discontent must affect performance.

A grievance is anything that an employee thinks or feels is wrong and is generally accompanied by an actively disturbing feeling. It does not to be justified.[2] There is a difference between the word 'grievance' and 'complaint'. A complaint is a discontent or dissatisfaction that has not, as yet, assumed a great measure of importance to the complainant.[3] Complaints are more in numbers than grievances at the workplace for example, its too hot in the shop, a colleague is not cooperating, etc. Often, the complaints are submitted in a very informal way. But a complaint becomes a grievance when the employee feels that an injustice has been done. When the supervisor or manager ignores the complaint and thereafter dissatisfaction that grows within the employee usually assumes the status of a grievance. A grievance is always expressed whether verbally or in writing. A grievance may be submitted by a worker or several workers. Where a grievance is transformed into a general claim—either by the union or by a large number of workers—it falls outside the grievance procedure and normally comes under the purview of collective bargaining.[4] In other words, where the issue is of a wider or general nature, or of general applicability then it will be outside the purview of grievance machinery.

CAUSES OF GRIEVANCE

The causes of grievance may broadly be classified in the following categories:

1. Working conditions

A large number of workers' grievances are related with the unhealthy and bad working conditions such as non-availability of proper tools, equipments and machines to perform the job, bad physical conditions in the factory, frequent breakdown of machines, tight production standards, more rejection of goods, unjustified and continuous cuts in wages, disruption in the supply of material, lack of proper discipline, etc.

2. Difference of opinion

The difference of opinion or thoughts on any particular point between workers and management also becomes a cause of grievance. Also, different interpretations of legal provisions lead to difference of thoughts.

3. Doubts and fears

In some cases, the doubts and fears in the minds of workers for any injustice to be committed to them may also give rise to grievances.

4. Management policy and practices

Various policies of management may contribute to grievances such as harsh supervision, victimisation, discrimination, ignoring suggestions from subordinates, authoritarian management style, promotion, transfer, demotion, discharge, leave, overtime, holidays, lack of career planning and employee development plan, non-recognition of trade union, hostility towards a trade union, non-adherence to policies or procedures, etc.

5. Status of trade unions

The age and status of trade union is also a leading factor in grievance bearing. If a trade union is comparatively young and it has substantial strength, naturally it will be more militant and it will give air to the slightest grievances of the workers in a big way.[5]

6. Social injustice

Grievances may be due to social injustice. For instance, a facility is provided in one department of the company, the employees of the other department where that facility is not provided may feel dissatisfied.

7. Personal maladjustment

Personal maladjustment may also give rise to grievances for example, excessive self-esteem, impractical attitude towards life, over-ambition, etc.

8. Violation

Grievances may be caused due to the alleged violation of central and state laws, collective bargaining agreement, past practice, company rules, etc.

9. Wages

Grievances may arise due to wage inequalities, payment system, complicated compensation systems, problems relating to calculation of incentives and overtime, fines, increments, stagnation and recovery of dues.[6]

IDENTIFICATION OF GRIEVANCES

The best approach towards grievances is to anticipate them well in advance and take suitable action before they assume some dangerous form. An ordinary manager just redresses grievances as and when they arise, however, a good manager anticipates and prevents them. Following methods may be used by the managers to know the grievances well in advance:

1. Observation

By simply observing the behaviour of the employees at work a supervisor or mangar may come to know of problems related with employee. For example, the employee usually remains absent, wasting more material, disobeying the instructions and orders, not getting along with the others, etc.

2. Exit interview

This is an excellent way to know what is the actual/real problem. Due to some dissatisfaction an employee may leave the organisation. The manager by properly conducting exit interview can obtain the valuable information and clearer picture.

3. Grievance procedure

There must be systematic grievance handling procedure in an organisation. This provides a mean to employees to highlight their grievances. Also, the management must encourage the employee to use this procedure whenever they want to say anything.

4. Opinion surveys

Management should conduct opinion surveys periodically to elicit the opinions of workers. This can be done through collective bargaining sessions, committee meetings, interviews, etc.

5. Gripe boxes

Workers can lodge their complaints in the gripe boxes. This is a good tool to know the real problem. In this the workers need not reveal their identity and they can express their feeling frankly. The gripe boxes should be kept at suitable places in the organisation.

6. Open door policy

In an open door policy, a worker can go to the manager's office at any time and talk about his or her grievances. This policy sounds very attractive, however, it suffers from some limitations, for example, a supervisor is totally bypassed in this policy, top managers are usually unfamiliar with the work situation, top management do not have sufficient time for this in their busy schedule, there are always some psychological and social barriers and it is suitable to smaller organisations.

NEED AND IMPORTANCE OF GRIEVANCE HANDLING MACHINERY

There is hardly a single organisation which functions absolutely smoothly at all times. Employees' grievances in any form will invariably always be there. For the maintenance of harmonious industrial relations, it is essential for the management to identify the causes of grievances and redress them in the best possible manner. Thus, setting up of proper grievance handling machinery is necessary for maintaining peace. The grievance machinery or procedure is a problem-solving or dispute-settling device. It has other benefits too. The mere fact that such a procedure exists is satisfying even though an employee never has an occasion to use it.[7] In brief, it can be said that a grievance handling procedure is essential in an organisation because of the following:

1. It encourages all the problems faced by workers should come out.
2. It provides a channel through which the aggrieved employee may put up his or her case forward.
3. It provides an opportunity to all workers to express their doubts, fears, feelings and dissatisfaction.
4. It improves the morale of the employees, as they know that if any injustice is done to them they will be listened by the authorities.
5. It helps the management in knowing the attitude and behaviour of the superior and supervisor towards their subordinates.

6. A proper and formal grievance handling procedure ensures that every grievance will be handled in a systematic manner.
7. It restricts the immediate boss and supervisors from acting in an arbitrary and autocratic manner.
8. It helps the management in knowing the drawbacks in the present practices, policies, procedures, styles of functioning, rules, etc.
9. It ensures that the supervisors and the management show more concern towards human aspects at workplace.

PRINCIPLES OF HANDLING GRIEVANCES

The following principles serve as guides for handling grievances:[8]

1. Principle of interviewing

To handle a grievance successfully and effectively, a manager or supervisor should talk in great length to the aggrieved workers. He should collect all the possible data and pass on the relevant information. It helps to remove misunderstanding and doubts.

2. Management's attitude towards employees

Management should develop positive attitude towards employees and their problems. Management should show a sincere interest in their grievances.

3. Management's responsibilities

Management should behave responsibly while handling grievances. Management should appear confident and accept their responsibilities of proper handling of workers grievances and should never make light comments on them.

4. Long-run principle

Grievances should not be handled keeping into consideration only their immediate or individual effect but also their long-term impact on the entire organisational climate because some time decisions on not so serious grievances have far-reaching effects on the organisation.[9] Thus, the following things should be taken into consideration:

(i) *Long run effects*

A solution to an employee's particular grievance is likely to set a precedent and the other employees will analyse its implications as in future all similar grievances are likely to settle in the same way.

(ii) *Danger of losing confidence*

Management should take utmost care and restrain while handling a grievance even if it is not so significant. A minor mistake on the part of management in handling a grievance could result in loss of worker's confidence that was gained after a long period of time.

(iii) *Effect-of-the past*

Not only the management should take into consideration the future impact of their decisions but also keep in view what has happened in the past. Grievances of today may have their roots in the acts of yesterday.

GRIEVANCE HANDLING PROCEDURE/MACHINERY

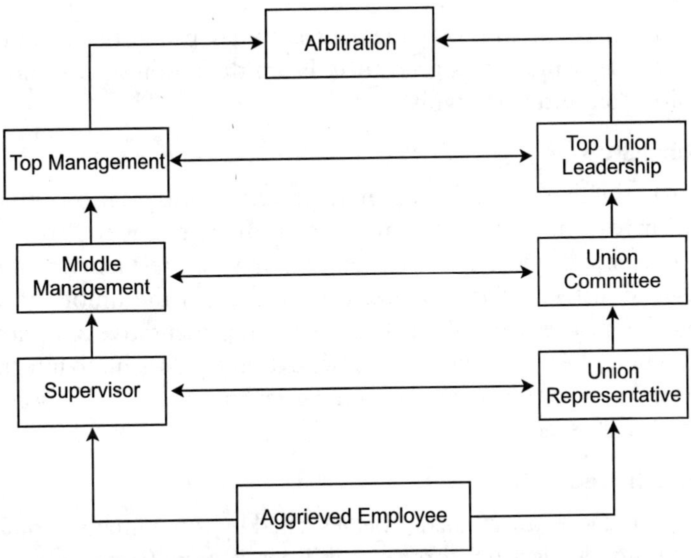

Fig. 20.1: A Grievance Handling Procedure

The details of a grievance handling procedure vary from organisation to organisation. Depending upon the size of an organisation, it may have as few as two steps or as many as ten steps. But the first and last steps are almost same for all organisations. Figure 20.1 shows four steps of the machinery. These are the following:

First Step

The first step in the grievance handling procedure in case of unionised organisation usually involves three persons. These are the aggrieved employee, a supervisor and a representative of the union. At this stage, the role of a supervisor is very important. He can play a significant role in reducing the number of grievances that get past to higher steps in the procedure because the higher the discontent rises through the organisation more difficult it becomes to resolve it. Hence, supervisor should be well-trained to deal with the employees with unresolved complaints.

Second Step

In the next step, middle level managers are made responsible to look into the grievances. At this stage, it is very important to ensure that the line management assumes prime responsibility for the settlement of a grievance. From the union side, usually a union committee is involved.

Third Step

In the final step, the top management representation and top union officials discuss the matter of grievance. From the management side, it may be president or Vice-president or a high-level industrial relations executive and from the union side, it may be the president of local union or a representative of national level union. At this stage, it becomes extremely difficult to integrate the interests of both parties, as the grievance has already become a political issue.

Fourth Step

If the grievance has not been settled by top management and top union leadership, three possibilities remain: (i) the union can temporarily or permanently drop the issue; (ii) the union can call a strike if the contract permits; or (iii) the case may be submitted to an impartial arbitrator.[10] In arbitration, services of an outside third party are sought to settle a dispute. The assumption behind arbitration is that an impartial, competent outsider can render a fair verdict not attainable from the parties themselves because of their prejudiced viewpoints or highly emotional stands.[11]

MODEL GRIEVANCE PROCEDURE

The National Commission on Labour suggested a model grievance procedure (Fig. 20.2). The model grievance procedure had successive time bound steps, with access to the next stage, if the satisfaction was not obtained. The stage or the level at which settlement takes place is an index of the climate or the spirit that prevails in the firm. The lower the level of settlement, the quicker the redressal of a grievance.[12] At the first stage, the supervisor is in position of give and take but at the subsequent stages he comes under the glare of publicity and thus his position is likely to harden. From the aggrieved employee's point of view, the delay would only increase his anxiety and frustration. In turn, this affects his morale and productivity. If an employee prefers this procedure for the redressal of his grievance then the formal conciliation machinery shall not intervene till all the stages outlined in this procedure have been exhausted. A grievance shall be presumed to take the form of a dispute only when the final decision given by the top management in respect of the grievance is not acceptable to the worker.

The grievance procedure shown in Figure 20.2 is as follows:

Stage I

Firstly, the aggrieved employee shall convey his grievance verbally in person to the officer designated by the management for this purpose. The officer has to answer within 48 hours of the presentation of the complaint.

Stage II

If the worker is not satisfied with the decision of this officer or he fails to receive the answer within the stipulated time, then, he shall along with his departmental representative, present his grievance to the head of the department. Usually, a fixed time is

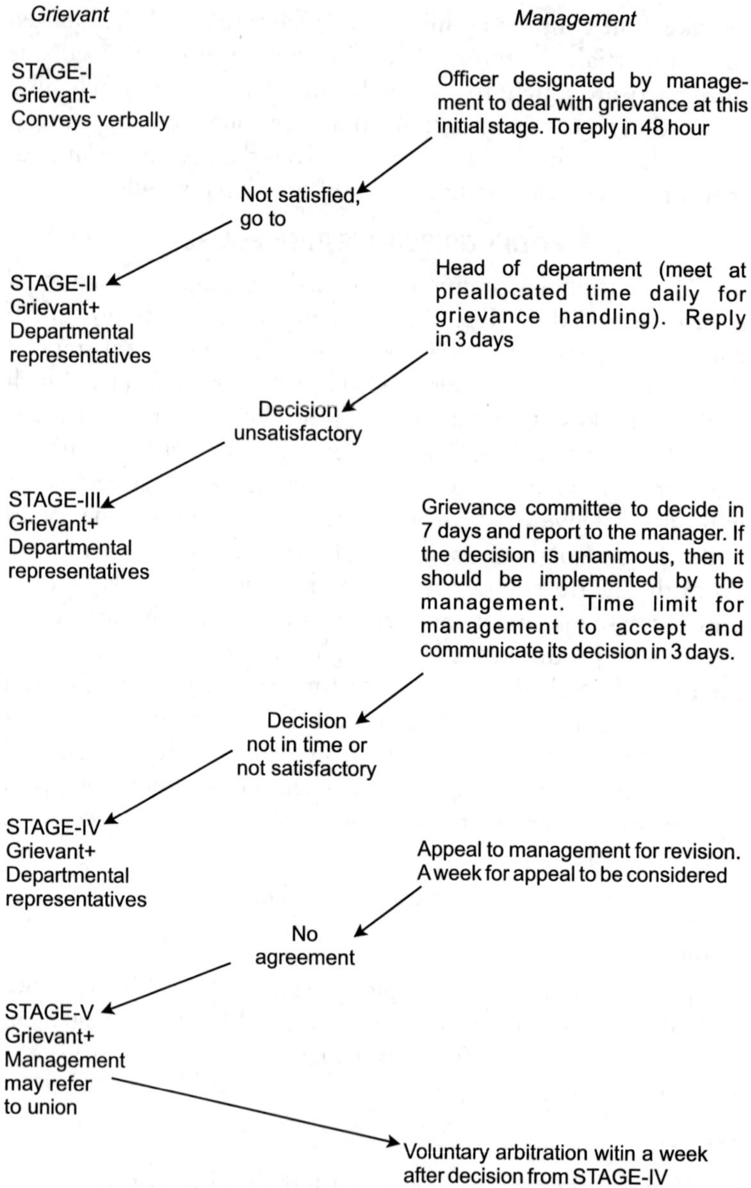

Fig. 20.2: Model Grievance Procedure

Source: Arun Monappa, *Industrial Relations*, Tata McGraw-Hill, New Delhi, 1995, p. 156.

specified during which an aggrieved employee could meet the departmental head. The head of the department shall give his answer within 3 days of the presentation of the grievance.

Stage III

If the decision of the head of department is unsatisfactory, then the aggrieved employee along with the departmental representative may forward his grievance to the grievance committee. The grievance committee shall make its recommendations to the manager within 7 days of the employee's request. If the recommendations of the committee are unanimous then the management shall implement it. If there are differences of opinion among the members of the committee then the views of all the members shall be placed before the manager for the final decision. In either case, the final decision of the management shall be communicated to the employee within 3 days from the receipt of the recommendations of the grievance committee.

Stage IV

If the decision of the management is not in time or unsatisfactory then the worker may appeal to the management for revision. The management shall communicate its decision on appeal within a week time.

Stage V

If still there is no agreement reached then the union and the management may refer the grievance to voluntary arbitration within a week after the decision of the management. In the model grievance procedure there is a time limit within which an appeal shall be taken from one stage to the other. Aggrieved workers shall within 72 hours of the receipt of the decision at one stage (in case no decision is received then on the expiry of the stipulated period), file his appeal with the authority at the next higher stage.

PRE-REQUISITES OF A SUCCESSFUL GRIEVANCE HANDLING PROCEDURE

1. Conformity with the prevailing legislations

The grievance procedure should be in conformity with the existing legislations. It should be designed in such a way that it supplements the statutory provisions.

2. Acceptability

The grievance procedure should be developed with the mutual consultation among management, workers and labour union. In other words, it must be acceptable to all the concerned parties.

3. Simplicity

It should be as simple as possible. It should involve steps only to encourage the employees. Otherwise if there are so many steps or stages this makes the procedure complex and the workers are discouraged.

4. Clarity

Each and every step in the procedure should be clear-cut and unambiguous. An aggrieved employee should be well-informed to whom he should make representation, the form of report, the time limit for making request appeal, etc.

5. Promptness

A grievance procedure must make speedy redressal of grievances as unnecessary delays just add to frustration of the workers.

6. Based on facts

At all the stages, the officer in charge of handling the grievance should make full search of facts and maintain his records properly. Getting the relevant facts is very essential and equally important is the analysis of the facts after taking into consideration the economic, psychological, social and legal issues involved in it.

7. Training

Proper training of supervisors and union representatives is essential for the effective working of grievance procedure.

8. Follow-up

The working of grievance handling procedure should be reviewed at periodical intervals. To make it more effective necessary improvements must be made.

GRIEVANCES OF MANAGEMENT

Employers and management too have grievances against their workmen and trade unions. These are generally the following:[13]

1. Indiscipline

This includes non-observance of the plant rules, disregard for supervisor's orders, non-observance for safety rules, absenteeism, late coming, irresponsible attitude, etc.

2. Output

This includes low speed of doing a work, less output, poor quality of work, etc.

3. Collective bargaining agreements

This includes wrong representation of the clauses of the contract, violation of contract, non-fulfilling of assurances by trade unions, etc.

4. Miscellaneous

This includes failure to take action by the trade unions for the acts of indiscipline by their members, misrepresenting management's actions and attitudes, undesirable methods of soliciting union members, irresponsible charges and statements by union leaders against management, inciting workers against management, illegal strikes, etc.

KEY TERMS

Complaint
Difference of opinion
Exit interview
Grievance
Grievance handling procedure
Gripe boxes
Open door policy
Opinion surveys

QUESTIONS

1. Define the term 'grievance'. Identify the causes of grievances.
2. Bring out the different ways of identification of grievances.
3. Describe the principles of handling grievances.
4. Describe the grievance handling procedure.
5. Describe the model grievance handling procedure as available in India.

6. Explain the pre-requisites of grievance handling procedure.

ENDNOTES

1. Edwin B. Flippo, *Personnel Management,* McGraw-Hill, Kogakusha Ltd, Tokyo, 1976, p. 429.
2. P. Calhoon, *Managing the Personnel*, p. 319.
3. Edwin B. Flippo, *Personnel Management*, Sixth Edition, McGraw-Hill, New York, 1984, p. 464.
4. Arun Monappa, *Industrial Relations*, Tata McGraw-Hill, New Delhi, 1985, p. 149.
5. D.C. Sharma and R.C. Sharma, *Personnel Management &Industrial Relations*, First Edition, S.J. Publications, Meerut, p. 435.
6. Ratna Sen, *Industrial Relations in India: Shifting Paradigms*, Macmillan, 2003, p. 462.
7. Edwin B. Flippo, op. cit., p. 465.
8. Michael J. Jucius, *Personnel Management,* Richard D. Irwin, Inc., Homewood, Illinois, 1975, pp. 465-467.
9. D.C. Sharma and R.C. Sharma, op. cit., p. 438.
10. Edwin B. Flippo, op. cit., p. 469.
11. Michael J. Jucius, op. cit., p. 471.
12. Arun Monappa, op. cit., p. 155.
13. D.C. Sharma and R.C. Sharma, op. cit., p. 436.

Employee Safety and Health

21

LEARNING OBJECTIVES

After studying this chapter, you should be able to:

1. Understand the importance of employee safety and health programmes
2. Understand the causes and costs associated with industrial accidents
3. Describe the procedure for the prevention of accidents
4. Describe the legal provisions related with employee safety and health

For a manager, employee safety and health must be a top priority in all he or she does. To ensure a safe working environment is also legally mandated. Moreover, it's an obligation for any socially responsible manager. It is very important that managers must understand the importance of health and safety issues and take steps to maintain a safe working environment at the workplace. An organisational culture that places a greater value on speed or saving money than on safety can result in the workplace accidents—some that involve the loss of human life.[1] Though line managers are primarily responsible for the maintenance of a safe and healthy work environment in the organisation but the human resource managers should provide staff expertise to help them deal with these issues.

MEANING

Before discussing safety and health issues in detail, first of all it is better to understand the nature and role of safety and health.

Safety involves protecting employees from injuries caused by work related accidents. Health refers to employees' freedom from physical or emotional illness.[2] Both health and safety programmes are concerned with protection against hazards. The achievement of the highest standards of health and safety in the workplace is important because the elimination or at least minimization of health and safety hazards and risks is the moral as well as the legal responsibility of employers.[3] Proper attention to safety and health of employees is important as illness and injuries cause suffering and loss to individuals and their dependents. Also it damages the organisation.

ACCIDENTS

An accident is an unplanned and uncontrolled event in which an action or reaction of an object, a substance, a person or a

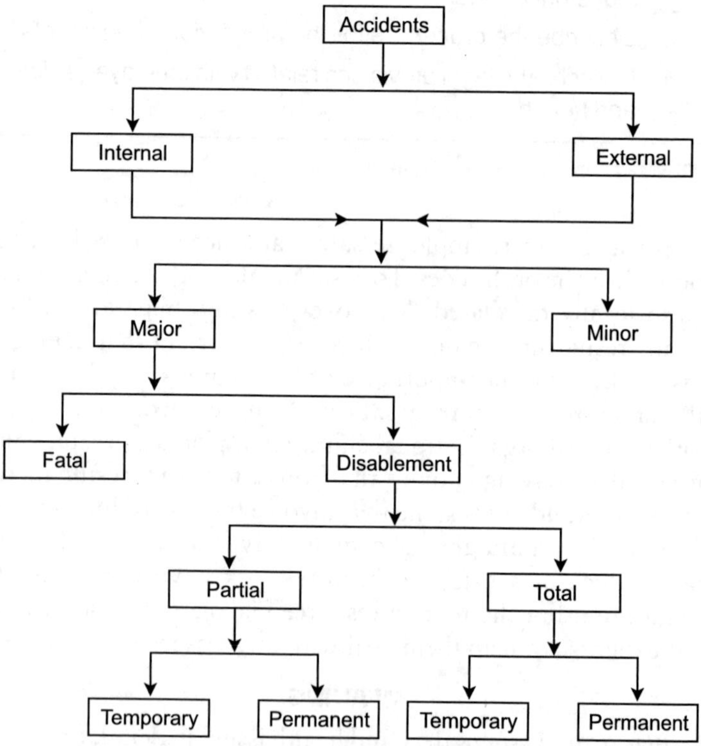

Fig. 21.1: Various Types of Accidents

radiation results in personal injury.[4] According to the Factories Act, 1948, an accident is an occurrence in an industrial establishment causing bodily injury to a person which makes him unfit to resume his duties in the next 48 hours.

TYPES OF ACCIDENTS

Accidents can be of different types. As Figure 21.1 displays, accidents can be classified into two categories, internal and external. An employee may fall from a height while engaged on a particular assignment, or he may be caught in a machine while working on it, or he may fall against a machine or parts of machine having a horizontal protruding motion may strike against him, or explosive used carelessly may explode and injure an employee.[5] This injury may be internal one, for example, a bone fracture, muscle is pull, etc. or external one which shows clearly the signs of injury. Further, these both kinds of injuries may be major or minor. Minor accident may result in a cut or a scratch, which is not a serious one. Whereas a major accident may be fatal or non-fatal. In other words, the major accidents may result in death or disablement.

According to the Workmen's Compensation Act, 1923, disablement means loss of capacity to work or to move. Disablement of a workman may result in loss or reduction of his or her earning capacity. In the latter case, he or she may not be able to earn as much as he or she used to earn before his or her disablement.

As Figure 21.1 shows that disablement may be partial or total. According to Section 2(1)(g) of the Workmen's Compensation Act, 1923, partial disablement means any disablement as reduces the earning capacity of a workman as a result of some accident. Partial disablement may be (i) permanent, or (ii) temporary. Temporary partial disablement means any disablement as reduces the earning capacity of a workman in any employment in which he was engaged at the time of accident which results in such disablement. On the other hand, permanent partial disablement is one, which reduces the earning capacity of a workman in every employment, which he was capable of undertaking at the time of injury. Finally, total disablement means such disablement, whether of a temporary or permanent nature, as incapacitates of a workman for all work which he was capable of performing at the time of the accident resulting in such disablement. In other words, this refers to that condition where a workman becomes unfit for every type of work and is not able to get job anywhere due to that disablement.

CAUSES OF ACCIDENTS

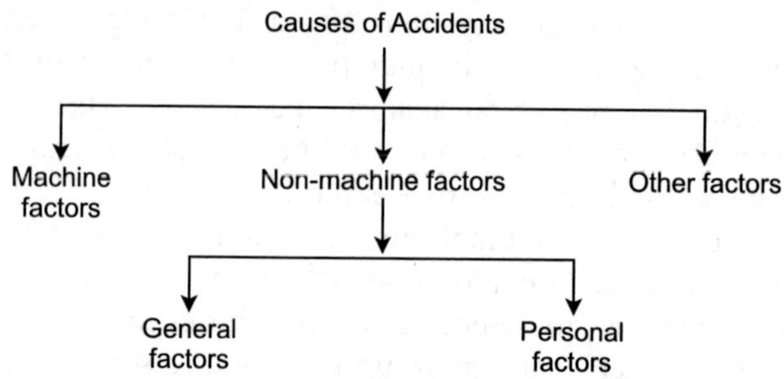

Fig 21.2: Various Causes of Accidents

The primary causes or factors responsible for accidents are as follows:

I. Machine Factors

These factors are also called as technical factors. Machine factors means the faulty mechanical or physical conditions. Although they are less in number but usually they are serious in nature, i.e. they normally result in injuries of serious or fatal nature. These include the following factors:

1. Improperly or inadequately guarded equipment
2. Defective equipment
3. Deficiencies in tools
4. Deficiencies in plant
5. Unsafely designed tools, machines, etc.
6. Insufficient lighting, glare, etc.
7. Improper ventilation, impure air source, etc.
8. Unsafe storage, overloading, congestion, etc.
9. Poor house-keeping

10. Lack of automatic quick stoppage devices
11. Inadequate fencing of machines
12. Wrong and faulty plant layout, bad location, etc.
13. Inadequate safety devices
14. Defective electrical fitting.

II. Non-Machine Factors

As per an estimate around 80% accidents occur due to non-machine factors. These factors can be divided into two categories as follows:

A. General factors

These include the following:[6]

1. Falling down from ladder or slipping of the ladder itself, especially in construction work/repairing/innovating/maintenance work, etc.
2. Prick of a wire nail carelessly thrown away by some one at the workplace.
3. Loading or unloading of heavy material without taking due care or without giving proper warning.
4. Improper foot rests or grips.
5. Non-wearing of right dress while working on or near an exposed moving part of a machine.
6. Not-using goggles especially in welding.
7. Flying-off of hammerheads or chisels, sometimes the whole hammer itself.
8. Lack of inspection of machines, etc. by experts.
9. Defective work methods.
10. Inefficient supervisor/leadership.

B. Personal factors

These factors relate to an individual's proneness to accident. There are few individuals who get involved in more accidents than others. An individual's proneness to accidents may be due to the following personal factors:[7]

1. Poor eye-sight

2. Poor physique
3. Nervousness
4. Fear complex
5. Suffering from diseases such as high blood pressure, fits, epilepsy, etc.
6. Immaturity, irresponsibility, etc.
7. Colour-blindness
8. Fatigue
9. Depression, worry, etc.
10. Ignoring safety instructions
11. Emotional instability, too much sensitiveness, etc.
12. Addiction to drugs, liquor, etc.
13. Day dreaming
14. Absentmindedness
15. Frustration.

III. Other Factors

Apart from the earlier discussed causes of accidents, there are few others, which are the following:[8]

1. Young, untrained and new workers generally sustain injuries more frequently than older, trained and experienced employees.
2. The way the management motivates employees affects the rate and frequency of accidents. For example, the tensions, which aggressive and negative supervisors generate among the employees, also tend to increase this rate and frequency.
3. Unmarried employees generally have more accidents than married employees.
4. Accidents are more frequent during the night shift.
5. Women employees have a better safety record than male counterparts.
6. Workers who work under stress, or who feel their jobs are threatened or insecure, seem to have more accidents than those who do not.

ACCIDENT COSTS

Accidents are generally costly, both to an employee as well as to an employer. Some losses are direct and some are indirect. Some losses are visible and some are invisible. From a worker's point of view, an accident creates pain for him and his family. From an employer's point of view, it disrupts production and also causes financial loss. From the employer's context the accident costs can be divided into two parts:

1. Direct costs

These include:

(i) Payment of wages to the injured worker during his period of absence due to injury.

(ii) Amount of compensation to be paid on the account of death, disablement, etc. The rates are decided as per the provisions of the Workmen's Compensation Act, 1923 or the Employees' State Insurance Act, 1948.

(iii) Cost of medical aid.

(iv) Cost of recruiting and training a substitute worker.

(v) Loss in production and quality due to lack of skill and experience of newcomer.

(vi) Loss due to waste of raw materials.

2. Indirect costs

The indirect costs of accidents are estimated to be all the way two to four times the direct costs. The indirect costs are the following:[9]

1. Cost of lost time of injured employee.
2. Cost of time lost by other employees who stop work out of curiosity and sympathy, to assist injured employee, etc.
3. Cost of time lost by foremen, supervisors in assisting injured employee, investigating the cause of the accident, arranging for the injured employee's production to be continued by some other employee, recruitment, selection and training of the new employee, preparing

state accident reports or attending hearings before industrial commissioner, etc.

4. Cost of time spent on the case by first-aid attendant and hospital staff when this is not covered by insurance.
5. Cost due to injury to the machine, tools, or other property, or to the material.
6. Cost due to interference with production, failure to fill orders on time, loss of bonuses, payments of forfeits and other similar causes.
7. Cost under employee welfare and benefit systems.
8. Cost in continuing the wages of the injured employees in full, after his return—even though the services of the employee (who is not yet fully recovered) may for the time be worth only about half his normal value.
9. Cost due to the loss of profit on the injured employee's productivity and on idle machines.
10. Cost of subsequent injuries that occurs in consequence of the excitement or weakened morale owing to the original accident.
11. Overhead cost—the expense of light, heat, rent, and other such items—that continues while the injured employee is a non-producer.

ACCIDENT MEASUREMENT

There are mainly two statistical ratios that are used to assess the accident rate, these are as follows:

1. Frequency rate

It is the number of time lost (or injuries which have disabled an employee) in accidents per million of man hours worked.

$$\text{Frequency Rate} = \frac{\text{Number of injuries} \times \text{One million}}{\text{Total number of man-hours worked}}$$

2. Severity rate

It is the total number of days lost because of accidents per million man-hours worked.

$$\text{Severity Rate} = \frac{\text{Number of man-days lost} \times \text{One million}}{\text{Total number of man-hours worked}}$$

PREVENTION OF ACCIDENTS

As per an estimate, 98 per cent of industrial accidents are preventable, if necessary preventive steps are taken.[10] Thus, it is essential for all concerned to take the necessary preventing steps. Following steps are taken for the prevention of accidents:

A. The Safety Programme

Once the management develops interest in promoting safety measures, then it should plan the safety programme. Any particular safety programme could be composed of one or more of the following elements:[11]

1. Support by top management

Top management's support is essential for the conduct and success of a safety programme. Management's support was characterized by personal attendance at safety meetings, periodic personal inspections, insistence on regular safety reports and inclusion of safety figures and achievements on the agenda of the company's board of director's meetings.[12]

2. Appointing a safety director

The next step is to appoint a safety director who shall be given the primary responsibility for the installation and maintenance of the safety programme. In case of a small organisation then this job can be assigned to any responsible line manager. However, in case of a larger organisation, staff safety director/safety engineer is usually appointed.

3. Engineering a safe plant and operation

A sound and forward-looking engineering is essential requirement for a safety programme. While preparing a safety programme all possible mechanical safety devices and human engineering should be thought of for application. Factory should be kept clean, well lighted, properly ventilated and free from dust. All dangerous parts of machines and equipments should be properly fenced.

4. Educating all employees to act safely

A good safety programme should have proper provision for educating the employees to act, think and work safely. This can be done through:

(i) Educating the new employees at the time of induction.

(ii) Give emphasis on safety point during training periods especially during the off-the-job training.

(iii) Special efforts to be made by first level supervisor.

(iv) Establishment of employee safety committees.

(v) Holding of employee safety meetings.

(vi) Usc of company periodical, if any.

(vii) Use of charts, posters and displays emphasising the need to act safely.

5. Record keeping

The employer should maintain a proper record showing the number of accidents, occupational illnesses and number of lost workdays.

6. Accident analysis

Even after taking all preventive measures, accidents occur. They should be thoroughly investigated in terms of both costs and causes. All sort of direct and indirect costs should be listed and the management should take a lesson from this.

7. Safety contests

Safety contests stimulates employees to think and act safely. These are a form of employee education. It has been observed that accident rate is lower in the pre-contest and during the contest period but once the period of contest is over the accident rates goes up again.

8. Enforcement

A safety programme should be enforced rigorously; only then the desired results can be obtained. Although the basic approach of a safety programme should be positive in nature but in some cases the negative approach by way of imposing fines, reprimands, discharge, lay-offs, etc. way also be necessary to enforce discipline in case someone deliberately violates the safety rules and instructions.

B. Legal Provisions Regarding Safety of Workers

The Factories Act, 1948 makes detailed provisions in regard to various matters relating to the safety of the worker. These provisions impose upon the occupiers or managers certain obligations to protect workers unwary as well as negligent from accident. Section 21 to 41 provides the safety provisions, which are absolute and obligatory in their character, and the occupier of every factory is bound to follow them.

1. Fencing of machinery (Sec. 21)

In every factory, every dangerous part of every machinery shall be properly fenced. Machineries include every moving part of a prime mover and every fly-wheel connected to a prime mover, the headrace and tailrace of every water-wheel and water-turbine, any part of a stock-bar which projects beyond the headstock of a lathe, every part of an electric generator, a motor or rotary converter and every part of transmission machinery.

2. Work on or near machinery in motion (Sec. 22)

In any factory, any examination, adjustment or lubrication of any part of operating machinery shall be carried out by trained adult male worker wearing tight fitting clothing. Women and young persons are not allowed to carry the above said task.

3. Employment of young persons on dangerous machines (Sec. 23)

There is a restriction on young persons to work on dangerous machines.

4. Striking gear and devices for cutting off power (Sec. 24)

Suitable striking gear to be provided, maintained and used. Also, suitable devices for cutting off power in emergencies from machinery should be provided and maintained in every workroom.

5. Self-acting machines (Sec. 25)

No traversing part of a self-acting machine in any factory and no material carried thereon shall be allowed to run on its outward or inward traverse within 45 centimeters from any fixed structure which is not part of machine.

6. Casing of a new machinery (Sec. 26)

All machinery driven by power shall be sunk, encased and effectively guarded to guard against danger/accidents.

7. Prohibition of employment of women and children near cotton-openers (Sec. 27)

No women or child shall be allowed in any part of the factory to press cotton when cotton-opener is at work.

8. Hoists and lifts (Sec. 28)

Hoists and lifts should be of good mechanical construction and should be properly maintained and examined once in every 6 months.

9. Lifting machines, chains, ropes and lifting tackles (Sec. 29)

Lifting machines, chains, ropes and lifting tackles should be of good construction and should be examined once in every 12 months. Also, cranes and lifting machines should not be loaded beyond safe working load.

10. Revolving machinery (Sec. 30)

Maximum safe working speed of grindstone or abrasive wheel, etc. should be clearly stated on a notice to be kept near machine.

11. Pressure plant (Sec. 31)

Safe working pressure should not be exceeded.

12. Floors, stairs and means of access (Sec. 32)

All floors, steps, stairs, passages and gangways should be of sound construction and properly maintained.

13. Pits, sumps, opening in floors, etc. (Sec. 33)

Every pit or opening in the floor should be properly covered or fenced.

14. Excessive weights (Sec. 34)

No person shall be employed in any factory to lift, carry or move any load so heavy as to be likely to cause him or her injury.

15. Protection of eyes (Sec. 35)

In every factory, screen or suitable goggles should be provided for the protection of persons who are employed in a work which involve danger or injury to the worker's eyesight.

16. Precautions against dangerous fumes (Sec. 36)

No person shall be allowed to enter any chamber, tank, pit, pipe, etc. in which any gas, dust or fume is likely to be present.

17. Precautions regarding the use of portable electric light (Sec. 36-A)

No portable electric light or any other electric appliance of voltage exceeding 24 volts shall be permitted for use inside any chamber, tank or pit unless adequate safety devices are provided.

18. Precautions against explosive or inflammable dust, gas, etc. (Sec. 37)

Effective measures should be taken to prevent explosion on ignition of gas, fume, etc.

19. Precautions in case of fire (Sec. 38)

Effective measures should be taken to prevent outbreak of fire and its spread. Workers should be familiar well in advance with the means of escape in case of fire.

20. Power to require specifications of defective parts or tests of stability (Sec. 39)

The inspector of the factory may ask the occupier or the manager or both to furnish drawings and specifications, which may be necessary to determine whether the buildings, ways, machinery or plant can be used with safety.

21. Safety of building and machinery (Sec. 40)

If any building or part of a building or machinery or plant in a factory is in such a condition that it is dangerous to human life or safety, then the inspector may serve on the occupier or the manager or both of the factory an order specifying the measures which in his opinion shall be adopted and requiring them to be carried out.

22. Maintenance of building (Sec. 40-A)

If it appears to the inspector that any building or any part of a building in a factory is in such a state of despair as is likely to lead to conditions detrimental to the health and welfare of the workers, then he may serve on the occupier or the manager or both of the factory an order specifying the measures which should be taken.

23. Safety Officers (Sec. 40-B)

In every factory (i) wherein 1000 or more workers are employed, or (ii) wherein, any manufacturing process or operation is carried on, which involves any risk of bodily injury, poisoning or disease, or any other hazard to health, to the persons employed in the factory, then the occupier shall appoint the required number of safety officer.

C. Other Voluntary Steps

In addition to adopting a safety programme and comply with the legal provisions, management can take other voluntary steps also. For example, it can ensure good working conditions with special emphasis on safety measures, pay attention to individual differences of employees, ensure proper speed of work, motivate safety attitudes, encourage safety habits, arrange strong motor tests, emotional stability tests, intelligence tests, etc.[13] Along with this, the workers and trade unions should also take voluntary steps in this regard, for example, guiding workers on safety measures, arranging lectures, publishes periodical/magazines, etc.

HEALTH

In the previous part of this chapter we had discussed the importance of prevention of accidents for the employee's well-being but this was just one part of the comprehensive programme. The employee's physical conditions can be harmed through diseases, stress and strain as well as through accidents.[14] Thus, it is also equally important for the organisation to be concerned with the general health, both physical and mental, of its employees for both economic and humanitarian reasons.

According to World Health Organisation (WHO) health is a state of complete physical, mental and social well-being and not merely an absence of disease or infirmity.

NEED AND IMPORTANCE OF INDUSTRIAL HEALTH

The need and importance of industrial health is clear from the following points:

1. It improves the efficiency and productivity of the workers.
2. It reduces absenteeism and labour turnover rate.
3. It reduces indiscipline.
4. It improves motivation and morale.
5. It lessens industrial discontentment.
6. It reduces occupational diseases.
7. It enables the workers to work for longer periods of work.
8. It reduces industrial unrest.
9. It reduces spoilage and cost of operation.

PHYSICAL HEALTH

Healthy employees are more safety conscious, more regular to work, more productive and more efficient. A healthy worker is confident, always happy and cheerful and a great asset for an organisation. Realising the significance of health generally the following measures are included under physical health programmes:[15]

1. A stated health and medical policy.
2. Pre-placement physical examination.
3. The performance of periodic physical examinations on all employees to health hazards.
4. The availability of facilities for voluntary periodic physical examinations for all employees.
5. A competent medical staff.
6. Systematic attention to sanitation, safety precautions and industrial hygiene.

7. A chief medical officer who reports to a responsible member of management.
8. A well equipped dispensary for emergency cases and physical examination.
9. Well qualified medical and nursing personnel.

STATUTORY/LEGAL HEALTH PROVISIONS

Sections 11 to 20 of the Factories Act, 1948 deals with the provisions related with the health of the workers in the factories. These provisions are the following:

1. Cleanliness (Sec. 11)

Every factory should be kept clean and free from effluvia and dirt. Effective means of drainage should be provided.

2. Disposal of wastes and effluents (Sec. 12)

In every factory effective arrangements should be made for the treatment of wastes and effluents due to manufacturing process carried on therein, so as to render them innocuous, and for their disposal.

3. Ventilation and temperature (Sec. 13)

Adequate ventilation and temperature should be maintained in every workroom of the factory.

4. Dust and fumes (Sec. 14)

Where dust or fumes or impurity of such a nature as is likely to be injurious to the workers is given off as a result of the manufacturing process being carried on in a factory, then effective measures shall be taken in the factory for prevention of inhalation or accumulation of dust and fumes in workrooms.

5. Artificial humidification (Sec. 15)

In respect of all the factories in which the humidity of the air is artificially increased, the state government may make rules prescribing the standards of humidification. The water used for this purpose should be taken from a public supply or other sources of drinking water.

6. Overcrowding (Sec. 16)

There should not be overcrowding in any room of the factory so as to be injurious to the health of the workers employed. There shall be at least 9.9 cubic meters (for the factories in existence at the time of the commencement of the Act) and 14.2 cubic meters (for the factories built after the commencement of the Act) space for every worker.

7. Lighting (Sec. 17)

There should be the provision of sufficient and suitable lighting in every part of the factory. All glazed windows and skylights used for the lighting of the workrooms should be kept clean on both the inner and outer surfaces and free from obstruction.

8. Drinking water (Sec. 18)

There should be the provision of suitable points for wholesome drinking water. All points for supply of drinking water shall be legibly marked 'drinking water' in a language understood by a majority of the workers employed in the factory. There should be the provision of cooling of drinking water where more than 250 workers are employed.

9. Latrines and urinals (Sec. 19)

Separate latrines and urinals for male and female workers should be provided. These should be conveniently situated and adequately lighted and ventilated.

10. Spittoons (Sec. 20)

In every factory sufficient number of spittoons should be provided in convenient places and also, they should be maintained in a clean and hygienic condition. Whoever spits in contravention of Section 20 shall be punishable with fine not exceeding Rs. 5.

MENTAL HEALTH

The rationale behind the organisation's mental health programme is the same as for programmes designed to maintain physical health. The aim of mental health programme is to help the employees to adjust themselves to the realties of actual life. Firstly, in modern life mental breakdown is common due to various tensions and pressure. Secondly, various types of mental difficulties are reflected in the lower productivity and lower profits of the organisation. Thirdly, mental illness takes its toll through alcoholism, high accident rates, high tardiness rates, high labour turnover and poor human relationships.[16] It has been reported that emotionally ill workers commit more safety violations, meet more number of accidents, file more grievances and are dismissed more than the sound and healthy employees. Despite its importance, mental health still ranks third behind safety and physical health. Following items can be included in a mental health programme:[17]

1. Availability of psychiatric counselling.
2. Cooperation with outside psychiatric specialists and institutions.
3. Education of company personnel concerning the nature and importance of mental health problems.
4. Development and maintenance of a proper human relations programme.

KEY TERMS

Accident	Non-machine factors
Accident costs	Physical health
Disablement	Safety director
Frequency rate	Safety contests
Machine factors	Severity rate
Mental health	

QUESTIONS

1. Bring out the significance of employee safety and health.
2. Bring out the various causes of accidents.
3. Describe the various types of accidents.
4. Describe a safety programme.
5. Describe the provisions of the Factories Act, 1948 in relation to employee safety and health.

ENDNOTES

1. Luis R. Gomez-Mejia, David B. Balkin and Robert L. Cardy, *Managing Human Resources,* Third Edition, Pearson Education, Delhi, 2003, p. 526.
2. R. Wayne Mondy and Robert M. Noe, *Human Resource Management*, Ninth Edition, Pearson Education, Delhi, p. 360.
3. Michael Armstrong, *A Handbook of Human Resource Management Practice,* Ninth Edition, Kogan Page, London, 2005, p. 828.
4. H.W. Heinrich, *Industrial Accident Prevention,* McGraw-Hill, New York, 1959, p.16.
5. C.B. Mamoria and S.V. Gankar, *Personnel Management*, Himalaya Publishing House, Mumbai, Twenty-fifth Edition, 2005, p. 790.
6. D.C. Sharma and R.C. Sharma, *Personnel Management &Industrial Relations*, First Edition, S.J. Publications, Meerut, p. 365.
7. *Ibid.*, p. 366.
8. C.B. Mamoria and S.V. Gankar, op. cit., p. 792.
9. H.W. Heinrich, op. cit., p. 50-52.
10. *Ibid.*
11. Edwin B. Flippo, *Personnel Management*, Sixth Edition, McGraw-Hill, New York, 1984, p. 523.
12. *Ibid.*
13. D.C. Sharma and R.C. Sharma, op. cit., p. 368.
14. Edwin B. Flippo, op. cit., p. 529.
15. *Ibid.*, p. 530.
16. *Ibid.*, p. 532.
17. *Ibid.*, p. 537.

Employee Welfare

22

LEARNING OBJECTIVES

After studying this chapter, you should be able to:

1. Understand the concept and importance of employee welfare work
2. Understand the aims and objectives of employee welfare work
3. Describe the various types of welfare work
4. Describe the various approaches to labour welfare
5. Describe the principles of a welfare programme
6. Describe the functions of a labour welfare officer

Once the employees are hired, trained and compensated, they also need to be maintained in order to serve the firm well. The aim of the welfare work is to preserve and improve physical, mental and economic conditions of the employees. Employee welfare includes both social and economic welfare. Social welfare aims at the social development through social legislation, social service, social reform and social work. The aim of economic welfare is to promote economic development by increasing production and productivity and through equitable distribution.

MEANING AND DEFINITION

Employee welfare can be defined as anything done for the comfort and improvement, intellectual and social, of the employees over and above the wages paid, which is not a necessity of the industry.[1]

According to The Labour Investigation Committee (1944–1946) employee welfare means anything done for the intellectual, physical, moral and economic betterment of the workers, whether by employers, by government or by other agencies, over and above what is laid down by law or what is normally expected as part of the contractual benefits for which the workers may have bargained.[2]

According to ILO's report at its Asian Regional Conference, labour welfare may be understood to mean such services, facilities and amenities, which may be established outside or in the vicinity of undertakings, to enable the persons employed therein to perform their work in healthy and congenial surroundings and to provide them with the amenities conducive to good health and high morale.

CONCEPT OF EMPLOYEE WELFARE

Employee welfare may be viewed as a total concept, as a social concept and as a relative concept. The total concept is a desirable state of existence involving the physical, mental, moral and emotional well-being.[3] These all four elements together constitute the structure of welfare, on which its totality is based. The social concept of welfare means the welfare of man, his family and the community. The relative concept of welfare refers to that welfare which is relative in time and place. It is a dynamic and flexible concept and hence the meaning and content differ from time to time, region to region, industry to industry, and country to country, depending upon the value system, level of education, social customs, political system, degree of industrialization and general standard of the socio-economic development of the people.[4]

IMPORTANCE OF LABOUR WELFARE WORK

In India labour welfare work assumes a great importance because of the following reasons:

1. Lack of strong trade union movement

In the absence of strong trade unions and effective leaders, welfare work help the workers in the industry to stand on their own feet, think properly and systematically of their interests, progress hand in hand and participate in the nation's development.

2. Poverty

Poverty is one of the main reasons behind the provisions of labour welfare activities. Indian workers in majority are poor, they are unable to provide a healthy living for their families and good education for their children.

3. Illiteracy

In India, the number of educated workers is low. Being illiterate, they are unable to receive advanced industrial training, understand the problems in industries, understand their own interests and those of nations.

4. Low level of health and nutrition

Due to poverty and illiteracy the Indian workers remain unhealthy and ill fed. This reduces their productivity and efficiency.

5. Lack of healthy recreation

Due to lack of healthy recreation, the workers indulge in crime and other wrong activities. The employer should provide means of healthy recreation in order to maintain their efficiency.

6. Lack of training

The number of trained workers in India is very low. Thus it is necessary to have training facilities for such a vast workforce.

AIMS AND OBJECTIVES OF EMPLOYEE WELFARE WORK

The main aims and objectives of employee welfare work are as follows:

1. Economic betterment of employees

This refers to increasing the efficiency and productivity of the workers, which raises their chances to earn more, and it aims at improving their standard of living.

2. Humanitarian consideration

This aims to enable workers to enjoy a fuller and richer life by providing them certain facilities and amenities.

3. Civic consideration

This aims to develop a sense of responsibility and dignity among the workers and thus, to make them worthy citizens of the nation.

CLASSIFICATION OF WELFARE WORK

Employee welfare work may be divided into three categories as follows:

1. Statutory welfare

This includes all those employee welfare activities, which are undertaken by employers because of legal requirements. The statutory welfare facilities are provided under the Factories Act, 1948, the Mines Act, 1952, the Plantations Labour Act, 1951, the Motor Transport Worker Act, 1961, the Contract Labour (Regulations and Abolition) Act, 1970, the Merchant Shipping Act, 1958, Dock Workers (Safety, Health and Welfare) Scheme, 1961 and Inter-State Migrant Workmen (Regulation of Employment and Conditions of Service) Act, 1979.

Exhibit 22.1: Provisions of Various Acts

The Factories Act, 1948

The welfare amenities provided under the Act are given below:

(a) Washing facilities (S. 42)

(b) Facilities for storing and dry clothing (S. 43)

(c) Sitting facilities for occasional rest for workers who are obliged to work standing (S. 44)

(d) First-aid boxes or cupboards—one for every 150 workers and ambulance facilities, if there are more than 500 workers (S. 45)

(e) Canteens if employing more than 250 workers (S. 46)

(f) Shelters, rest rooms and lunch rooms, if employing over 150 workers (S. 47)

(g) Crèche, if employing more than 30 women (S. 48)

(h) Welfare officer, if employing 500 or more workers (S. 49)

The Mines Act, 1952 and the Mines Rules

The main obligations of the mine owners regarding health and welfare of their workers are as follows:

(a) Maintenance of crèches where 550 women workers are employed

(b) Provision of shelters for taking food and rest if 150 or more persons are employed

(c) Provision of a canteen in mines employing 250 or more workers

(d) Maintenance of first-aid boxes, and first-aid rooms in mines employing more than 150 workers

(e) Provision in coal mines of (i) pit head baths equipped with shower baths; (ii) sanitary latrines and (ii) lockers, separately for men and women workers

(f) Appointment of a Welfare Officer in mines employing more than 500 or more persons to look after the matters relating to the welfare of the workers

The Plantations Labour Act, 1951

The following welfare measures are to be provided to the plantation workers:

(a) Canteens in plantations employing 150 or more workers (S. 11)

(b) Crèches in plantations employing 50 or more women workers (S. 12)

(c) Recreational facilities for the workers and their children (S. 13)

(d) Educational facilities in the estate for the children of workers, where there are 25 workers' children between the age of 6 and 12 (S. 14)

(e) Housing facilities for every worker and his/her family residing in the plantation. The standard and specification of the accommodation, procedure for allotment and rent chargeable from workers, are to be prescribed in the rules by the State Governments (S. 15 and 16)

(f) The State Government may make rules requiring every plantation employer to provide the workers with such number and type of umbrellas, blankets, raincoats or other like amenities for the protection of workers from rain or cold as may be prescribed (S. 17)

(g) Appointment of a Welfare Officer in plantations employing 300 or more workers (S. 18)

The exact standards of these facilities have been prescribed under the rules framed by the State Governments.

The Motor Transport Workers Act, 1961

The Motor Transport Undertakings are required to provide certain welfare and health measures given as follows:

(a) Canteens of prescribed standard, if employing 100 or more workers (S. 8)

(b) Clean, ventilated, well-lighted and comfortable restrooms at every place wherein motor transport workers are required to halt at night (S. 9)

(c) Uniforms, raincoats to drivers, conductors and line checking staff for protection against rain and cold. A prescribed amount of washing allowance is to be given to the above-mentioned categories of staff (S. 10)

(d) Medical facilities are to be provided to the motor transport workers at the operating centres and at the stations as may be prescribed by the State Governments (S. 11)

(e) First-aid facilities equipment with the prescribed contents are to be provided in every transport vehicle (S. 12)

The Contract Labour (Regulation and Abolition) Act, 1970

The following welfare and health measures are to be provided to the contract workers by the contractor:

(i) A canteen in every establishment employing 100 or more workers (S. 16)

(ii) Rest rooms or other suitable alternative accommodation where the contract labour is required to halt at night in connection with the work of an establishment (S. 17)

(iii) Provision for a sufficient supply of wholesome drinking water, sufficient number of latrines and urinals of prescribed types and washing facilities (S. 18)

(iv) Provision for first-aid boxes equipped with the prescribed contents (S. 19)

The Act imposes liability on the principal employer to provide the above amenities to the contract labour employed in his other establishment, if the contractor fails to do so.

The Merchant Shipping Act, 1958

Provisions in the Act relating to health and welfare cover:

(i) Crew accommodation

(ii) Supply of sufficient drinking water

(iii) Supply of medicines, medical stores, and provision of surgical and medical advice

(iv) Maintenance of proper weights and measures on board, and grant of relief to distressed seamen aboard a ship.

(v) Every foreign-going ship carrying more than the prescribed number of persons, including the crew, is required to have on board, as part of her complement, a qualified medical officer

(vi) Appointment of a Seamen's Welfare Officer at such ports in or outside India as the government may consider necessary

(vii) Establishment of hostels, clubs, canteens, and libraries

(viii) Provision of medical treatment and hospital

(ix) Provision of educational facilities

The governments have been authorized to frame rules, *inter alia,* for the levy of fees. Payable by owners of ships at prescribed rates for the purpose of providing amenities to seamen and for taking other measures for their welfare.

Dock Workers (Safety, Health and Welfare) Scheme, 1961

A comprehensive Dock Workers (Safety, Health and Welfare) Scheme, 1961 has been framed for all major ports and is administered by the Chief Advisor, Factories (Factory Advice Service and Labour Institutes). It is framed under the Dock Workers (Regulation of Employment) Act, 1948. Amenities provided in the port premises include provision of (i) urinals and latrines; (ii) drinking water; (iii) washing facilities; (iv) bathing facilities; (v) canteens; (vi) rest shelters; (vii) call stands; (viii) first-aid arrangements.

Other welfare measures provided are (i) housing; (ii) schools; (iii) educational facilities; (iv) grant of scholarships; (v) libraries; (vi) sports and recreation; (vii) fair price shop; and (viii) co-operative societies.

Cost of amenities, welfare and health measures and recreation facilities for registered workers shall be met from a separate fund called the Dock Workers Welfare Fund which shall be maintained by the Board. Contributions to this Fund shall be made by all registered employers at such a rate as may be determined by the Board. The Board shall frame rules for contributions for the maintenance and operation of the Fund. Different ports have been fixed.

Inter-State Migrant Workmen (Regulation of Employment and Conditions of Service) Act, 1979

Section 16 of the Act stipulates that every contractor employing inter-state migrant workmen in connection with the work of an establishment to which this Act applies will have to provide the following facilities:

(a) To ensure regular payment of wages to such workmen (at least minimum wages have to be paid as fixed under the Minimum Wages Act, 1948)

(b) To ensure equal pay for equal work irrespective of sex

(c) To ensure suitable conditions of work to such workmen having regard to the fact that they are required to work in a state different from their own state

(d) To provide and maintain suitable residential accommodation to such workers working during the period of their employment

(e) To provide the prescribed medical facilities to the workmen, free of charges

(f) To provide such protective clothing to the workmen as may be prescribed

(g) In case of fatal accident or serious bodily injury to any such workman, to report to the specified authorities of both the states and also the next of kin of the workmen.

With regard to labour welfare, the Act contains provisions for:

1. Appointment of a labour welfare officer; and
2. Welfare of workers.

Source: K. Aswathappa, *Human Resource and Personnel Management*, Fourth Edition, Tata McGraw-Hill, 2006, pp. 452-454.

2. Voluntary welfare

This includes all those welfare activities, which are undertaken by the employers at their own, for example, provision of educational facilities, medical facilities, transport facilities, recreational facilities, housing facilities, etc.

3. Mutual welfare

This includes all those activities which are undertaken by the workers themselves through the platform of their trade unions, for example, reading rooms, sports, indoor games, etc.

Labour welfare work can also be classified as follows:

1. Intra-mural welfare activities (within the organisation)

This includes all those activities, which are undertaken inside the factories. For example, medical facilities, canteens, crechès, rest rooms, washing and bathing facilities, provision of safety measures (such as fencing of exposed moving parts of machines, protective clothing, fire-fighting measures), supply of drinking water, spittoons, cleanliness, sanitary conditions, lavatories, wash basins, waste disposal, etc.

2. Extra-mural welfare activities

This includes all those welfare activities or services or amenities, which are undertaken outside the factories. For example, proper housing accommodation, facilities for recreation (clubs, gymnasium, etc.), amusement and sports, educational facilities for adults and children, etc.

AGENCIES OF LABOUR WELFARE ACTIVITIES

The main agencies engaged in labour welfare activities are as follows:

1. Government

The Government of India has enacted numerous laws in order to make it mandatory for employers to provide certain welfare facilities to their employees. These include the Factories Act, 1948, the Mines Act, 1952, the Plantations Labour Act, 1951, the Motor Transport Worker Act, 1961, the Contract Labour (Regulations and Abolition) Act, 1970, the Merchant Shipping Act, 1958, Dock Workers (Safety, Health and Welfare) Scheme, 1961 and Inter-State Migrant Workmen (Regulation of Employment and Conditions of Service) Act, 1979. In addition, the Central Government has constituted welfare funds for the benefits of employees. These funds are constituted in mica, coal, iron-ore, limestone and dolomite mines. These funds are meant for providing medical, housing, educational and recreational facilities.

2. Employers

At present, the employers have to provide the various welfare activities as per the norms set by government under the various legislations. It has become obligatory on the part of employers to provide welfare facilities for example, canteens, dispensary, etc. Most of the employers still consider the expenditure on labour welfare activities as a mere wastage of money rather than an investment.

3. Trade unions

Trade unions in India have also rendered welfare services for the benefit of their members. These welfare activities are provided out of their own resources and also administered by them. Although limited in extent and scope but certain trade unions have undertaken great interest in various social welfare programmes. Some of these programmes include adult literacy programme, leadership training programme, publication and research activities, establishment of libraries, establishment of schools and even traded union colleges. Some of the important workers' organisations' are Textile Labour Association (TLA) of

Ahmedabad, Mill Mazdoor Union, Indore, Rashtriya Mill Mazdoor Sangh (RMMS) of Mumbai, Mill Mazdoor Sabha of Mumbai and Transport and Dock Workers' Unions of Mumbai. The services offered by TLA for its members are the following:

1. Schools for workers' children
2. Pre-natal and maternal care through a maternity home and dispensary
3. Cultural and religious centers
4. Gymnasiums, libraries and reading centers
5. Legal aid in civil as well as in criminal matters
6. Vocational training like radio repairing, sewing, typewriting, etc.
7. Formation of community development centers
8. Blood banks
9. Workers' cooperative banks
10. Publication of a bi-weekly, *Mazdoor Sandesh*
11. Attending to civil and municipal problems
12. Hostels for students
13. Girls' hostel for backward communities
14. Celebration of national festivals.

4. Other Agencies

There are various voluntary agencies who are doing good labour welfare work. These include the philanthropic charitable and social service organisations such as Bombay Social Service League, the Maternity and Infant Welfare Association, the Seva Sadan Society and the Women's Institute of Bengal. These agencies provide educational facilities, medical aid, libraries, recreational facilities, etc.

APPROACHES TO LABOUR WELFARE

The main theories of or approaches to labour welfare are the following:[5]

1. The police theory

This theory is based upon an assumption that without policing, i.e. compulsion, the employers do not provide even the minimum facilities for their employees. At least provision of minimum standard of welfare is essential for the workers. The owners and managers of industrial undertakings get ample opportunities for the exploitation of the workers. This is done by paying workers low wages, keep them for long hours, keeping workplace in an unhygienic condition, by ignoring the health and safety provisions, etc. Hence, the state has to intervene in order to provide minimum standard of welfare to the workers. State enacts a number of legislation, which compels the management to provide basic amenities to the employees. So, the state assuming the role of a policeman and compels the owners and managers to provide the various welfare facilities.

2. The religious theory

This theory is based upon two aspects. One aspect of this theory is investment aspect. According to this theory, any good work is considered as an investment by which both the benefactor and the beneficiary are rewarded. Man is considered to be a religious animal. Many acts of man are related with the religious sentiments and beliefs. These religious beliefs sometimes prompt an employer to take up the welfare activities in the expectations of future emancipation either in this life or after that. Another aspect of this theory is the atonement aspect. This aspect implies that the current disabilities of a person are the result of the sins committed by him/her earlier. Thus, he/she should take up welfare work now to atone or compensate for his/her sins. So, the benevolent acts of welfare are treated as either an investment or atonement.

3. The philanthropic theory

In Greek “philos” implies loving and “anthropes” implies man. So, philanthropic refers to affection for mankind. According to this theory a philanthropist strives to remove the sufferings of others and promotes their well-being. The labour welfare movement began in the early years of the industrial revolution with the support of philanthropists such as Robert Owen. According to this theory the employers provides crèches, hostels, canteens, good working conditions, etc. to remove the disabilities of the workers.

4. The trusteeship theory

This is also known as paternalistic theory of labour welfare. According to this theory the industrialist or employer holds the total industrial estate, properties and profits accruing from them in trust. In short, the employer should hold the industrial assets for himself, for the society. This theory was strongly advocated by Mahatma Gandhi. As per this theory, the labour welfare work depends entirely on the initiative of the top management. Also, as there is no legal sanction, so its value is related to the moral conscience of the industrialist. This theory puts emphasis on the employers to provide funds on an on going basis for the well-being of their workers.

5. The placating theory

This theory is based on the fact that workers are becoming more organised and militant. They are now more conscious of their rights and privileges than ever before. So, timely and periodical acts of labour welfare can appease the workers. They are some kind of pacifiers.

6. The public relations theory

This theory provides the basis of an atmosphere of goodwill between the management and labour and also between management and the public outside. Under this theory, the labour welfare work is used as a tool of advertisement to project the organisation's good image/impression on the minds of public. Usually, the employers take their visitors on the round of the organisation to show the various welfare activities organised by them.

7. The functional theory

This is also known as efficiency theory. Under this theory, the welfare work is used as a means to secure, preserve and develop the efficiency and productivity of workers. This theory emphasizes that the employer should take good care of his workers. So, they become more efficient and productive. The higher production will benefit both the labour and the management.

8. The social theory

This theory emphasizes that an organisation is morally bound to improve the conditions of the society in addition to improving the conditions of its workers. Hence, the labour welfare work is gradually taking the form of social welfare.

PRINCIPLES OF A WELFARE PROGRAMME

For the successful implementation of any welfare programme, the following principles should be kept in mind:[6]

1. The labour welfare activities should provide the entire hierarchy of an organisation. In other words, the employer should be welfare-oriented at every level.
2. The employer should not bargain labour welfare as a substitute for wages, or monetary incentives. Workers have a right to adequate wages in addition to welfare measures.
3. The employer should look after the welfare of his employees as a matter of social obligation.
4. Labour welfare must aim at helping employees to help themselves in the long run. Self-help principle will enable them to become more responsible and efficient.
5. There should be proper coordination, harmony and integration of all labour welfare services in an undertaking.
6. The labour welfare work of an organisation must be administratively viable and essentially development oriented.
7. The management should ensure cooperation and active participation of unions and workers in formulating and implementing labour welfare programmes.
8. There should be periodical assessment or evaluation of welfare measures and necessary timely improvements on the basis of the feedback.

LABOUR WELFARE OFFICER

Realising the importance of labour welfare officer in Indian industry, the Royal Commission on Labour in 1931 recommended their appointment in order to protect the workers from the evils of jobbery and indebtedness, to act generally as a spokesman of labour and to promote amicable relations between workers and management. According to Section 49 of the Factories Act, 1948, in every factory wherein 500 or more workers are ordinarily employed, the occupier shall employ in the factory such number of welfare officer as may be prescribed. The State Government may prescribe the duties, qualifications and conditions of service of a welfare officer.

The main functions or duties of labour welfare officers are the following:[7]

1. Supervision of
   - (i) Health, safety and welfare programmes
   - (ii) Working of joint committees
   - (iii) Redressal of workers' grievances
2. Counselling of workers on
   - (i) Personal and family problems
   - (ii) Adjustment to their work environment
   - (iii) Undertaking their rights and privileges
3. Advising management on the matters of
   - (i) Formulating labour and welfare policies
   - (ii) Apprenticeship training programmes
   - (iii) Meeting statutory obligations of workers
   - (iv) Developing fringe benefits programme
   - (v) Workers' education
   - (vi) Use of communication media
4. Establishing liaison with workers so that they may
   - (i) Understand the various limitations under which they work
   - (ii) Appreciate the need for harmonious industrial relations in the plant
   - (iii) Interpret company policies clearly
   - (iv) Come to a settlement in case of disputes
5. Establishing liaison with management so that they may
   - (i) Appreciate workers' point of view on various matters in the plant

Exhibit 22.2: Authority and Responsibilities of the Factory Labour Welfare Officer in India

Authority	Area of Responsibility
1. *Advisory:* — to advise — to suggest — to encourage — to promote — to secure	In the formulation of company labour policies, he should promote training and apprenticeship programmes; induction programmes; improve working condition; welfare programmes; housing, recreational and educational and methods of communication with workers.
2. *Service:* — to help — to explain	(a) To workers: (i) In personal and family problems; (ii) To adjusting to work environment; (iii) In understanding their rights and privileges; (iv) In making application for leave. (b) To management By helping workers understand various problems. (i) Welfare and benefit programmes. (ii) Health and safety programmes. (iii) Joint Committees. (iv) Paid vacations.
3. *Supervisory:* — to supervise — to inspect — to regulate	(i) Implementations of labour laws. (ii) Wages and employment.
4. *Functional:* — to ensure — to deal with	(i) To bring to notice of factory of management the workers' grievances; (ii) To watch industrial relations with a view to influencing both factory management and workers when a dispute arises between them; (iii) To exercise restraining influence on workers and management for illegal strikes and lockouts;
5. *Police:* — to watch — to bring to notice — to restraint — to prevent	(i) To establish contact and hold consulations for building harmonious relations between management and labour; (ii) To secure expeditious redressal of workers' grievances; (iii) To help bring about settlement of industrial dispute by persuasive efforts; (iv) To maintain a neutral attitude during strikes or lockouts and to help in bringing about a peaceful settlement.

Source: C.B. Mamoria et al, *Dynamics of Industrial Relations*, Himalaya Publishing House, Mumbai, 2005, p. 563.

(ii) Maintain harmonious industrial relations in the plant

6. Working with management and workers in order
   (i) To maintain harmonious industrial relations in the plant
   (ii) To arrange for the prompt redressal of grievances and speedy settlement of disputes
   (iii) To improve productivity and efficiency of the enterprise

7. Working with outside public in order
   (i) To ensure the proper enforcement of various Acts that are applicable to the plant by establishing contact with factory inspectors, medical officers and other authorities
   (ii) To assist other agencies to help workers to make use of community services.

The above-said functions of labour welfare officer highlights that welfare officer act as a counsellor, advisor, mediator and liaison-man between labour and management.

KEY TERMS

Employee welfare	Statutory welfare
Extra-mural	Voluntary welfare
Intra-mural	Welfare officer
Mutual welfare	

QUESTIONS

1. Define the term 'employee welfare' and discuss its importance.
2. What are the aims and objectives of employee welfare work?
3. Describe the various agencies of employee welfare activities.
4. Describe the various theories of labour welfare.
5. What are the main duties of a labour welfare officer?

ENDNOTES

1. Arthur James Todd, *Industry and Society—A Sociological Appraisal of Modern Industrialism*, pp. 250-251.
2. Report of the Labour Investigation Committee, 1946, p. 345.
3. A.M. Sarma, *Understanding Wage System*, Himalaya Publishing House, Bombay, Third Edition, 1992, p. 3.
4. *Ibid.*, p. 4.
5. M.V. Moorthy, *Principles of Labour Welfare*, Gupta Brothers, Visakkapatnam, 1968, p. 28.
6. A.M. Sarma, op. cit., pp. 11-12.
7. Report of the Labour Welfare committee, 1964.

Collective Bargaining

23

LEARNING OBJECTIVES

After studying this chapter, you should be able to:

1. Understand the concept and nature of collective bargaining
2. Describe the features and objectives of collective bargaining
3. Describe the collective bargaining process
4. Understand the various types of bargaining

Industrial peace is vital for the economic progress of a nation. In order to maintain industrial harmony, it is essential that industrial disputes should be prevented first and if disputes happen then it should be settled down quickly and amicably. One of the best ways for the prevention and settlement of industrial disputes is collective bargaining. It is an essential element of industrial democracy. It is a two-party procedure for arriving at a mutually agreed solution.

MEANING AND DEFINITION

The term collective bargaining was coined by Sydney and Beatrice Webb. They defined collective bargaining as a method by which trade unions protect and improve the conditions of their members.[1] Collective bargaining is a procedure by which employers and a group of employees agree upon the conditions of work.[2] The term collective bargaining is extended to all negotiations between employers and workers' organisation's, for (1) determining working conditions and terms of employment, (2) regulating relations between employers and workers, and

(3) regulating relations between employers or their organisation's and a workers' organisation or between workers' organisation.[3]

MAIN CHARACTERISTICS/FEATURES OF COLLECTIVE BARGAINING

The main features of collective bargaining are the following:

1. It is a group action as opposed to individual action. The representatives of both labour and management act in this process.
2. It is flexible in approach and not rigid or static.
3. It is a two-party process. Collective bargaining can work only with thc acceptance by labour and management of their appropriate responsibilities. It can succeed only when both labour and management want it to succeed.[4]
4. It is based on the principle of mutual give and take rather than take-it or leave-it approach of settlement of a dispute.
5. It is a continuous and dynamic process. Preparation for the next round of negotiations often begins the moment a contract is ratified.
6. It is a sort of industrial democracy at work. Collective bargaining is democratic in nature. It is a joint formulation of an organisation's policy on all matters which directly affects the workers in a plant.
7. It is an advanced form of human relations.
8. It is essentially a complementary process and not a competitive process.

OBJECTIVES OF COLLECTIVE BARGAINING

The main objectives of collective bargaining are the following:

1. To establish and maintain cordial relations between management and labour.
2. To prevent and settle industrial disputes.
3. To protect the interests of workers through collective/joint action and prevent the unilateral action on the part of employer.

4. To ensure the participation of labour unions in industry.
5. To promote industrial democracy.

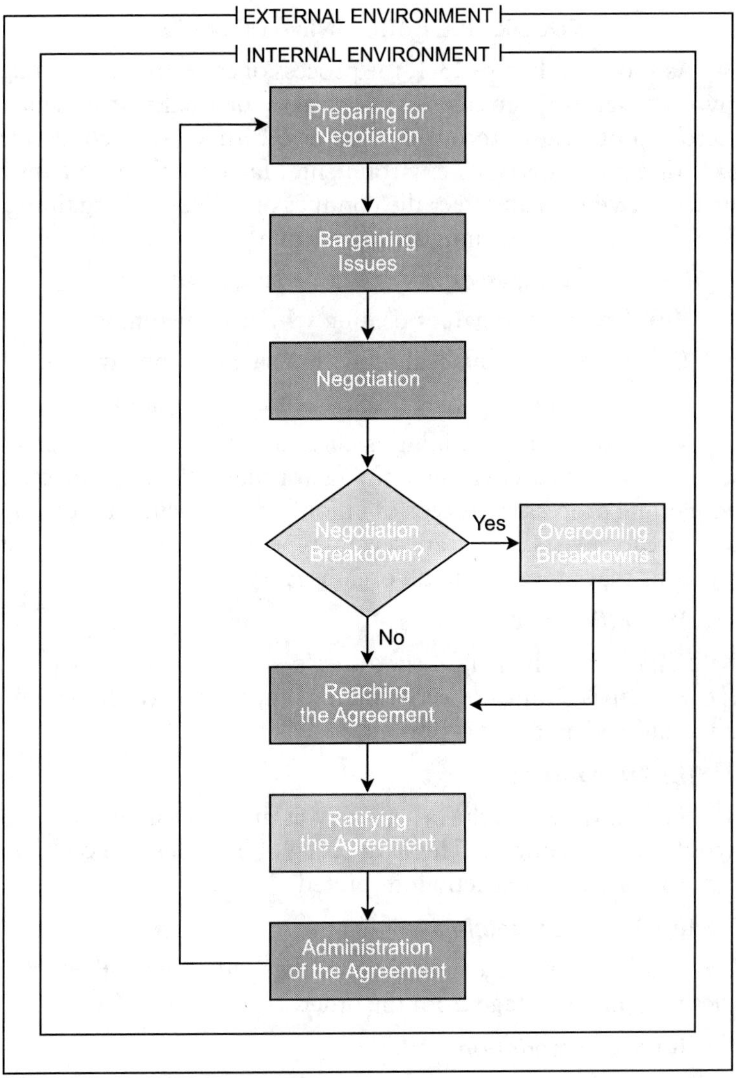

Fig. 23.1: The Collective Bargaining Process

Source: R.W. Mondy and R.M. Noe, *Human Resource Management*, Pearson Education, Delhi, 2005, p. 428.

6. To avoid the need of state intervention in industrial disputes.
7. To resolve the disputes by voluntary negotiations.

COLLECTIVE BARGAINING PROCESS

As shown in Figure 23.1, the process of collective bargaining involves mainly seven steps in a logical sequence. Environmental factors, both the internal and external affects the collective bargaining process. One environmental factor is the bargaining structure, which can affect the conduct of collective bargaining. The four major bargaining structures are:[5]

(i) One company dealing with a single union;
(ii) Several companies dealing with a single union;
(iii) Several unions dealing with a single company; and
(iv) Several companies dealing with several unions.

Most contract bargaining is carried out in the first type of structure. Another environmental factor that influence collective bargaining process is the type of union-management relationship that already exists. There are several types of union-management relations that may exist in an organisation:[6]

(i) *Conflict*

Each party challenges the other's actions and motivation, cooperation is totally non-existent, uncompromising attitudes and trade unions militancy is present.

(ii) *Armed truce*

Each party views the other party as antagonistic but tries to avoid head-on conflict. The bargaining obligations and contract provisions are very strictly interpreted.

(iii) *Power bargaining*

In this the management accepts the trade union. Each side tries to gain advantage from the other.

(iv) *Accommodation*

Each party tolerates the other in a live and let live atmosphere and attempts to reduce conflict without eliminating it.

(v) *Cooperation*

Each party accepts the other and both work together to resolve the human resource and production problems as they occur.

(vi) *Collusion*

In this, both the parties cooperate to the extent of adversely affecting the legitimate interests of employees, other businesses in the industry and the consuming public, this involves convincing to control markets, supplies and prices illegally or unethically.

1. Preparing for negotiation

This is the first step in the collective bargaining process. Advance preparation by both the parties is essential. The parties should know thoroughly about the history, culture, climate, present economic state, wage and benefit structure of the organisation and also of the similar organisations. The success of collective bargaining is directly proportional to the thoroughness of the preparations made by the negotiators. Advance preparation is necessary for both the parties because of the following reasons:

1. To substantiate its positions by gathering the relevant facts and figures.
2. To understand the complex issues and estimate the costs of innovative proposals and programmes.
3. To create confidence with in the bargaining team.

The negotiators from management side are required to:[7]

1. Prepare the specific proposals for changes in the contract language.
2. Determine the general size of the economic package, which the company proposes to offer.
3. Prepare statistical displays and related data for uses in negotiation.

The negotiators from employees' side should collect the information in the following areas:[8]

1. The financial position of the company and its ability to pay.
2. The attitude of the management towards various issues, as shown in the past negotiations or inferred from negotiations in similar companies.

3. The attitude and desires of the employees.

2. Bargaining issues

The major issues/topics that are included in collective bargaining agreements are the following:

(i) *Recognition*

Usually, this section appears in the beginning of the labour agreement. Its purpose is to identify the union that is recognised as the bargaining representative and to describe the bargaining unit, that is, the employees for whom the union speaks.[9]

(ii) *Management rights*

This section spells out the rights of the management in the labour agreement. The contents of management rights section vary by industry, organisation and union. Generally, management rights include following areas:[10]

1. Freedom to select the business objectives of the company.
2. Freedom to determine the use to which the material assets of the enterprise will be devoted.
3. Power to discipline for cause.

(iii) *Compensation and benefits*

This section covers a large part of most of labour agreements. This includes topics such as basic wage rates, cost of living allowance, wage differentials, overtime pay, pension plans, paid vacations, paid holidays, layoff or severance pay, unemployment pension, retrenchment pay, health insurance plans, etc.

(iv) *Employee security*

This includes establishment of procedures that cover job security for individual employees. A key topic related with employee security is the seniority, i.e. the length of service of an employee in the organisation. Agreement on seniority is important because the person with the most seniority, as defined in the labour agreement, is typically the last to be laid off and the first to be recalled.[11]

(v) *Union security*

This is one of the most important item negotiated during collective bargaining agreements. The main objectives of union security provision are to ensure that the union continues to exist and perform its various functions. Some basic forms of union security clauses are the following:

(a) Closed Shop

In this arrangement a worker must be the member of the union at the time of his employment and continue to do so in order to retain his job.

(b) Union Shop

In this arrangement a worker would become a member of the union within a specified period of his employment in that enterprise and that he would continue his membership in order to retain his job.

(c) Membership Shop

In this arrangement all the employees who are members of the union on a specified date or who become members after that date are obligated to maintain their memberships until the termination of the agreement, as a condition of employment.

(d) Agency Shop

An agency shop provision does not require employees to join the union, however, the labour agreement requires that, as a condition of employment, each non-union member of the bargaining unit pay the union the equivalent of membership dues as a kind of tax, or service charge, in return for the union acting as the bargaining agent.[12]

(e) Open Shop

This arrangement shows the absence of union security, rather than its presence. The open shop is employment that has equal terms for the union members. In this arrangement, no employee is required to join or contribute to the union financially.[13]

(f) Checkoff of Dues

In this arrangement, the organisation agrees to withhold the union dues from their members' paychecks and to forward the money directly to the union.

(vi) *Job-related factors*

These factors include safety issues, work rules, work standards, etc.

(vii) *Grievance procedure*

A part of labour agreements is also devoted towards the grievance procedure. This includes the grievance redressal procedure through which the employees can express their dissatisfaction and appeal for action.

3. Negotiation

Once the preparations have been made and issues have been identified, the next logical step is negotiating the agreement. This phase of collective bargaining takes few days until the final agreement is reached out. Negotiations should be conducted in a private conference room, not openly. There is a need to develop and maintain clear and open lines of communication between the two parties. This phase involves a certain amount of give and take, its success depends upon the skills, tactics and abilities of the negotiators (see Exhibit 23.1).

Exhibit 23.1: The Guidelines for Negotiations

The "Dos" of Negotiations:

1. Do seek more (or offer less) than you plan to receive (or give).
2. Do negotiate in private, not through the media.
3. Do let both sides win. Otherwise the other side may retaliate.
4. Do start with easy issues.
5. Do remember that negotiations are seldom over when the agreement is concluded. Eventually the contract will be renegotiated.
6. Do resolve deadlocks by stressing past progress, another point, or counter proposals.
7. Do enlist the support of the Federal Mediation and conciliation service if a strike seems likely.

The "Don'ts" of Negotiations:

1. Do not make your best offer first; that is so uncommon that the other side will expect more.

2. Do not seek unwanted changes; you may get them.
3. Do not say "no" absolutely, unless your organisation will back you up absolutely.
4. Do not violate a confidence.
5. Do not settle too quickly. Union members may think a quick settlement is not a good one.
6. Do not let the other side bypass your team and go directly to the top management.
7. Do not let the top management actually participate in face-to-face negotiations. They are often inexperienced and poorly informed.

Source: William B. Werther and Keith Davis, *Human Resources and Personnel Management,* McGraw-Hill, New York, 1993, p. 574.

4. Breakdown in negotiations

Sometimes the negotiations may break down, even though both labour and management sincerely want to arrive at an amicable settlement. In order to remove breakdown following measures are generally used:

(a) Third party intervention such as mediation and arbitration;
(b) Union strategies such as strikes and boycotts; and
(c) Management strategies such as lockout and hiring replacement (in case of strike) either temporarily or permanently.

5. Ratifying the agreement

After the negotiators reached on a tentative agreement on all the contract terms, then they prepare a written agreement covering all these terms along with the effective and termination dates. Now the two sides usually return to their constituencies for approval. Often, the approval process is easier for the management than for the labour. In case of labour side, the approval process is complex. Until and unless a majority of members voting in a ratification election approve it, the proposal or tentative agreement is not final.

6. Administration of the agreement

Perhaps this is the most important part of the collective bargaining process. The main problem encountered in the contract administration is uniform interpretation and application of the contract's terms.[14] Contract administration is a day-to-day activity. The aim of both the parties should be that to make the agreement work for the benefit of all concerned. But this is not an easy job. The management is primarily responsible for implementing the agreement. This may include meetings not only to point out significant features but also to provide clause-by-clause analysis of the contract terms. Supervisors, especially, need to know their responsibilities and what to do in case disagreements arise. Also, the HR manager plays a crucial role in the day-to-day administration of the contract. The HR manager gives advice on the matters of discipline, resolve the grievances arising out of the agreement. Also, he or she should help the first line supervisors in establishing good working relationships within the terms of the agreement.

TYPES OF BARGAINING

A collective bargaining process generally consists of following types of activites:[15]

1. Intra-organisational bargaining

In this type of bargaining, both the employers' and unions' executives discuss the general demands/strategies and arrive at a consensus of approach among themselves before parties meet at the bargaining table.

2. Attitudinal structuring

It implies an approach to the collective bargaining as an ongoing relationship, rather than as a piecemeal, adhoc settlement. Here, the focus shifts from a mere settlement of issues to evolving long-term bipartite relationships whereby two parties live and work together.

3. Distributive bargaining

In this one party gains and the other loses. For the management, labour is a cost and must be curtailed, for the labour they must win as many concessions or demands as is possible. It is, therefore, a 'zero sum' game, i.e. one party's gain is another's loss.[16]

4. Integrative bargaining

This is perhaps the most desirable form of bargaining. It aims at expanding the size of the cake with both parties getting a continuously bigger share. In this type of bargaining, productivity aspects are taken into account and through a process of mutual problem-solving the sum total of the gains can be increased. The problem of distribution does come up, but where the approach is one of concern for the viability of the enterprise, as also with one's own growth, then the reconciliation of interests is much greater. Therefore, this becomes a 'non-zero sum game' with a more open and acceptable approach to productivity increase and sharing of such gains in a mutually satisfactory manner.[17]

PRE-REQUISITES OF SUCCESSFUL COLLECTIVE BARGAINING

The prerequisites of successful collective bargaining process are the following:

1. There should be a truly representative, enlightened and strong trade union.
2. There should be progressive and strong management, which is conscious of its obligations, duties and responsibilities to the employers, employees, consumers and the nation.
3. It is essential for the management to recognise a trade union.
4. The negotiating team should be properly selected. It should have a mixed composition of experts of different key areas, for example, finance, industrial relations, production, etc.
5. Both the parties should bring change in their attitudes towards each other. There is a need to have open minds, listen and appreciate the other party's concern and point of view and have some flexibility in making adjustments.
6. Collective bargaining is best conducted at plant level.
7. Both the parties should rely on facts and figures to support point of view during collective bargaining.
8. Unfair labour practices should be avoided and abandoned by both sides.

9. Both the parties should enter upon negotiations on points of difference with a view to reach on agreement.
10. Once the collective agreement has been reached, it must be put down in writing.
11. The agreement should be honoured and fairly implemented.

KEY TERMS

Agency shop
Armed truce
Attitudinal structuring
Bargaining issues
Checkoff of dues
Closed shop
Collective bargaining
Collusion
Distributive bargaining
Integrative bargaining
Management rights
Membership shop
Negotiation
Power bargaining

QUESTIONS

1. Define the term 'collective bargaining'. What are the features of collective bargaining?
2. Describe the objectives of collective bargaining.
3. Discuss in detail the collective bargaining process.
4. What are the various types of bargaining?
5. What are the prerequisites for a successful collective bargaining?
6. Define the following:
   (a) Agency shop
   (b) Closed shop
   (c) Membership shop

ENDNOTES

1. S. Webb and B.P. Webb, *Industrial Democracy*, Longman Green & Co., London, 1920, p. 185.
2. *Encyclopedia of Social Sciences*, Vol. III, 1951, p. 628.
3. B.R. Patil, *Collective Bargaining: Perspectives and Practices*, University Press, 1993.

4. C. Kerr, "Employer Polices Towards Industrial Relations", *Year Book of American Labour*, Vol. II.
5. R. Wayne Mondy and Robert M. Noe, *Human Resource Management*, Ninth Edition, Pearson Education, Delhi, p. 427.
6. A.A. Sloan and F. Witney, *Labour Relations*, Fourth Edition, Prentice Hall, Englewood Cliffs, NJ, 1981, pp. 28-35.
7. R.S. Schuler et al., *Effective Personnel Management*, West Publishing, New York, 1989, p. 589.
8. *Ibid.*
9. R. Wayne Mondy and Robert M. Noe, op. cit., p. 432.
10. *Ibid.*, p. 433.
11. *Ibid.*, p. 435.
12. A. Gregg, "The Constitutionality of Requiring Annual Renewal of Union Fee Objections in an Agency Shop", *Texas Law Review*, 2000 April, pp. 1159-1180.
13. S. Winston, "Labour: When Contractors are Organised", *ENR* (Dec. 20, 1999), pp. 30-32.
14. R. Wayne Mondy and Robert M. Noe, op. cit., p. 441.
15. R.E. Walton and R.B. McKersie, *A Behavioural Theory of Labour Negotiation*, McGraw-Hill, New York, 1965.
16. Arun Monappa, *Industrial Relations*, Tata McGraw-Hill, New Delhi, 1985, p. 111.
17. *Ibid.*, p. 111.

Global/International Human Resource Management

24

LEARNING OBJECTIVES

After studying this chapter, you should be able to:

1. Understand the concept of GHRM/IHRM
2. Describe the various modes of entering foreign market
3. Describe the process of GHRM
4. Understand the types of global staff
5. Understand the approaches to global staffing

Globalisation, as defined by the IMF, is the growing economic interdependence of countries worldwide through increasing volume and variety of cross-border transactions in goods and services and of international capital flows and also through the more rapid and widespread diffusion of technology. All institutions have to make global competitiveness a strategic goal. No institution, whether a business, a university or hospital, can hope to survive, let alone to succeed, unless it measures up to the standards set by the leaders in its field, any place in the world.[1]

EVOLUTION OF GLOBAL BUSINESS

For many companies to grow in today's domestic economic environment, they must expand overseas because often the market has been saturated at home.[2] Generally, companies evolve to the point of being truly global over an extended period. Some of the different modes of entering foreign market are as follows:

1. Exporting

This is one of the oldest and common way of entering the foreign market. In this kind of market entry strategy, a company may do the complete manufacturing of the product domestically and export it to the foreign market.

2. Licensing

Under licensing agreement, a company in one country (the licensor) grants company in another country (the licensee) the right to use its intellectual properties (such as patents, trade marks, copyrights, technology, technical know-how, marketing skill, manufacturing process, etc.) for a specific period of time.

3. Franchising

It is a form of licensing in which a parent company (the franchiser) grants another independent entity (the franchisee) the right to do business in a prescribed manner. This right can take the form of selling the franchiser's products, using its name, production and marketing techniques, or general business approach.[3] Usually, licensing is limited to manufacturers, whereas franchising is popular with service firms like hotels and restaurants. Also, franchisees must follow stricter operational guidelines than do licensees.

4. Joint ventures

This refers to sharing of ownership and management in an enterprise. In other words, ownership and management are shared between a foreign firm and a local firm. Sometimes, there may be more than two parties involved.

5. Mergers and acquisitions

Mergers and acquisitions provide an instant access to markets and distribution network. A large number of Indian companies are using this route of entering foreign market (see Exhibit 24.1).

Exhibit 24.1: The Tata-Corus Deal

Victory of ethical business

It is natural for the Tata-Corus deal to provoke parallels with the Mittal-Arcelor merger. Since the Tata are known to be a benevolent employer and reputed for honesty in business, there have been no howls of protest or arguments of national pride getting hurt—as it was in the Arcelor case—against the Rs. 9,100 crore takeover, the largest by an Indian company. Mittal Steel was seen as a friendly business rival. The Tatas will retain, at least for the time being, the present Corus identity. The British reaction to the deal has been low key, though company workers in the UK and the Netherlands fear job losses in restructuring. Compared to Corus, Tata Steel is a low-cost producer of steel and the integration will benefit both.

Raising money for the prized acquisition will not be a problem. Problem, if any, may come from rival Brazilian firm CSN which has appointed a noted banker, Lazards, as an adviser to snatch the deal from the Tatas. If a bidding war breaks out, the Tatas have made it known that they would withdraw. That is typical of the Tata mindset. The group is reputed for not getting what they want. That is saying a lot in the Indian work culture. That is what commands respect at home and abroad.

Mergers and acquisitions are common in steel. The past two years have seen 305 such deals. After taking over a company three times its size, Tata Steel will become the sixth largest global producer of steel with Arcelor-Mittal occupying the top slot and featuring in the Fourtune 500 list. The Tatas began their acquisitions with Daewoo of South Korea and include British tea giant Tetley and NetSteel of Singapore. How many such deals prove beneficial in the long run remains to be seen. But the regret remains why for so long Indian enterprise had remained tied in chains. By breaking shackles that had bound industry for decades, globalisation has allowed Indian ambition to spread.

Source: *The Tribune*, 24th October, 2006.

Indian companies hunting for assets across the globe have acquired 307 companies worth over $ 20 billion, i.e. over Rs. 90,000 crore. Acquisitions rose from 46 in 2004 to a whopping 130 in 2005. According to Anji Reddy, Chairman of Dr. Reddy's Laboratory, "India is unstoppable. What is driving the acquisitions is the fact that we have grown gusty". Their ambitions are driven by the need for global scale and are fuelled by a new confidence. According to Nanadan Nilekani, CEO, Infosys technologies, "Having survived domestic competition, Indian companies are now learning to be globalised." Commenting upon latest Tata-Corus deal, Tata Sons chairman Ratan Tata said, "Acquisitions for the sake of acquisitions will often not yield the necessary results. We need to link each acquisition with the industry in which a company is operating and the strategic context of that industry. The ultimate objective is to leverage opportunities and resources, wherever in the world they may be resident, to improve the competitiveness of our companies".[4]

Depending upon their degree of global involvement, the companies may be of following types:

Multinational Corporation (MNC)

According to ILO report, "the essential nature of the multinational enterprise lies in the fact that its managerial headquarters are located in one country (parent or home country) while the enterprise carries out operations in a number of other countries as well (host countries)".[5]

Global Corporation

A global corporation views the entire world as one entity. This type of organisation has corporate units in a number of countries that are integrated to operate as one organisation worldwide.

GLOBAL/INTERNATIONAL HUMAN RESOURCE MANAGEMENT (GHRM/IHRM)

GHRM is the utilization of global human resources to achieve organisational objectives without regard to geographic boundaries.[6] GHRM is the process of procurement, allocation and effective utilization of human resources in international business. As Figure 24.1 shows GHRM is the interplay among the three dimensions. These are human resource activities, types of employees and countries of operation. In other words, the basic human resource processes such as HR planning, procurement, training and development, induction, compensation, performance management and industrial relations are influenced by two other groups of variables. First group of variables consists of types of employees; these may be host-country nationals, parent-country nationals and third-country nationals. Second group of variables consists of countries involved, these are the host country where a subsidiary may be located, the home country where the company has its headquarters and the other countries that may be the source of finance or labour.

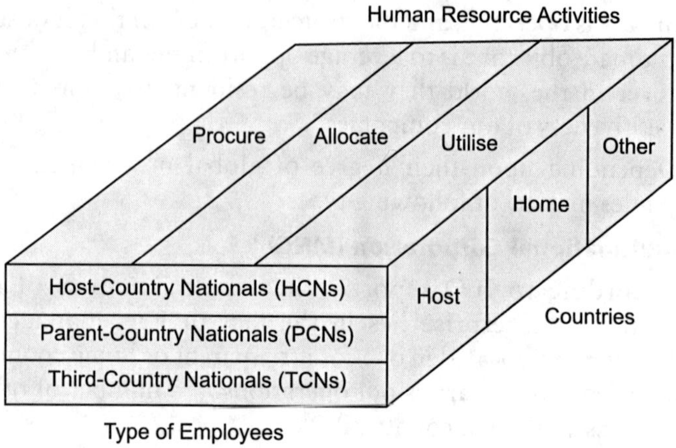

Fig. 24.1: A Model of GHRM

Source: Cited in SC Gupta, *Textbook of International HRM*, Macmillian, New Delhi, 2006, p. 3.

DIFFERENCES BETWEEN GLOBAL AND DOMESTIC HRM

The practice of HRM in the international context is different from its domestic counterpart in following number of ways:[7]

1. Being responsible for a greater number of functions and activities, such as the selection, training and management of international assignees.
2. Having to expand one's area of expertise to include a much broader knowledge of foreign country employment laws and global organisation designs.
3. Having to get much more closely involved with employees' lives as the firm moves employees to foreign assignments. For example, collecting information and furnishing to visa authorities about aids or martial status of employees.
4. Being involved with a greatly expanded and constantly changing mix of employees (from the host country and foreign locales), adding considerable diversity and complexity to the HR tasks.

5. Having to cope with more external influences, for example, having to consider the impact of foreign cultures and laws.
6. Having to face greater exposure to problems and liabilities (for example, making mistakes in expatriate assignments can cost as much as US$ 4 million per assignee). The accumulated direct and indirect costs can be huge.
7. Additional responsibilities like translation of language, both at headquarters and at the subsidiary level, organising schooling and housing for expatriates and providing administrative services.
8. Management of differential compensation due to variety of allowances and adjustments.
9. More emphasis on activities like international relocation and orientation, both pre-departure and post-departure cultural training. Knowledge of international taxation, rate of inflation and cost of living, including currency fluctuation.
10. Diversity management, like managing people from different cultural and political backgrounds and gender differences.
11. More contacts with government officials for obtaining visas, tax certificates, fixing of meetings and so on.
12. More coordination and travel to assess performance of expatriates and solve problems.
13. More risk management as threats from terrorists, kidnappers and protecting intellectual property rights of firms.
14. More public relations work to enhance the multinationals image and deal with human rights and other NGOs and interest groups operating in different countries.

THE PROCESS OF GHRM

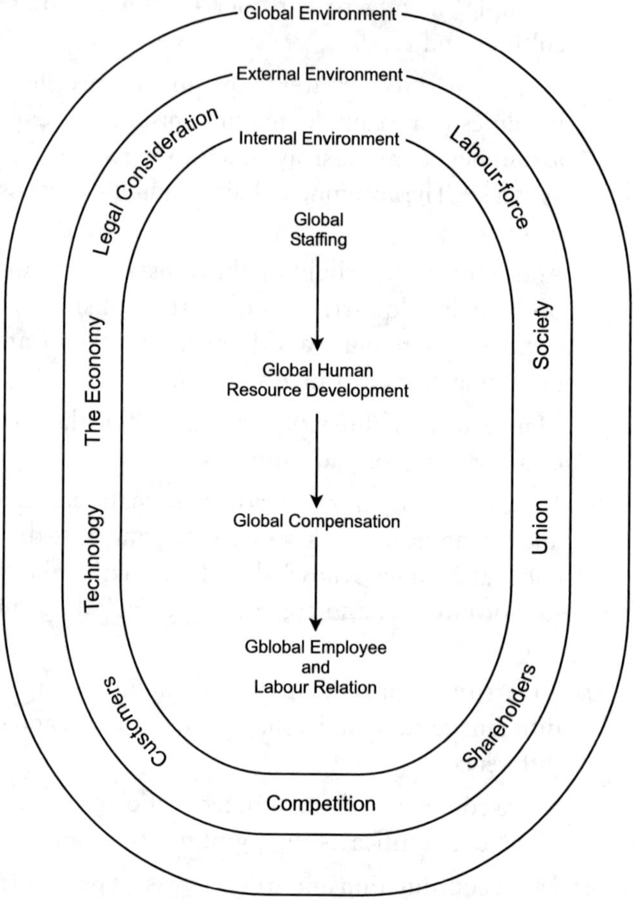

Fig. 24.2: The HRM in the Global Environment

Source: Adapted from Mondy, R.W. and Noe, R.M., *Human Resource Management*, 9th Edition, Pearson Education, Delhi, p. 484.

The Figure 24.2 depicts that the functional areas associated with global human resource management are the same as those experienced domestically. Those engaged in the management of global human resources develop and work through an integrated international human resource management system similar to the one they experience domestically. Though the functional areas are same, but how they are implemented may differ.

1. Global staffing

The global staff members may be of three types:

(i) *Expatriate*

An expatriate is a person employed in a foreign country. In other words, it is an employee who is not a citizen of the country in which the organisation's operation is located but is a citizen of the country in which the organisation is headquartered.

(ii) *Host-Country National (HCN)*

HCN refers to an employee who is a citizen of the country where the subsidiary is located, for example, an Indian citizen working for a Japanese company in India.

(iii) *Third-Country National (TCN)*

TCN refers to a citizen of one country, working in a second country and employed by the firm headquartered in a third country, for example, an Indian citizen working for a German company in England. Table 24.1 presents the advantages and disadvantages of each choice.

Staffing policy/approaches

There are four major approaches to global staffing. These are the following:

(i) *Ethnocentric staffing*

This staffing policy means hiring home country individual for higher/senior level foreign positions. The major logic behind this staffing policy is that the managers are well aware of the organisation's policies and programmes and they can implement these policies and programmes efficiently. Japanese managers have shown their success in implementing their home country policy. The expatriate selection criteria should include cultural adaptability, strong communication skills, technical competence, professional or operational expertise, global experience, country-specific experience, interpersonal skills, language skills, family flexibility and country or region-specific consideration.[8]

The difficulty in adjusting to a foreign country by managers often leads to 'culture shock', which means that the expatriates feel uncomfortable in a foreign country environment that changes

Table 24.1: The Advantages and Disadvantages of Using PCNs, TCNs and HCNs

	Advantages	Disadvantages
PCNs	• Familiarity with the home office, goals, objectives, policies and practices. • Easy organizational control and coordination. • Promising managers are given international exposure. • PCNs are the best people for assignment because of special skills and experiences.	• Difficulty in adapting to the foreign language and the socio-economic, political, cultural and legal environment. • Excessive cost of selecting, training and maintaining expatriate managers and their families abroad. • Promotional opportunities for HCNs are limited. • PCNs may impose an inappropriate HQ style. • Compensation for PCNs and HCNs may differ. • Family adjustment problems, especially concerning the unemployed spouses.
HCNs	• Familiarity with the socio-economic, political and legal environment and with business practices in the host country. • Lower cost incurred in hiring as compared to PCNs and TCNs • Promotional opportunities to locals and consequently their motivation and commitment. • Responds effectively to the host country's demands for localization of the subsidiary's operations. • Languages and other barriers are eliminated. • Continuity of management improves, since HCNs stay longer in positions.	• Difficulty in exercising effective control over the subsidiary's operations, • Communication difficulties in dealing with home office personnel. • Lack of opportunity for the home country's nationals to gain international and cross-cultural experience. • HCNs have limited career opportunity outside the subsidiary. • Hiring HCNs may encourage a federation of nationals rather than global units.
TCNs	• Salary and benefit requirements may be lower than for PCNs. • TCNs may be better informed than PCNs about host country environment. • TCNs are truly international managers.	• Host country government may resent hiring TCNs. • TCNs may not want to return to their own countries after assignment. • Host country's sensitivity with respect to nationals of specific countries. • HCNs are impeded in their efforts to upgrade their own ranks and assure responsible positions in the multinational subsidiaries.

Source: K. Aswathappa, *Human Resource and Personnel Management*, Tata McGraw-Hill, New Delhi, 2006, p. 648.

their psychological orientation and makes them irritable, home sick and low performing.[9] In other words, culture shock means the problems faced while working in a foreign country. In cases where expatriates are able to adapt themselves to the local environment in the host country and find themselves unsuitable for the home country environment after working abroad for some time, they prefer to stay abroad. In case the company compels them to return home, they suffer from 'reverse culture shock'.[10]

(ii) *Polycentric Staffing*

This staffing policy means that in foreign operations, more host country nationals are used throughout the organisation, from top to bottom.

(iii) *Regiocentric Staffing*

This policy is based upon the logic that regional insiders know what neighbouring countries want. An organisation implements a regional staffing strategy when synergistic benefits can be obtained by sharing functions across regions. For example, a regiocentric firm might select an Indian subsidiary to manage its Asian operations and a German subsidiary to manage its European operation.

(iv) *Geocentric Staffing*

This staffing approach uses a worldwide-integrated business strategy. The ultimate objective of the organisation is to hire the best person available for a position, regardless of where the individual comes from.

Table 24.2 shows the relationship among the above-discussed staffing approaches.

2. Global HRD

After selecting the staff for the foreign assignment, the next step in GHRM is their training and development. Global training and development is needed because people, jobs and organisations are often quite different globally.[11] The training and development programme should start as soon as employees are selected, definitely before beginning the global assignment. Organisations are recognising that expatriate employees and their families face special situations and pressures that training and development

Table 24.2: Relationships among Strategic Mode, Organisational Variables and Staffing Approaches

	Orientation			
Aspects of the Enterprises	Ethnocentric	Polycentric	Regiocentric	Global
Primary strategic orientation/stage	International	Multi-domestic	Regional	Trans-national
Perpetuation (recruiting, staffing, development)	People of home country developed for key positions everywhere in the world	People of local nationality developed for key positions in their own country	Regional people developed for key positions anywhere in the region	Best people everywhere in the world developed for key positions everywhere in the world
Complexity of organisation	Complex in home country, simple in subsidiaries	Varied and independent	Highly interdependent on a regional basis	"Global Web": complex, independent, worldwide alliances/network
Authority; decision making	High in headquarters	Relatively low in headquarters	High regional headquarters and/or high collaboration among subsidiaries	Collaboration of headquarters and subsidiaries around the world
Evaluation and control	Home standards applied to people and performance	Determined locally	Determined regionally	Globally integrated

(*Contd...*)

Aspects of the Enterprises	Ethnocentric	Polycentric	Regiocentric	Global
Rewards	High in headquarters; low in subsidiaries	Wide variation; can be high or low rewards for subsidiary performance	Rewards for contribution to regional objectives	Rewards to international and local executives for reaching local and world-wide objectives based on global company goals
Communication; information flow	High volume of orders, commands, advice to subsidiaries	Little to and from headquarters; little among subsidiaries	Little to and from corporate headquarters, but may be high to and from regional headquarters and among countries	Horizontal; network relations
Geographic identification	Nationality of owner	Nationality of host country	Regional company	Truly global company, but Identifying with national interest ("glocal")

Source: D.A. Heenan and H.V. Perlmutter, *Multinational Organisation Development,* Reading MA: Addison-Wesley, 1979, pp. 18-19.

activities must prepare them to deal with.[12] Figure 24.3 shows the expatriate preparation and development programme.

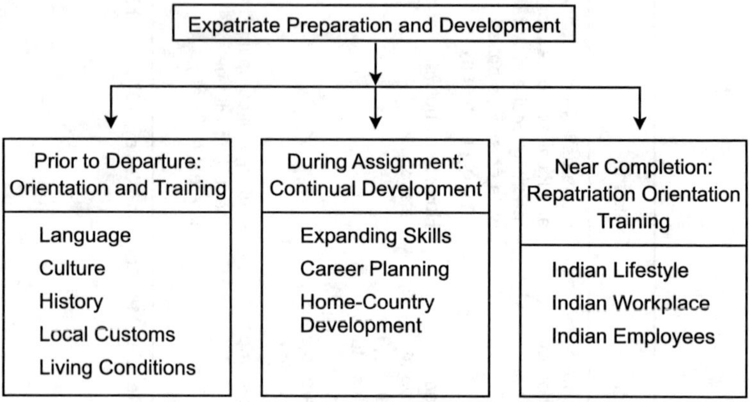

Fig. 24.3: The Expatriate Preparation and Development Programme

Source: Adapted from Mondy, R.W. and Noe, R.M., *Human Resource Management,* 9th Edition, Pearson Education, p. 487.

As the Figure 24.3 illustrates, expatriate preparation and development involves pre-departure orientation and training, continual development and repatriation orientation and training. The pre-move orientation involves training and familiarization in language, culture, history, living conditions, and local customs and peculiarities.[13] Specifically, the training programme concentrates on cultural training, language training and practical training.[14] Cultural training acquaints the employees regarding the host country's culture, which helps them to deal with the person there. Although English is a language of international business but employees are also taught about the language of the host country. Practical training provides the employees ease in day-to-day activities in the host country.

Continual development involves expanding both professional and operational skills when appropriate, comprehensive career planning and involvement in home-country development programme.[15] Repatriation refers to the process of bringing expatriates home. Prior to repatriation, training and orientation is also essential. This training is required to prepare the worker and his/her family for a smooth return to the home-country culture and to prepare the expatriate's new subordinates and supervisor for the return. This training ensures preparing the individual and the family for returning to the Indian lifestyle.

3. Global compensation

Variations in laws, living costs, tax policies and other factors all must be considered when a company is establishing global compensation packages.[16] The issues that should be considered while establishing appropriate pay package for a country are: minimum wages, working time information such as annual holidays, vacation time and pay, paid personal days, standard weekly working hours, probation periods and overtime restrictions and payments covering severance practices.[17] Both internal as well as external factors affect expatriate compensation. Figure 24.4 shows these factors, which are self-explanatory.

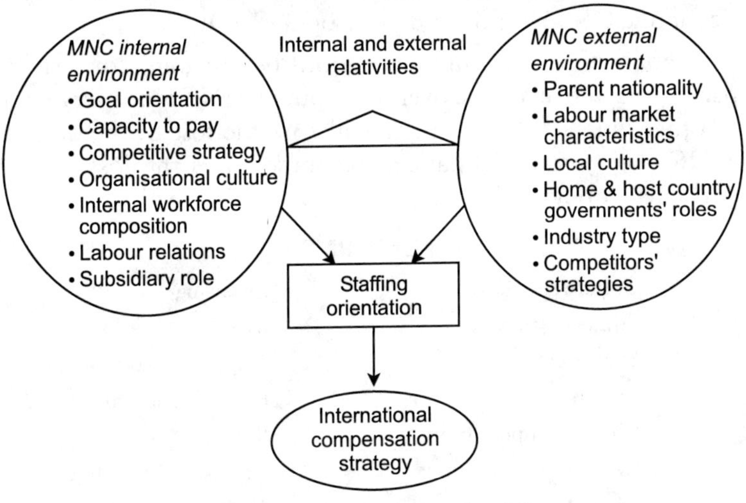

Fig 24.4: The Factors Affecting International Compensation

Source: Anne-WilHarzing, et al., *International Strategic Human Resource Management*, p. 311.

4. Global employee and labour relations

This is the last component of GHRM. An organisation's desire and ability to integrate its operations worldwide can be halted by labour unions. The nature and strength of unions differ from one nation to another, with labour unions ranging from non-existent to relatively strong. For instance, labour unions in Italy virtually shut down the entire country, protesting the government's plan that would, for the first time, allow companies to layoff workers.[18] Whereas in some South American countries such as Chile, collective bargaining for textile workers, miners and carpenters is prohibited, all negotiations are limited to the individual company and the unions are generally allowed only in companies of 25 workers or more.[19] Keeping in mind that above discussed instances, most of MNC's allow their subsidiaries considerable autonomy in managing labour relations as these subsidiaries are more capable of solving the local problems. The commonly adopted tactics of unions are strike, formation of International Trade Secretariats (ITS) (these function as a loose confederation to provide links for the national unions in a specific trade or industry) and seek intervention from International Labour Organisation (ILO), European Union (EU) and Organisation for Economic Co-operation and Development (OECD).

Labour unions should be cautious before going for a strike because its impact on the overall output of MNC is not very large as other units of the company make up the loss of the output. MNCs enjoy strong financial resources thus the loss at one particular foreign subsidiary can be easily absorbed.

KEY TERMS

Culture shock
Ethnocentric staffing
Expatriate
Franchising
Global compensation
Geocentric staffing
GHRM
HCN
Licensing
MNC
Polycentric staffing
Regiocentric staffing
Repatriation
Reverse culture shock
TCN

QUESTIONS

1. What is GHRM/IHRM? How does it differ from domestic HRM?
2. Describe the different modes of entering a foreign market.
3. Give different types of global staff.

4. What are the approaches for global staff?
5. Define the following:
   (a) Culture shock
   (b) Reverse culture shock
   (c) Expatriate training and development

ENDNOTES

1. P. Drucker, *Management Challenges for the 21st Century*, Harper Business, New York, 1999, p. 61.
2. M. Prewitt, "Global Expansion Requires World of Planning, Panelists Agree", *Nation's Restaurant News*, 21st October, 2002, p. 58.
3. D.W. Hackett, "The International Expansion of US Franchise System", in W.J. Keegan and C.S. Mayers (Eds.) *Multinational Product Management*, AMA, Chicago, 1979, pp. 61-81.
4. Ratan Tata, "Overseas Acquisitions", *India Today*, November 6, 2006, p. 42.
5. ILO, *Multinational Enterprises and Social Policy*, Geneva, 1973, p. 3.
6. R. Wayne Mondy and Robert M. Noe, *Human Resource Management*, Ninth Edition, Pearson Education, Delhi, p. 483.
7. S.C. Gupta, *Textbook of International HRM*, Macmillan, New Delhi, 2006, p. 4.
8. C.M. Soloman, "Success Aboard Depends on More Than Job Skills", *Personnel Journal*, April 1994, 73, pp. 51-59.
9. V. Sharan, *International Business*, Second Edition, Pearson Education, Delhi, p. 413.
10. *Ibid.*
11. K. Roberts, E. Ernst and C. Ozeki, "Managing the Global Workforce: Challenges and Strategies", *The Academy of Management Executive"*, November 1, 1998, p. 93.
12. J. Britt, "Expatriates Want More Support From Home", *HR Magazine*, 47, July 2002, p. 21.
13. M.E. Mendelhall and C. Wiley, "Strangers in a Strange Land: The Relationship between Expatriate Adjustment and Impression Management", *American Behavioural Scientist*, March/April 1994, pp. 605-621.
14. P.J. Dowling and R.S. Schuler, *International Dimensions of HR Management*, 1990, PSW-Kent, Boston.
15. R. Wayne Mondy and Robert M. Noe, op. cit., p. 487.

16. *Ibid.*, p. 488.
17. N.B. Krupp, "Global Compensation Planning—Establishing and Maintaining a Competitive Edge in the International Market Place", *Compensation and Benefits Management*, 18 Spring 2002, pp. 54-56.
18. K. Rankin, "European Labor Laws No Solution to American Retail Strugglers", *DSN Retailing Today*, June 24, 2002, p. 14.
19. R. Wayne Mondy and Robert M. Noe, op. cit., p. 490-491.

Small HR Dictionary

Accident. An accident is an unplanned and uncontrolled event in which an action or reaction of an object, a substance, a person or a radiation results in personal injury.

Achievement Tests. These tests measure applicant's abilities that have already been acquainted by training or experience.

Agency Shop. An agency shop provision does not require employees to join the union, however, the labour agreement requires that, as a condition of employment, each non-union member of the bargaining unit pay the union the equivalent of membership dues as a kind of tax, or service charge, in return for the union acting as the bargaining agent.

Alternate/Parallel/Equivalent-Form Method. This method also uses a test-retest approach, but instead of using the same test for the second time, an alternate/similar form of the test is administered.

Application Blank/Form. The form that gives information on education, experience and skills.

Appraisal Interview. This is a discussion, following a performance appraisal, in which the supervisor and employee discuss the employee's rating and possible remedial actions.

Apprenticeship. A programme in which an individual is considered to be learning a skill.

Aptitude Tests. These tests are designed to measure specific abilities like mechanical aptitude, numerical aptitude, clerical aptitude and dexterity.

Arbitration. This is the last step in the dispute settlement procedure. The decision of the arbitrator, who is a neutral individual, is binding on both the parties.

Attitudinal Structuring. It implies an approach to the collective bargaining as an ongoing relationship, rather than as a piecemeal, adhoc settlement.

Attrition. A policy of an organisation to reduce the company's workforce by not refilling job vacancies that are created by turnover.

Autonomous Work Groups. A team responsible for the 'whole and meaningful' work. Team members plan, execute and control the work processes together.

Bandhs. This means closed or locked. This conveys the idea that everything is to be closed or blocked.

Bargaining Issues. The major issues/topics that are included in collective bargaining agreements.

Bargaining Unit. It is a group of employees the trade union will be authorised to represent.

Behaviour Modeling. This is structured approach to teach specific supervisory skill. This is based on the social learning theory in which the trainee is provided with a specific model of behaviour and is informed in advance of the consequences of engaging in that type of behaviour.

Behavioural Interview. These interviews ask interviewees to describe how they reacted to actual situations in the past.

Behaviourally Anchored Rating Scales (BARS). It attempts to evaluate job performance in terms of key/specific behaviours that are important to success or failure on the job. BARS are produced by merging critical-incident method with the graphic rating concept.

Boycott. The aim of boycott is to disrupt the normal functioning of the organisation. It is appeals for the workers to voluntary withdraw the cooperation.

Brainstorming. This is creativity-training technique, it helps people to solve problems in a new and different way. In this technique, the trainees are given the opportunity to generate ideas openly and without any fear of judgement.

Burnout. It is condition of physical, emotional and mental exhaustion caused by excessive striving to reach an unrealistic work-related target.

Business Process Reengineering (BPR). A fundamental rethinking and redesign of business processes to achieve improvements in cost, quality, speed and service.

Cafeteria Programme/system. This system allows employees to choose from a variety of benefits that are most valuable to him or her.

Career Counselling. Assisting employees to find suitable and best career goals and paths.

Career Development. A deliberate, formal and ongoing effort that focuses on developing capable and enriched employees.

Career Goals. These are the future positions an individual strives to reach.

Career Path. It shows the possible directions and opportunities available to an individual in an organisation.

Career. A career can be defined as a sequence of separate but related work activities that provides continuity, order and meaning in a person's life.

Checklist. A checklist is prepared in which several questions in relation to a particular job are included. The rater has to simply mark the tick against the column of yes or no.

Checkoff of Dues. In this arrangement, the organisation agrees to withhold the union dues from their members' paychecks and to forward the money directly to the union.

Closed Shop. In this arrangement a worker must be the member of the union at the time of his employment and continue to do so in order to retain his job.

Coaching. It refers to meetings and discussion between a manager and his or her employees regarding the latter's career development. Coaching involves setting of conducive environment, actively listen to employee, ask questions and provide useful feedback.

Coinsurance. These are the payments made to cover health care expenses.

Collective Bargaining. Collective bargaining is a procedure by which employers and a group of employees agree upon the conditions of work.

Compulsory Arbitration. Compulsory arbitration implies when the parties are required to accept arbitration without any willingness on their part.

Concurrent Validity. A way to establish criterion-related validity that involves administering a test to employees on the job and correlating their scores with job performance data.

Construct Validity. It refers to the extent the test measures the psychological characteristics such as intelligence, motivation, emotional stability, etc.

Content Validity. This means how well the contents/items of the test, as a sample, represent all the situations that could have been included.

Contributions. This refers to the payment made for the benefits coverage.

Criterion-related Vaildity. This is concerned with the relationship between test scores and the subsequent job performance.

Critical Incidents. Critical incidents refer to certain key acts of behaviour that make the difference between success and failure on a job.

Demotion. Demotion is just the opposite of promotion. It means shifting an employee to a lower level where responsibilities and wages are less.

Discharge. Discharge also means termination from services of an employee, but not necessarily as a punitive measure.

Dismissal. Dismissal takes place when the employer terminates the services of the employee.

Distributive Bargaining. In this one party gains and the other loses. For the management, labour is a cost and must be curtailed, for the labour they must win as many concessions or demands as is possible. It is, therefore, a 'zero sum' game i.e., one party's gain is another's loss.

Dry Promotion. This type of promotion involves increase in responsibilities and status without any increase in pay.

Employee Benefits. Employee benefits or indirect compensation are group membership rewards that provide security for employees and their family.

Employee Compensation. Employee compensation refers to all forms of pay or rewards going to employees and arising from their employment.

Employee Health. Health refers to employees' freedom from physical or emotional illness.

Employee Safety. Safety involves protecting employees from injuries caused by work related accidents.

Employee Security. This includes establishment of procedures that cover job security for individual employees.

Employee Welfare. Employee welfare can be defined as anything done for the comfort and improvement, intellectual and social, of the employees over and above the wages paid, which is not a necessity of the industry.

Ethnocentric staffing. This staffing policy means hiring home country individual for higher/senior level foreign positions.

Exit Interview. This is conducted when an employee leaves the organisation. The aim of the exit interview is to select information about the job, supervisor or other related matters.

Expatriate. An expatriate is a person employed in a foreign country.

Exporting. A kind of market entry strategy, in which, a company may do the complete manufacturing of the product domestically and export it to the foreign market.

Extra-mural Welfare Activities. This includes all those welfare activities or services or amenities, which are undertaken outside the factories.

Extrinsic Motivation. It is concerned with what is to be done for the employees in order to motivate them.

Face Validity. Face validity is not a statistical measure but a subjective expression of how well the test items seem to be related to the job in question.

Fair Wage. A wage rate is fair in the narrower sense when it is equal to the rate current for similar workmen in the same trade and neighbourhood and fair in the wider sense when it is equal to the predominant rate for similar work throughout the country and in the generality of traders.

Field Review. In this method, the evaluator, usually HR specialist, asks/interviews supervisors questions about their subordinates.

Franchising. It is a form of licensing in which a parent company (the franchiser) grants another independent entity (the franchisee) the right to do business in a prescribed manner.

Free Essay Method. In this method, the evaluator, usually supervisor, writes a report about employees performance.

Frequency Rate. It is the number of time lost (or injuries which have disabled an employee) in accidents per million of man-hours worked.

Geocentric Staffing. The ultimate objective of the organisation is to hire the best person available for a position, regardless of where the individual comes from.

Gherao. This refers to the encirclement of the employers or managers or supervisory staff with intention to criminally intimidate them to accept the demands of workers.

Global/International Human Resource Management (GHRM/ IHRM). It is the utilisation of global human resources to achieve organisational objectives without regard to geographic boundaries.

Grading. In this method certain categories of grades are established well in advance. After this, employee performance can be compared with these grades and the person is allocated the suitable grade, i.e. the grade that best represents him or her performance.

Graphic Rating Scales. This approach is similar to person-to-person comparison but the difference is that the degrees on the factor scales are represented by definitions rather than by key people.

Grievance Disputes or Legal Disputes. These disputes arise when the workers feel that their rights have been violated or an act of injustice has been done to them.

Grievance Interview. The general purpose of a grievance interview is resolution of the controversy to the satisfaction of both the employee and the company.

Grievance Procedure. This includes the grievance redressal procedure through which the employees can express their dissatisfaction and appeal for action.

Grievance. A grievance can be any discontent or dissatisfaction, whether expressed or not, whether valid or not, arising out of anything connected with the company that an employee thinks, believes or even feels is unfair, unjust or inequitable.

Halo Effect/Error. This occurs when the rater is influenced by ratee's specific qualities (good or bad) and he evaluates the entire performance accordingly.

High-performance Job Design. It concentrates on setting up working groups in environments where high levels of performance is required. It starts from the principle of autonomous group working and develops an approach which enables groups to work effectively together in situations where the role of innovation is high.

Horizontal Promotion. This type of promotion includes an increase in responsibilities, pay and a change in designation. However, the employee doesn't shift the job classification.

Host-country National (HCN). HCN refers to an employee who is a citizen of the country where the subsidiary is located.

Human Resource Accounting (HRA). HRA is the process of identifying and measuring data about human resources and communicating this information to interested parties.

Human Resource Management. Human resource management is the planning, organising, directing and controlling of the procurement, development, compensation, integration, maintenance and separation of human resources to the end that individual, organisational and social objectives are accomplished.

Human Resource Planning. Human resource planning is the process by which an organisation ensures that it has the right number and kind of people, at the right place, at the right time, capable of effectively and efficiently completing those tasks that will help the organisation achieve its overall objectives.

Human Resources. Human resources are the people who work in an organisation.

Incentive System. Incentive system is related with wage payment plans, which tie wages directly or indirectly to standards of productivity or to the profitability of the organisation or to both criteria.

Individual Disputes. The disputes about the compensation for wrongful dismissal, reinstatement, etc. are individual disputes.

Induction. Induction is the process of receiving and welcoming employees when they first join a company and giving them the basic information they need to settle down quickly and happily and start work.

Industrial Disputes. It means any dispute or difference between:

(i) Employers and employers, or

(ii) Employers and workmen, or

(iii) Workmen and workmen, which is connected with

- (a) The employment or non-employment,
- (b) The terms of employment, or
- (c) The conditions of labour of any person.

Industrial Relations. It is the relationship between management and employees or among employees and their organisations that characterise or grow out of employment.

Integrative Bargaining. In this type of bargaining, productivity aspects are taken into account and through a process of mutual problem-solving the sum total of the gains can be increased.

Intelligence Tests. Intelligence tests are defined as the capacity for abstract thinking and reasoning.

Interest Disputes or Economic Disputes. These disputes usually come up when trade unions demand improvement in their wages, dearness and other allowances, fringe benefits and other terms of employment.

Interest Tests. These tests attempt to measure interests and preferences of people. These are mainly used in career counselling.

Interviewing. An interview refers to conversation with a purpose.

Intra-mural Welfare Activities (within the organisation). This includes all those activities, which are undertaken inside the factories.

Intra-organisational Bargaining. In this type of bargaining, both the employers' and unions' executives discuss the general demands/strategies and arrive at a consensus of approach among themselves before parties meet at the bargaining table.

Intrinsic Motivation. It is concerned with self-generation factors that influence individuals to behave in a particular way.

Job. It is defined as the collection or aggregation of tasks, duties and responsibilities which as a whole, are regarded as a regular assignment to individual employees.

Job Analysis. Job analysis is the process of studying and collecting information relating to the operations and responsibilities of a specific job. The immediate products of this analysis are job description and job specification.

Job Description. Job description is an organised factual statement of the duties and responsibilities of a specific job.

Job design. Job design has been defined as the specification of the contents, methods and relationships of jobs in order to satisfy technological and organisational requirements as well as the social and personal requirements of the job holder.

Job Enlargement. It refers to the expansion of job content to include a wider variety.

Job Enrichment. Job enrichment puts specialised tasks back together so that one person is responsible for producing a whole product or an entire service.

Job Evaluation. It is a formal and systematic comparison of jobs to determine the worth of one job relative to another and eventually results in a wage or salary hierarchy.

Job Rotation. It refers to systematic movement of workers from one job to another without disrupting the flow of work.

Job Specification. Job specification is a statement of the minimum acceptable human qualities necessary to perform a job properly.

Job-posting. This refers to the announcement of job openings in the company either posting on bulletin board, or in a company's newsletter.

Job-related Interview. In this interview, a number of job related questions are asked that just focus on relevant past job-related behaviours.

Joint Ventures. This refers to sharing of ownership and management in an enterprise.

Lay-offs. Lay-offs means the failure, refusal or inability of an employer to give employment to a worker whose name is borne on the muster rolls of his industrial establishment and who has not been retrenched.

Learning. Learning is the process by which a person acquires new knowledge, skills and capabilities.

Licensing. Under licensing agreement, a company in one country (the licensor) grants company in another country (the licensee) the right to use its intellectual properties (such as patents, trade marks, copyrights, technology, technical know-how, marketing skill, manufacturing process, etc.) for a specific period of time.

Living Wage. This is the highest level of wages and obviously it would include all amenities, which a person living in a modern civilised society is entitled and expects when the economy of the country is sufficiently advanced and the employer is able to meet the expanding aspirations of his workers.

Lockout. According to Section 2(l) of Industrial Disputes Act, 1947, lockout means the temporary closing of a place of employment or the suspension of work, or the refusal by an employer to continue to employ any number of persons employed by him.

Management by Objectives. MBO refers to joint setting of specific measurable goals and periodical review of the progress made.

Mass Interview. In this, a panel interviews several candidates simultaneously.

Membership Shop. In this arrangement all the employees who are members of the union on a specified date or who become members after that date are obligated to maintain their memberships until the termination of the agreement, as a condition of employment.

Mentor. A mentor is an older and respected manager or professional who counsels and listens for feelings as well as facts and stimulates people through ideas and information.

Mentoring. Mentoring is a developmentally oriented relationship between senior and junior colleagues or peers that involves advising, role modeling, sharing contacts and giving general support.

Minimum Wage. Minimum wage refers to that amount which not only provides for the bare sustenance of life but also for the preservation of the efficiency of the worker.

Motivation. Motivation can be defined as the willingness to exert high levels of effort to reach organisational goals, conditioned by the effort's ability to satisfy some individual need.

Mutual Welfare. This includes all those activities which are undertaken by the workers themselves through the platform of their trade unions.

Occupation. An occupation is a group of jobs that are similar as to kind of work and are found throughout the industry or the entire country.

Open Shop. In this arrangement, no employee is required to join or contribute to the union financially.

Outplacement. Outplacement is an HR programme created to help separated employees' deal with the emotional stress of job loss and provide assistance in finding a new job.

Paired Comparison. This method compares the performance of each worker with that of every other worker in the group or section.

Panel Interview. In this a panel (or group) of interviewers ask questions to the candidates.

Performance Appraisal. Performance appraisal is the periodic, formal evaluation of employee performance for the purpose of making career decisions.

Personality. Personality refers to the dynamic organisation within the individual of those psychophysical systems that determine his unique adjustments to his environment.

Picketing. This means watching and dissuading those who go to work during a strike.

Placement. Placement refers to the determination of the job to which an accepted candidate is to be assigned and his assignment to that job.

Polycentric Staffing. This staffing policy means that in foreign operations, more host country nationals are used throughout the organisation, from top to bottom.

Position. A position is a group of tasks assigned to one individual. There are as many positions in a firm as there are personnel.

Predictive Validity. An approach to establishing criterion-related validity in which a new test is administered to all job applicants and all applicants are hired, regardless of test scores. Later, when a measure of job performance can be obtained, test scores are correlated with job performance to see how well the test predicted job success.

Preliminary Interview. This is an introductory interview, which is quite short and just aims at elimination of the obviously unqualified.

Programmed Instruction/learning. This is step-by-step self-learning method where the medium may be a textbook, computer or the internet.

Promotion. Promotion refers to advancement to position of increased responsibility.

Psychological Appraisals. Psychological appraisals are conducted to assess the future potential of the employees. In this method, the past and actual performance is not assessed. The focus is on the future potential.

Ranking. In this method one person is compared with all other employees for the purpose of placing them in a simple rank order of worth.

Rational Validity. This is the type of validity that relates to the nature, properties and content of a test, independent of its relationship to job performance measures.

Realistic Job Previews. Realistic job previews can help prospective employees more accurately gauge whether the job is indeed for them and particularly whether a job's demands are a good fit with a candidate's skills and interests.

Recognition Disputes. These disputes arise due to reluctance or refusal shown by the employers in recognizing the worker's union.

Recruitment. It is the process of searching for prospective employees and stimulating them to apply for jobs in the organisation.

Regiocentric Staffing. This policy is based upon the logic that regional insiders know what neighbouring countries want.

Reliability. Reliability refers to the degree of consistency of results obtained.

Retrenchment. It refers to termination of the services of an employee by the employer because of economic reasons. This includes rationalisation in organisation, installation of new machines that replaces the labour, etc.

Role-playing. In this method, the trainees are assigned a role, which they have to play in an artificially created situation.

Selection. It is the process of screening job applicants to ensure that the most appropriate candidates are hired.

Selection/Employment Interview. Here the interviews are used as a key selection device.

Self-managing Teams/Autonomous Work Teams. An autonomous or self-managing team is allocated an overall task. This technique focuses on giving a team, rather than an individual, a whole and meaningful piece of work to do.

Separation. It means termination of an employee's association or membership in an organisation.

Sequential Interview. In this, several persons interview the candidate, in sequence before a final decision is made.

Severity Rate. It is the total number of days lost because of accidents per million man-hours worked.

Simple Ranking System. In this method of job evaluation, the committee evaluates the job description and ranks the jobs in the order of their importance.

Situational Interview. In this the interviewer asks the candidate what his or her behaviour would be in a given situation.

Split-halves Method. In this method, the test is divided into two equivalent halves and the correlation found for these halves-tests.

Standardisation. Standardization refers to the consistency or uniformity of the conditions and procedures for administering a psychological test.

Statutory Welfare. This includes all those employee welfare activities, which are undertaken by employers because of legal requirements.

Stereotyping. This type of error arises when the interviewers have already formed some associations between a particular trait, origin and particular type of personality.

Stress Interview. The aim of this interview is to identify sensitive candidates and those with low or high stress tolerance.

Strike. According to Section 2(q) of Industrial Disputes Act, 1947, strike means:

(i) a cessation of work by a body of persons employed in any industry acting in combination, or

(ii) a concerted refusal of any number of persons who are or have been so employed to continue to work or to accept employment, or

(iii) refusal under a common understanding of any number of such persons to continue to work or to accept employment.

Structured or Directive Interview. In this type of interview, a set sequence of questions is followed.

Suspension. Suspension means prohibiting an employee from attending work, stopping him from performing the duties assigned to him and withholding the remuneration payable to him.

Test-retest (Repetition) Method. In this, a test is administered twice to the same group of people and correlating the two sets of scores.

Third-country National (TCN). TCN refers to a citizen of one country, working in a second country and employed by the firm headquartered in a third country.

360-degree Feedback. 360-degree feedback can be defined as the systematic collection and feedback of performance data on an individual or group derived from a number of the stakeholders on their performance.

Training. Training refers to any process by which the aptitudes, skills and abilities of employees to perform specific jobs are increased.

Transfer. A transfer refers to a movement of an employee from one job to another with no change in salary, status and responsibilities.

Understudy. In this the employee is trained by his or her supervisor.

Union Security. The main objectives of union security provision are to ensure that the union continues to exist and perform its various functions.

Union Shop. In this arrangement a worker would become a member of the union within a specified period of his employment in that enterprise and that he would continue his membership in order to retain his job.

Unstructured or Non-directive Interview. Opposite to structured interview, in unstructured interview there is no set format of questions followed.

Validity. Validity refers to the extent to which a test measures what it is designed to measure.

Vertical Promotion. In this type of promotion, an employee is moved to higher level in the hierarchy. This involves increase in pay, status and responsibilities.

Voluntary Arbitration. Voluntary arbitration implies when the parties are unable to solve their dispute by themselves or through conciliation decided to submit the dispute to an impartial authority whose decision they are ready to accept.

Voluntary Welfare. This includes all those welfare activities, which are undertaken by the employers at their own.

Work Simplification. In this, the work is broken down into simple and repetitive tasks that maximize efficiency.

Subject Index